Women in
Twentieth-Century
Europe

D1596970

Gender and History

Series Editors: Amanda Capern and Louella McCarthy

Published

Ann Taylor Allen
WOMEN IN TWENTIETH-CENTURY EUROPE

Trev Lynn Broughton and Helen Rogers (eds)
GENDER AND FATHERHOOD IN THE NINETEENTH CENTURY

Rachel G. Fuchs and Victoria E. Thompson
WOMEN IN NINETEENTH-CENTURY EUROPE

Angela Woollacott
GENDER AND EMPIRE

Forthcoming

Shani D'Cruze and Louise A. Jackson
WOMEN AND CRIME SINCE 1660

William Foster
GENDER, MASTERY AND SLAVERY
The Atlantic World Experience

Perry Wilson
WOMEN IN TWENTIETH-CENTURY ITALY

Gender and History Series
Series Standing Order ISBN 1–4039–9374–2 hardcover
ISBN 1–4039–9375–0 paperback
(*outside North America only*)

You can receive future titles in this series as they are published by placing a standing order. Please contact your bookseller or, in case of difficulty, write to us at the address below with your name and address, the title of the series and the ISBN quoted above.

Customer Services Department, Macmillan Distribution Ltd, Houndmills, Basingstoke, Hampshire RG21 6XS, England

The Library
St. Mary's College of Maryland
St. Mary's City, Maryland 20686

Women in Twentieth-Century Europe

Ann Taylor Allen

© Ann Taylor Allen 2008

All rights reserved. No reproduction, copy or transmission of this
publication may be made without written permission.

No paragraph of this publication may be reproduced, copied or transmitted
save with written permission or in accordance with the provisions of the
Copyright, Designs and Patents Act 1988, or under the terms of any licence
permitting limited copying issued by the Copyright Licensing Agency,
90 Tottenham Court Road, London W1T 4LP.

Any person who does any unauthorized act in relation to this publication
may be liable to criminal prosecution and civil claims for damages.

The author has asserted her right to be identified
as the author of this work in accordance with the Copyright,
Designs and Patents Act 1988.

First published 2008 by
PALGRAVE MACMILLAN
Houndmills, Basingstoke, Hampshire RG21 6XS and
175 Fifth Avenue, New York, N.Y. 10010
Companies and representatives throughout the world

PALGRAVE MACMILLAN is the global academic imprint of the Palgrave
Macmillan division of St. Martin's Press, LLC and of Palgrave Macmillan Ltd.
Macmillan® is a registered trademark in the United States, United Kingdom
and other countries. Palgrave is a registered trademark in the European
Union and other countries.

ISBN-13: 978–1–403–94192–3 hardback
ISBN-10: 1–403–94192–0 hardback
ISBN-13: 978–1–403–94193–0 paperback
ISBN-10: 1–403–94193–9 paperback

This book is printed on paper suitable for recycling and made from fully
managed and sustained forest sources. Logging, pulping and manufacturing
processes are expected to conform to the environmental regulations of the
country of origin.

A catalogue record for this book is available from the British Library.

A catalog record for this book is available from the library of Congress.

10   9   8   7   6   5   4   3   2   1
17   16   15   14   13   12   11   10   09   08

Printed and bound in China

To my students,
with thanks for all they have taught me

Contents

Acknowledgments

Many people helped me to write this book. First, I would like to thank the University of Louisville, and particularly my colleagues in the Departments of History and of Women's and Gender Studies. Ever since 1974, when I developed the University's first course in women's history, they have encouraged my teaching and scholarship in this exciting field. My colleagues Julia Dietrich, Nancy Theriot, and Mary Ann Stenger read and commented on portions of this manuscript. Sonya Barker, Amanda Capern, Rachel Fuchs, and Michella Marino were sympathetic but demanding critics. My parents, Ann Updegraff Allen and Franklin G. Allen, gave me many kinds of support for this and all my other endeavors.

I also owe an enormous debt of gratitude to all the authors whose works I have used. Though I have acknowledged many of them, the format of this book does not allow for extensive citations, so there are some that I have not mentioned. Without their painstaking research and valuable insights, I could not have written this book.

Most of all, I thank the students whom I have taught at the University of Louisville and elsewhere. Their questions have helped me to clarify my thoughts; their interest and enthusiasm have motivated me to expand my knowledge; their friendly spirit has brightened my days. They are people of the twenty-first century. I hope that they will learn from the past as they go forward into the future.

Introduction: The Best of Times, the Worst of Times

"It was the best of times, it was the worst of times."[1] The words in which Charles Dickens described the age of the French Revolution could also be used to sum up the history of women in the twentieth century. Women in Europe and throughout the Western world lived through a process of change that was probably the most rapid and thorough in all of human history. Not only were the material conditions of women's existence transformed by medicine and technology, but they also gained some of the rights for which their foremothers had vainly contended: the status of citizens, legal equality in the marital relationship, access to higher education and professions, increases in earning power, and expanded opportunities to work, to create, and to live as they chose. Impressed by all these gains, popular culture and history usually portray this as a period of progress and emancipation. But to take this optimistic view would be to overlook the massive suffering inflicted by war, political oppression, and other calamities in a century that was among history's most tragic. In the twentieth century, women experienced both liberation and oppression, and confronted both new opportunities and new hardships.

This book will provide an overview of the history of women in Europe during this eventful era. As a basis for this complex story, we need to define a few basic concepts and themes that will run through the chapters that follow.

As the title indicates, the geographical area covered by this book is Europe and its time period is the twentieth century. Histories of Europe have traditionally focused chiefly on the "great powers," which during this era included Britain, France, Germany, Italy, and Russia. At certain points in our narrative— for instance, in the chapters on the First and Second World Wars—these countries will legitimately claim most of our attention. But in most of the book, the perspective will be as broad as possible, including all the nations of Europe. The book will begin with the outbreak of the First World War in 1914, partly because the authors of the previous volume in this series, Rachel Fuchs and Victoria Thompson, end their book on the nineteenth century at this point.[2] But a more important reason for this chronological break is that the First World War marked a crucial stage in the integration of women, as citizens, mothers, and workers, into the national state—a process that shaped their material conditions and mentalities throughout the twentieth century. The book ends around 2000, as women of many nations attempted to transcend national identities and to create a broader, transnational European community.

Throughout the story that this book will tell, there will be several recurring themes. We will constantly be reminded of the century's most fundamental changes—those that transformed women's life expectancy, fertility, health and material circumstances. Traditionally, female biology—menstruation, sexuality, pregnancy, childbirth—had been associated with so much suffering that religious authorities saw it as a divine punishment for Eve's transgressions in the Garden of Eden. Twentieth-century advances in medicine and rising standards of living transformed the female condition from a curse to an advantage. Life expectancies for both sexes increased dramatically, but those of women more than those of men. As of 1900, the average woman in the richer countries of Europe could expect to live about 50 years, and in the poorer countries about 38; by 2000 these figures had increased to 80 and 75 years.[3] At the same time as their life spans increased, women's fertility dropped, from an average of about four children apiece in 1900 to less than two in 2000.[4]

These changes provided the basis for broader transformations in women's material lives and ways of thinking about themselves and their possibilities. The combined effect of longer life expectancy, more robust health, and lower fertility enabled women to develop new interests, abilities, and life plans. Expectations in the areas of education, career success, financial independence and personal freedom that had in the past been confined to a privileged few were now shared by the majority. But in every area—the family, the labor market, the political arena—women's new aspirations met obstacles raised by men's defense of their privileges as well as by poverty, political oppression, or disadvantages arising from ethnicity, race, religion, or sexual orientation. Therefore, our story will emphasize not only progress, but also its price: bitter struggles, harsh confrontations, backlash, and misogyny in old and new forms.

This book will also look at changes in the prevailing gender ideology—that is, in ways of thinking about gender. The nineteenth-century gender ideology had been based on difference and separation. Legal systems emphasized women's subordination to men, and culture assigned them a separate sphere of domesticity. In the twentieth century, women won formal and legal equality in many areas—politics, the family, and the workplace—and the ideal of "separate spheres" declined, to make way for a new norm that promoted the integration of men and women. Of course, this transition was more in ideology than in practice—the genders had not, in fact, been entirely separate in the nineteenth century, nor were they entirely integrated in the twentieth. Nonetheless, the change was striking. In 1900, women were still excluded from most areas of politics, government, and military service, and from many educational institutions, professions, and occupations. By 2000, women had joined men in all these areas. In 1900, women were visibly different from men in their clothing, manners, and recreational interests; by 2000, these cultural differences had narrowed.

We will look at many forms of gender integration and its effects on the lives of women. The entry of women into areas that were traditionally defined as male was often equated with emancipation or liberation. In each case, we will assess this claim critically. Sometimes, integration into a formerly male area provided new opportunities, enhanced earning power, and greater personal freedom. Sometimes, however, the appearance of progress masked continuing inequality, and exposed women to new forms of discrimination and subordination.

In the twentieth century, the lives of women were more than ever shaped by the governments under which they lived, and therefore the relationship of women to the state will be an important theme of this book. Among women's major achievements was their acquisition of the rights of citizenship. To be sure, the ideology that had defined the public sphere of politics and government as a male realm did not disappear, and men kept most leadership positions. Nonetheless, women entered politics—though chiefly at low levels—gaining the right to vote, to run for office, to join and lead political parties, and to serve the state in appointed and elected positions. Of course, this process took longer in some countries than in others. Finnish women began to vote in 1906, Swiss women not until 1971.

We will not regard the admission of women to the rights of citizenship simply as a step toward emancipation, for in fact its consequences were very mixed. Governments accepted women as citizens primarily because the state needed their support and service. The expansion of government, first driven by the pressures of total war, continued in peacetime, eventually placing many areas of life—education, social welfare, public health, and the labor market, to name only a few—wholly or partially under state control. Along with new rights, women acquired new responsibilities and burdens as servants of the state in many areas—politics, labor, military service, and so on. Governments reconfigured even the most intimate areas of life, such as sexuality, reproduction, and childbearing, as public concerns over which the state exercised control. This book will look at the different forms of the state that arose in the twentieth century—the democracies, the inter-war authoritarian and totalitarian states, the post-war communist and post-communist states, and the integrated states of the European Union—and the ways in which these states defined the status and shaped the lives of women.

The book will tell the story of women's everyday lives, which despite ideological and national differences developed in many similar ways. During the twentieth century, the labor force participation of women increased, but as many women had worked for pay in earlier periods, this was not the most important change. What was new was the relationship of paid labor to the female life cycle. In 1900, women who held full-time jobs were predominantly young (many were teenagers) and single. Culture still defined marriage and waged work as incompatible and associated the employment of married women chiefly with poverty, low educational levels, and subordination, for many wives worked on farms and in businesses owned by their husbands. By 2000, not only did more married women work for pay, but many regarded their work as a means to independence and self-realization. As their educational attainments and other qualifications increased, women moved into some occupational areas that had previously been chiefly or wholly male.

But despite these advances, we will see that these women workers were still disadvantaged by gender. The entry of women into traditionally male work was not paralleled by any similar movement of men into female work, especially housework and child rearing. The household was not, as it is so often pictured, a "traditional" realm—in fact, maternity and domestic work changed as much as any other occupation. But these remained unpaid jobs that culture and custom still assigned to women. The so-called "double burden" of paid work and domesticity cut back many women's career prospects and earning potential. By 2000, this was a major cause of a persistent disparity in male and female wages, occupational choices, and access to leadership positions across the European Union.

Feminist movements will also have a prominent place in the chapters that follow. We will see that the size, popularity, and success of these movements varied greatly over time and space. Traditional histories identify two separate "waves" of feminism: the "first women's movement," which began in the mid-nineteenth century, peaked around 1900, and declined in the 1920s; and the "second women's movement" which began around 1968, peaked in the mid-1970s, and has continued in many forms until the present. The earlier movement focused on winning legal equality in areas such as suffrage, the family, and education, and worked chiefly through large national organizations in which policy was set by a small elite of leaders. The later movement, which was far less centralized, derived its major energies from small groups, many of which were less concerned with legal equality than with the myriad social, psychological, and cultural dimensions of female identity and gender relations. The historian Karen Offen objects to the metaphor of "waves," which pictures the history of feminism as a series of brief and dramatic surges punctuated by long troughs of inactivity. She proposes another metaphor—a volcano, in which feminism is the magma that seethes below the surface and seeks opportunities to erupt.[5] In ways that were sometimes quiet and inconspicuous and sometimes noisy and sensational, feminists continued their work in all the times and places that will be depicted here.

To be sure, feminist movements never gained the support of the majority of women, many of whom preferred other forms of organization and political self-expression. Like the advocates of other forms of social change, moreover, feminists were deeply divided by class, ethnicity, religion, and political alignment. And the goal of these diverse feminisms—gender equality—had no simple and obvious definition. Some feminists asserted that both men and women shared the same basic abilities and aspirations, and therefore deserved the same rights and opportunities. Others asserted that women were different from men but entitled to equal power and respect.

Despite all their disagreements, feminists shared a passionate commitment to improving the lives and expanding the rights of women in whatever ways seemed possible and appropriate. They encouraged women to define their goals and to work to realize them in many different times, places, and situations. And many feminists were also scholars, journalists, authors, and artists. They found vivid words and images to depict women's experience, to analyze contemporary issues, to expose injustice and abuse, and to imagine a better future. The works of feminists provide both a theoretical framework and invaluable documentation for the history of women in the twentieth century.

This book will look at women of many nations—rich and poor, married and single, religious and secular, feminists and antifeminists, militarists and pacifists. Like other historical accounts, it will deal with both change and continuity—changes in technology, political systems, reproductive patterns, and standards of living, continuity in many basic forms of gender inequality. Because the lives of women were bound up as never before with the state, politics and the ongoing struggle for equality will be a major theme of our story. But we will also consider many other aspects of women's lives: work, culture, sexuality, intellectual and artistic creativity, and parenthood. As women were and are a very diverse group, we will pay close attention to individual stories, some told by famous and others by unknown women. Of course, this brief volume can provide only an introduction to this rich and complex history, but if it encourages further study and research, it will have served its purpose. .

1

Women and the First World War, 1914–1918

The First World War took Europe by surprise. The public knew little of the diplomatic crisis caused by the assassination of Franz Ferdinand, the heir to the Austrian throne, on June 28, 1914. As they made the decisions that would plunge Europe into war, the ruling elites of Austria, Russia, Germany, France, and Britain did not consult their people, who were more preoccupied with the summer heat than with international tensions. When the German army's crossing of the Belgian frontier set off hostilities in the first days of August, prominent feminist leaders vied with their male compatriots in expressions of patriotism and earnest resolve. "The greatest crisis known in all our national history is upon us ... Now is the time for resolute effort and self-sacrifice on the part of every one of us to help our country," proclaimed Millicent Garrett Fawcett, the head of the British NUWSS (National Union of Woman Suffrage Societies the main organization that worked toward woman suffrage). "Let us show ourselves worthy." And Helene Lange, the most prominent figure in the German women's movement, declared that "the enormous importance of these recent events has overwhelmed us. . . . Today, the spiritual progress of the women's movement must show itself in the clarity and seriousness, with which we women respond to this time."[1] But Vera Brittain, a young Englishwoman who was preparing for her first year at Oxford and absorbed in an exciting new romance, was more irritated than inspired. "When the Great War broke out, it came to me not as a superlative tragedy but as an interruption of the most exasperating kind to my personal plans."[2]

All of these women were soon caught up in events that were far more catastrophic than any of them could have imagined in August, 1914. This chapter will look at the pre-war debates on the duties of women in wartime, female military personnel and nurses at the front, work on the so-called "home front," conditions of life during the war, women's pacifist movements, and the war's various effects on the position of women in the belligerent countries. The central question will concern the effect of women's wartime activities—did they raise the status of women, or did they provoke chiefly anti-feminist backlash?

In fact, both of these things happened. At the outset of hostilities, women who rallied enthusiastically to their nations' war effort assumed that their male fellow citizens would show their gratitude by granting women the full rights of citizenship. And indeed, in wartime women gained some rights and benefits for which they had struggled vainly in peacetime. However, when the initial popular enthusiasm for the war gave way to skepticism and then to sullen revolt, the woman who took the place of an absent worker or father became the visible symbol of wartime hardship, separation, and bereavement. Therefore, women's efforts often earned them more hostility than praise.

Military service and the female citizen

In response to the outbreak of war in 1914, activists of women's movements throughout Europe proclaimed that they were the equals and the comrades of men. The immediate pre-war era had seen a massive growth in women's organizational activities, which included not only suffrage movements but also labor unions, civic groups, and many others. Though most conspicuous in Western Europe, where women's educational and occupational status was relatively high, feminist activity had also gained increased visibility in the poorer eastern regions. In Russia's 1905 Revolution, working-class women had participated in strikes, and middle-class women launched huge demonstrations for woman suffrage.

Though women's movements had an international dimension, most were primarily nationalist and patriotic. They claimed for women not only the rights of citizenship—among them the right to vote—but also its responsibilities. Chief among these was military service, which in all major European countries except Britain was required of men of all classes. Enemies of feminism often linked the right to vote to military service, claiming that only those who paid the "tax of blood" were qualified to govern. Women responded that they, too, performed services for the nation, and that though they were most skilled in the arts of peace, they were also ready to come to the nation's defense.

But what form should women's patriotic service take? Political, military, and medical elites defined women's service to the nation chiefly as child-bearing. Throughout Western Europe birthrates had fallen dramatically in the immediate pre-war years. This was a period when the effectiveness of armies depended chiefly on the number of bodies that could be put into the field, and thus on the numbers of the younger generation. Regarding this so-called "population crisis" as a threat to national security, pre-war governments blamed it on feminism, which allegedly had encouraged women to refuse motherhood in order to pursue educational and career ambitions. Feminists responded by indignantly denying these accusations, and asserting that the modern woman desired nothing so much as to be a mother. What deterred her from child-bearing was her disadvantaged status, which forced her into the subordination of marriage or the outcast disgrace of single motherhood. To give women equal rights in marriage and in the state would thus be the best way to raise birth rates. Some expressly compared the mother to the soldier: she too deserved pay and the rights of citizenship. "The mother who assures the perpetuation of the species," wrote the prominent French suffrage leader Hubertine Auclert, "should be treated like the soldier who assures the security of the territory: that is, she should be lodged and nourished during the period of her maternal service."[3]

Though affirming motherhood as an important form of patriotic service, pre-war women's movements also urged young childless women to take their place alongside men on the battlefield. To be sure, few agreed with the unconventional French physician Madeleine Pelletier, who seriously proposed that women who truly wished to shoulder the responsibilities of citizens should fight alongside men. Most feminists defined nursing, an activity that combined feminine gentleness with masculine courage and patriotism, as women's most appropriate military service.

When war broke out, the political leaders of the belligerent nations called on all men to forget their political differences and join in a patriotic coalition that the French called *Union sacrée* and the Germans, *Burgfrieden*. Women's organizations too resolved to unite. Everywhere they abandoned their struggles for suffrage and for other rights. In Germany the National Woman's Service (*Nationaler Frauendienst*), in France the French Women's Alliance (*Éffort féminin français*), in Italy the Italian Women's Committee (*Comitato nazionale femminile*), and in Britain a diverse group of old and new organizations proclaimed the readiness of women to serve. "The British Lion is awake, so is the Lioness," signaled a British newspaper headline. In Russia, the leadership of the League for Women's Equality called upon its members "come out of the narrow confines of the family" and to devote all their "energy, intellect and knowledge" to their country.

"Willing to do anything": women at the front

At the first news of war in 1914, many young women envied their male contemporaries. They, too, longed to escape the routine of civilian life and to be "off to the field." As her fiancé, Roland, departed for the front, Vera Brittain entered nursing training. "Not being a man and able to go to the front," she wrote to her parents, "I wanted to do the next best thing. I do not agree that my place is at home doing nothing... for I consider that the place now of anyone who is young and strong and capable is where the work that is needed is to be done."[4]

The largest number of military women served as nurses. At first, armies were reluctant to employ female nurses in war zones, but by 1915 that policy had changed and women of all nations worked near the front lines. The first nurses to appear in military hospitals were volunteers, organized chiefly under the auspices of the Red Cross and various patriotic women's organizations. Most of these volunteer nurses came from upper-class families and could afford to work for nominal wages. As the number of the sick and wounded increased, armies hired additional nurses, but at a rate of pay that was often too low to attract many of the working-class women who now had the opportunity to work in well paying and less hazardous military jobs. Thus, volunteers continued to predominate on the staffs of military hospitals in every war zone.

The British volunteers were uniformed and organized as Voluntary Aid Detachments (VADs) under Katherine Furse, their Commandant in Chief.

Furse exhorted her troops to combine martial courage with feminine propriety. "Willing to do anything" was the motto that she chose for her service.[5]

War propaganda depicted the volunteer nurse as a pure and dainty "white angel of the battlefield." Nothing could have been further from the bloody and stinking reality. Women trained to treat minor injuries were shocked by the sight of bodies shattered by artillery fire. "The wounded men, with their bodies shot to pieces, would like to lie on something soft, but we do not have enough straw," wrote a German nurse who worked in a typically improvised and under-equipped military hospital. "They are sticky with blood and dirt . . . We have not water, no basins, no soap or towels—nothing. Many die without our being able to do anything to ease their pain. . . . I was on night watch today . . . So many died in the night. . . . It is so terribly cold and frightful here."[6] Vera Brittain, who had joined a VAD, remembered "the queer, frightening sensation . . . of seeing the covered stretchers come in, one after another, without knowing . . . what fearful sight or stench, what problem of agony or imminent death, each brown blanket concealed."[7] Nurses faced disease, infection, and enemy fire. After the Germans defeated an Italian army at Caporetto (1917), Italian volunteer nurses refused to abandon their patients and were taken as prisoners of war. Twenty French Red Cross nurses were killed; 1000 received their nation's highest military decoration, the Croix de Guerre.

As the war continued and casualties mounted, women volunteered for other duties at the front. The British military leadership founded three women's auxiliary services: the Women's Royal Naval Service (WRENS), the Women's Auxiliary Army Corps (WAAC), and the Women's Royal Air Force (WRAF). In the armed forces of all the belligerent nations, women performed non-combat tasks as clerks, cooks, electricians, code breakers, and ambulance drivers (to mention only a few). The most remarkable military deployment of women was in Russia, where Maria Bochkareva, a woman from a peasant family in Tomsk, joined the army in 1914. At first, her comrades assumed that she was a "loose-moraled woman who had made her way into the ranks for the sake of carrying on her illicit trade," but she won their respect for her bravery. In August 1917, a Women's Military Congress met to coordinate the deployment of several women's military units. In all, about 6000 Russian woman served in combat.

In other ways, too, women won fame as war heroes. Edith Cavell was a British nurse who ran a hospital in Brussels, Belgium. When the Germans conquered Belgium, Cavell remained there, taking care of soldiers of all nationalities. In secret, she helped to organize a Belgian resistance network that assisted British, French, and Belgian soldiers to escape German-occupied territory. In 1915, she was arrested along with 30 other Belgian agents, condemned to death for espionage, and executed by firing squad. The Belgian Louise de Bettignies worked as a courier for the Red Cross and as a secret agent of the British Intelligence Service, gathering important information about German military operations. When the Germans captured her in 1915, they held her as a prisoner but—probably deterred by the international outcry over Cavell's execution—did not sentence her to death. However, she died in prison in Germany in 1918.

In their relationships to soldiers, some women acted as surrogate mothers and tried to add spiritual comfort to their physical ministrations. Many others aspired to a more comradely relationship with their male age-mates. First overwhelmed with embarrassment by the sight of naked male bodies, Vera Brittain soon lost her shame—even her attitude toward her fiancé and approaching marriage became "less romantic and more realistic."[8] When 18 British WAAC members were killed in France, their leader, Helen Gwynne-Vaughan, discouraged newspapers from making too much fuss. The women were soldiers, and their deaths were only to be expected.

But the era's popular media did not portray military women as the brave soldiers that they were, but instead according to stereotyped notions of female personality and behavior. Some of these were sentimental and idealized, as in the image of the nurse as "white angel" or Edith Cavell as a saintly martyr rather than the tough, resourceful patriot that she was. More often, however, the images were of a less exalted kind. Popular fiction and visual arts often portrayed the relationship between the nurses and their patients as romantic and sexual, and the nurses themselves as frivolous society women who went to the front in search of male companionship. Likewise, British newspapers claimed that the women of the WAAC associated too freely with soldiers and that many were sent home pregnant—a story that a senior member of the Corps had to deny. The military woman thus became the butt of popular anger against a war that, by separating married couples and breaking up families, had disrupted many traditional standards of behavior.

"The mother-side of humanity": women and pacifism

When war broke out in 1914, small groups of women in all countries refused to rally around their nations' flags. Since the nineteenth century, international women's organizations such as the International Council of Women had striven for understanding among nations and had rejected war as an instrument of national policy. Many members of these organizations succumbed to the war fever, but some continued to work for peace. In 1915, the Dutch physician and suffrage leader Aletta Jacobs Gerritsen summoned women who wished to "protest together against the horrors of war" and perhaps even to "find a way to end the hostilities" to a meeting in the Hague.[9] The national feminist associations in the belligerent countries refused to send delegates, but small groups from Germany, Italy, Belgium, and Great Britain, as well as from such neutral nations as Sweden, the Netherlands, the United States, and Canada attended. The meeting was chaired by a woman of great international prestige, the American Jane Addams.

These peace activists claimed that women's innate motherly nature predisposed them to pacifism. "Every man killed or mangled in war has been carried for months in his mother's body," wrote a British participant, Helena Swanwick. "He is the work of women; they have rights in him and in what he does with the life that he has given and sustained."[10] The delegates formed an organization known as the International Committee for a Permanent Peace (a name that was later changed to the Women's International League for Peace and Freedom). The document that emerged from the 1915 conference proposed ways to prevent war by resolving disputes peacefully, and influenced the Fourteen Points that were later proposed by the American President Woodrow Wilson. When they returned home from the conference, delegates set up branches of the International Committee in their own countries and also worked for peace through organizational work and journalism.

Though most socialist women refused to cooperate with the International Committee, which they associated with a middle-class feminist movement, they held their own peace conference in Switzerland in 1915. Among the participants were the French socialists Helène Brion and Louise Saumoneau, and the Russian Bolsheviks Nadezhda Krupskaya (wife of Lenin) and Inessa Armand. Another Bolshevik activist was Alexandra Kollontai, who spread anti-war propaganda in Norway and the United States. The Bolsheviks, who worked for the violent overthrow of governments, soon split from other socialists who were committed to non-violent methods. Brion, a leader of a socialist teachers' union, was arrested in France for anti-war activities in 1917. At her trial, she declared herself both a socialist and a feminist. "And it is because of my feminism," she testified, "that I am an enemy of war."[11]

However, the pacifists' appeal to female solidarity found little resonance. For most women, nationality transcended gender as a focus for loyalty. National feminist organizations rejected pacifism and supported their countries' war efforts. Unless German women protested their own government's violations of international law, stated the National Council of French Women, any cooperation with them would amount to treachery. Marianne Hainisch, the head of the League of Austrian Women's Associations, likewise declared that support for the peace movement was a betrayal of the Fatherland.[12] Like the young Vera Brittain, many women aspired to share men's lot rather than to assert a separate female or feminist identity. Only later did Brittain and many others regret their initial support for a war that blighted the future of their generation.

"It is jolly worth while": women on the home front

The War's first effect was to increase female unemployment. Just when the departure of breadwinners made it necessary for many women to support their families, the conversion of factories to military production eliminated many civilian jobs. Women's organizations rushed to provide services—child-care, employment agencies, emergency assistance—for these destitute or disrupted households. In Russia, the Empress headed a Supreme Council for the Care of Soldiers' Families and of the Families of the Dead and Wounded. When Italy entered the war in 1915, women activists formed an association known as the National Committee to Assist the Families of Servicemen. In Britain, France, and Germany, women's organizations across the political spectrum gathered money and oversaw social services.

But by 1915, when hopes for a quick end to the conflict were disappointed, government and military leaders who had at first contemptuously refused women's offers of help summoned them to support the troops on what was called the "home front." Feminist leaders played a conspicuous role in recruiting female workers into wartime industries. In Britain, the representatives of several suffrage organizations attended the National Conference on War

Service for Women headed by Arthur Henderson, the head of the War Cabinet. In France, prominent leaders participated in a Committee on Women's War Work, summoned by the Ministry of Munitions in 1915. In 1916 Marie Elisabeth Lüders, a leader of the League of German Women's Organizations, was appointed by the War Office to be head of a "Women's Department" that was charged with administering the work of women in wartime industries. The Russian suffragist and reformer Anna Shabanova worked with her country's War Industries Committee. These were the most conspicuous political roles that women had ever held in any of these countries.

The widely publicized image of the woman industrial worker in boots and overalls suggested that women had moved massively into men's jobs. And indeed, there was an enormous increase in the number of women who worked in a few formerly all-male industries. In Britain during the years from 1914 until 1918, the number of women engaged in building trades rose by 320 percent; in metal industries, 249 percent; in chemical industries, 158 percent. In the German state of Bavaria, the number of women employed in metal trades rose by 319 percent. In Italy, the female workforce in war-related industries numbered 23,000 in 1914 and 200,000 by 1918. Russian women poured into industrial employment, where their numbers rose 38 percent between 1914 and 1918.[13] Women also appeared in unaccustomed roles as postal clerks, mail carriers, bus drivers, and administrators at all levels of government. Many of these women took over the jobs that their husbands had left. But the impact on women's overall employment patterns was limited. Relatively few of the women who entered war industries had been full-time housewives; most were already employed and merely changed their workplace. And many wartime jobs involved work—sewing, office work, cooking, medical and social services—that was already stereotyped as female.

The feminists press in all countries spoke optimistically of the new respect for women workers, many of whom cheerfully accepted the double burden of work and family. Jane Misme, editor of *La Française*, reported that a boss had praised his new employees. "With some exceptions, they are wonderful," he said, "After ten hours of work per day, they find ways to keep a perfect house."[14] However, the real conditions of wartime work were often far from this optimistic assessment. Women representatives to government commissions insisted that men and women must receive equal pay for equal work, and male trade unionists who were concerned to prevent a disastrous fall in wages usually supported this demand. The wages paid to women in formerly all-male industries were in fact often much higher than they had received in earlier jobs. However, many employers justified paying women less than men by arguing that women's work was less productive. And with lower wages came longer hours and increased workloads.

Women often learned new skills easily, but men perceived their competence more as a threat than as a benefit. By invalidating the "apprenticeship myth"—the assumption that skilled work required long training periods—women workers placed male trade unionists' claim to high wages in jeopardy. Men often protested against of women's presence in the workplace by stealing the women's tools, messing up their desks, or emptying their drawers. A British munitions worker, Peggy Hamilton, remembered "showers of steel shavings pouring down on me from the gallery above as I worked at my lathe. Another time, as I was bending over my machine, a great wad of cotton waste, stuck with shavings and dripping with oil, caught me right in the face."[15] Men also resented wartime policies that placed women in civilian jobs in order to "free up" more men for the front. In Germany, women workers who replaced men were often known as "gravediggers."

Although certainly much safer than combat, women's jobs were often dangerous. The official concern for preserving femininity and protecting mothers did not extend to the workplace. Most of the protective legislation that had limited the hours and regulated the working conditions of women, teenagers, and mothers-to-be was suspended for the duration. Many munition workers handled sulphur without protective clothing, and their skin turned yellow. In Britain, they were called "canaries." As the drive for munitions intensified, women workers worked ever-longer hours. The resulting exhaustion increased the number of accidents, some of them fatal. Work with explosives was particularly risky. In a poem entitled "Munition Wages," a woman worker anticipated that she would one day be "blown to the sky," but reflected that, in the meantime, the opportunity to earn high wages and enjoy unaccustomed luxuries made her work "jolly worth while."[16]

In the countryside as well as the city, women replaced their absent men. The French Prime Minister René Viviani called upon women to "replace in the work of the fields those who are on the fields of battle! Prepare to show them, tomorrow, the soil cultivated, the crops harvested, the fields sown. . . . Tomorrow, there will be glory for everyone."[17] But the requisitioning of horses and vehicles for the war effort crippled food production. The resulting shortages were blamed on rural women, whose public image changed from "heroine of the harvest" to idler, even to deserter. In Russia, too, peasant women took over the heavy field labor that had been done by men, and in their husbands' absence their power in the assemblies that regulated village life increased.

In 1916, when German submarine attacks threatened Britain's food supply— a great deal of which was imported from overseas—the British government resolved to make the country self-sufficient in food. To that end, the government created the Women's Land Service Corps—in 1917 re-named the Women's Land Army (WLA)—to replace the male agricultural workforce. This was a uniformed service, and its members wore brown corduroy trousers, green jerseys, a WLA hat, and work boots. In order to save fuel for the war effort, the use of tractors and other machinery was restricted, and most of the work was done by hand. Sent out to live in remote rural areas and constrained by strict rules of conduct that forbade them to enter pubs or to go out in the evening, these young women often led hard and lonely lives. And farmers were often reluctant to accept the help of women, preferring instead to hire boys or old-age pensioners.

Opportunities for educated professional women widened during the war. Even men who had previously opposed the admission of women to the medical profession now clamored for the services of female physicians. Women teachers appeared in girls' schools, and in many civil service and clerical jobs. Some authority figures resented these ambitious women. German military commanders called for the closing of universities in order to prevent women from taking advantage of men's absence to gain professional qualifications. But others encouraged them. Count Ignatev, the Russian Minister of Education, increased the number of women who were admitted to universities, broadened the opportunities available to women teachers, and recruited women into the engineering profession.

Among the most essential war workers was the prostitute. Though military leaders passed harsh judgment on women who were unfaithful to their soldier husbands, armies provided brothels for their men. Prostitutes faced difficult working conditions. "50 to 60 men of every color to do per day, under the constant threat of the planes, the bombardments . . . eighteen hours' hard work a day," wrote a French prostitute. But there were compensations: "you earned 400 to 500 francs a day, and that was almost a fortune."[18] The prostitute was perhaps the only woman war worker who was not surprised when her hard work for the Fatherland earned her more contempt than praise.

The women workers themselves were often proud of their achievements. "What millions of women have done behind the front, since the beginning of the war, day in and day out," asserted an editorial in the periodical of the League of Austrian Women's Associations, "is as important and indispensable for the war effort as the sacrifice of millions of heroes at the Front."[19] But many observers found the spectacle of the woman worker more disturbing than inspiring, and feared for the future of marriage and motherhood. Hands "coarsened in munitions factories," lamented the British poet Mary Gabrielle Collins, were better suited to "guide the rosy teat swelling with milk to the eager mouth of the suckling babe."[20] A popular song complained that everything was "topsy-turvy since the war began." Prominent women responded to these concerns by reassuring the public that this "topsy-turvy" gender order was temporary, and then when the men returned women would gladly revert to more appropriate behavior. Indeed, many had signed contracts that committed them to give up their jobs at the war's end.

The war and the family

Though far from the battlefield, the home too was mobilized for the war effort. The household became a public sphere, in which consumption, recreation, and social behavior were subject to governmental regulation. Even private functions such as sexuality and reproduction did not escape mobilization. Mothers, after all, produced the most important resource of all—the next generation of citizens and soldiers.

In the pre-war era, military, political, and medical elites had warned that falling birthrates threatened military readiness. In wartime, the pressure on mothers became more open. It was up to women, said the German Dr. Hugo Sellheim in a speech that he gave to women Red Cross volunteers in 1915, to "make up for all our losses and . . . to ensure the survival of our nation."[21] The many organizations that promoted increased birthrates (natalism) grew, and new ones arose. In France, the League for Life (*Ligue pour la vie*); in Germany the Society for Population Policy (*Gesellschaft für Bevölkerungspolitik*), both of which were founded in 1916, conducted propaganda campaigns that linked reproduction to military service. For example, French post-cards that were risqué by the standards of this period showed three babies hanging by their swaddling bands from a soldier's bayonet with the caption "a good thrust." On another card, a pregnant women encouraged her compatriots to "work for France."[22]

Feminist leaders patriotically accepted the challenge of encouraging motherhood and combating the high infant mortality rates that deprived their nation of so many potential soldiers. Shrewdly adapting their rhetoric to the times, they recast many of their long-standing demands as responses to the current emergency. For example, British, German, and French feminists of the pre-war era had vocally protested the plight of unmarried mothers, who as a result of their disadvantaged legal and outcast social status saw their children die at much higher rates than those of married parents. In Britain, child-welfare activists characterized the so-called "War Babies," or soldiers' illegitimate offspring, as precious "children of the state." In wartime, many governments included the unmarried partners and "illegitimate" children of soldiers in familial support and survivor benefits. Other measures that raised the status of unmarried mothers and their children, such as laws permitting fathers to marry the mothers of their children in absentia and to recognize their children from the front, were also passed in several countries. But many other reforms—such as, the right of "illegitimate" children to belong to their fathers' families—still met with strong opposition from conservative and religious groups.

Women social reformers succeeded in realizing another aim for which they had worked during the pre-war era: the public provision of health-care and social services to mothers and their children, and particularly to those who were poor or deserted. At the war's outset, women's organizations provided charitable services to the many families whom the departure of male breadwinners had plunged into crisis. At the same time, their leaders insisted that charity was not sufficient. If the state now regarded children as its most important resource, then it should support the mothers who produced them. Since the 1880s, German state-sponsored workers' insurance funds had financed leaves for certain categories of women workers. During the war, the state lengthened the period of coverage, increased the payments, and extended the eligible group. In Britain, the Maternity and Child Welfare Act of 1918 created an extensive network of publicly supported health centers.

Some reformers took advantage of the wartime emergency to create a new relationship between state and family. All national governments made support payments to the families of servicemen. In most cases, these payments were inadequate. In Russia, they were more promise than reality; in Germany and France, they were so low that they hardly enabled families to subsist. But in Britain, which in 1914 had no system of military conscription, payments were set at a higher level in order to motivate men to volunteer.

Eleanor Rathbone was a British socialist whose wartime job was in the Soldiers' and Sailors' Family Association, a private organization that distributed benefits to soldiers' families. She chose (in the words of the historian Susan Pedersen) to "misread" a benefit that was intended to reward the nation's fighting men as a form of state support for women, and more specifically for mothers.[23] Rathbone observed that the women who received support payments were in some ways better off than before the war, when they and their children had depended on male breadwinners. Along with some other women's organizations, including the socialist Women's Cooperative Guild, Rathbone and her colleagues urged the state to continue these payments in peacetime. Mothers, she insisted, performed an essential service for the state, and the state should reward their contribution through subsidies—first called the "endowment of motherhood" and subsequently "family allowances"—that enabled them to raise their children without sacrificing their financial independence.

The Women's Cooperative Guild, a British organization made up chiefly of working-class women, took up the cause of mothers in a sensational book entitled *Maternity: Letters from Working Women*, which appeared in 1915. The contributors, all members of the organization, recounted their experiences of motherhood, which they claimed was a contribution to the nation that was equivalent in risk, hardship, and sacrifice to men's military service. The editor, Margaret Llewelyn Davies, summed up the mother's lot as "perpetual overwork, illness, and suffering." One mother wrote that she had "six children, all living, and what a terrible time it is, to be sure, especially during the last two months—only just enough to live on and another coming. . . . The mental strain in addition to bodily labour must surely affect the child."[24] Another had lost six children before she reared one. "I was very unfortunate in my married life," she recalled, "and at one time thought that I was not going to rear any children."[25] Most of the contributors agreed that "the state . . . if it wants citizens, and healthy citizens . . . must make it possible for men and women to have families while living a full life themselves and giving a full life to their children . . . The first requirement is, then, the improvement of the economic position of the family."[26] But Davies added that the mother needed not only material benefits, but also individual freedom and dignity— "the means and the leisure to live a life of her own without which she is unfit to give life to her children and to direct it during their most impressionable years."[27]

Women's organizations in all countries also aimed to enable women to combine motherhood with work outside the home—an issue that wartime mobilization had brought to the forefront of public attention. A French law of 1917 guaranteed working mothers regular breaks and rooms in which they could nurse their babies in the workplace. The members of the Italian Women's National Committee set up kindergartens and day-care centers, some of them in the mansions of noble families. In Germany, private organizations founded "war kindergartens" for the children of working mothers. As head of the Women's Department of Germany's War Office, Marie-Elisabeth Lüders developed an elaborate plan to provide child-care to all such mothers, but because of the catastrophic financial state of local governments and the lack of sympathy of her male superiors, this ambitious scheme could not be implemented. Margaret McMillan, a British socialist and early childhood educator, set up a kindergarten for munitions workers at Deptford with financing from the British Ministry of Munitions.

But these wartime measures did nothing to raise birthrates, which were the lowest ever recorded. Of course, the main reason was the absence of men; but another could have been a widespread reluctance to bring children into a world of privation, violence, and chaos. In Britain and Germany, knowledge and use of contraception increased during the war years, and the rate of abortions also increased. Wartime governments concluded that if women could not be persuaded, they must be forced to bear and rear children for the nation.

In Germany in 1918, the Imperial government introduced three legislative proposals into the national parliament (or *Reichstag*): the first stepped up penalties for abortion; the second forbade the sale or advertising of contraceptives; and the third tightened control over prostitution and the reporting of venereal disease. The main German feminist organization, the League of German Women's Associations (*Bund Deutscher Frauenvereine*, or BDF), supported some of these provisions, but defended the sale (though not the advertisement) of contraceptives. Socialist feminists spoke out more openly against what they called "*Gebärzwang*" (or compulsory child-bearing). Because of the collapse of the German monarchy in 1918, these laws were never passed.

In France, a draft law of 1916 criminalized not only the sale, but also the spread of information about contraception, and sharpened penalties for performing, seeking, or advocating abortion. Caught up in the wartime emergency, some prominent feminists defended this law. In an article for the French feminist newspaper *La Française*, Marguerite de Witt-Schlumberger, who was the head of the French Union for Woman Suffrage, proclaimed that "mothers owe service to the country just as do soldiers at the front," and that "young married people in good health who refuse to give a child to the Fatherland in the first year of peace should be considered deserters."[28] Historians speculate that Schlumberger's statement may have been part of a "deliberate political trade-off" in which feminists consented to the restriction of women's reproductive liberty in return for male politicians' support of woman suffrage. The 1916 draft became the model for a law that was finally passed in 1920. In Britain, the Defense of the Realm Act, passed in 1914, was designed to protect the troops and their offspring against venereal infection by reintroducing the inspection of prostitutes and punishing diseased women for sexual relations with servicemen.

The connection between reproduction and war became clear in the controversy that arose over the tragic situation of the French and Belgian women who had become pregnant as a result of rape by German invaders in August and September of 1914. Many prominent French journalists and literary figures incited these women to abortion or even infanticide. Appealing to racism to justify wartime hatred, these propagandists claimed that hereditary taint of German blood marked these children of rape as outcasts. Some also attacked the women themselves for not preferring death to dishonor. A French woman who was on trial for infanticide and claimed that the murdered baby was the child of a German rapist was acquitted.

The housewife as revolutionary

Like motherhood, housework was also organized to serve military needs. As entire economies were restructured to serve the needs of the armed forces, food products were among the first commodities to be rationed. Patriotic women's organizations urged housewives to conserve resources and organized cooking courses and educational programs for children. Due to shortages caused by the absence of many agricultural workers, the disruption of food imports, and the priority given to military over civilian needs, the prices of food and other necessities rose steadily. In France, for example, the price of coal had tripled by 1917, that of many food products had doubled, and milk was rationed. In Britain, ration cards were needed to purchase bacon, butter, meat, and bread. In both countries, housewives waited for hours to obtain scarce and necessary supplies.

Food shortages were far more catastrophic in Germany, Austria, and Russia. As a volunteer for the German National Women's Service, the social worker Alice Salomon produced pamphlets that urged housewives to conserve food. By 1916 the effects of the British blockade of the German coastline combined with the demands of the army and the shortage of agricultural workers to produce a crisis in civilian food supplies. "Rationing cards, endless queues in front of shops, and the turnip curse: turnips as vegetables, turnips as meat, marmelade, bread, even cake made out of turnips. . . . Those of us who didn't want to buy supplies on the black market were threatened by malnutrition," Salomon recollected.[29] The housewife's burdens increased. Urban women often tried to feed their families by planting their own gardens, by traveling to the countryside in search of food, or by resorting to theft, barter, or illegal black markets. Children often helped their mothers to scavenge for food.

Under these desperate circumstances, urban housewives became revolutionaries. In Germany, working-class women's showed their resentment by smashing store windows, looting markets, and attacking police. These actions were not simply motivated by the wartime food crisis, but expressed a growing political consciousness as well. German women protested against their government's disrespect for their contributions to the war effort by complaining that they seldom received the increased food ration allotted to manual laborers. In a series of noisy demonstrations, these women called for a government that responded to the needs of its people. Their actions helped to overthrow the monarchy and to make way for a new German democracy, the Weimar Republic.[30]

In Russia, urban women began their raucous and violent "food pogroms" in 1915. In solidarity with the protesters, women workers engaged in strikes and demonstrations. On February 23, 1917—International Woman's Day—women massed in Petrograd and began to wreck streetcars and to loot shops. The arrival of striking women workers from the trolley-car park and from local factories transformed the riot into a massive protest march. Eventually, the women joined a popular demonstration in the center of the city. They fearlessly faced the soldiers who had been sent out to disperse them. They "go up to the cordons more boldly than men," reported an observer, the prominent Bolshevik Leon Trotsky, "take hold of the rifles, beseech, almost command: 'Put down your rifles and join us.' "[31] Thus began the Russian Revolution of 1917—a revolution that would eventually topple the Russian monarchy and enable a new party, the Bolsheviks, to seize power.

War and suffrage

In 1914, feminist leaders had temporarily called off their campaigns for woman suffrage. But they had not forgotten their goal. They continued to hope that their governments would recognize women's patriotic sacrifice by finally granting to them the rights of citizens. In the closing months of the war, suffrage movements were resurrected. In some countries, these movements achieved the goal toward which they had worked for many decades, and women won the right to vote.

Because it occurred during or after the First World War, it was easy to assume that the enfranchisement of women expressed gratitude for women's wartime work and a new vision of gender equality. The story of the Representation of the People Act—the legislation through which some British women won the right to vote in 1918—casts doubt on this optimistic interpretation. During the war, a parliamentary committee decided finally to abolish property qualifications and to give all adult men the right to vote. The same committee decided to enfranchise some women, but not on the same terms as men—an action that they feared might give women, who due to wartime losses now outnumbered men, an electoral majority. The compromise was to give suffrage rights to men over 21 (19 if they had served in the military), but to women over 30 years of age who owned property or were the wives of property-owners. As the House of Commons debated this bill, a bitter backlash against the supposed gains made by women in wartime forced many women out of their jobs—hardly a sign of appreciation for their patriotism. Indeed, the higher female voting age excluded most of the young women whose services as nurses and industrial workers had been most crucial to the war effort. Fear of a new outbreak of suffragist violence rather than enthusiasm for gender equality may have motivated the majority of the House of Commons to approve this measure. But suffragists professed themselves happy to accept this incomplete but nonetheless significant gain. In Germany, where the revolution that was sparked by urban women's uprisings also toppled the monarchy, women gained the right to vote in the new Weimar Republic, the country's first experience of democracy. In 1919, about 90 percent of the newly enfranchised women turned out to elect the National Assembly that wrote the Republic's constitution. Twenty-four delegates to the Assembly were women. In France, however, a revived suffrage movement failed. One of France's two parliamentary chambers, the Chamber of Deputies, voted for woman suffrage, but the second chamber, known as the Senate, opposed it, and French women did not win the vote until the end of another war in 1944. The rise of a Fascist movement and a totalitarian state in Italy also thwarted Italian women's aspirations to equal citizenship.

In Russia, the popular demonstrations in which working-class women played such an important role eventually led to the overthrow of the monarchy and the assumption of power by a Provisional Government composed chiefly of politicians from the liberal and progressive parties. Feminists created a new national organization—the All-Russia Women's Society—and renewed the campaign for woman suffrage that they had abandoned in August of 1914. Support also came from women's trade unions, organized into the Republican Union of Democratic Women's Organizations. The Provisional Government granted the right to vote to all adults over the age of 20. Other legislation gave women the right to practice law, to serve on juries, and to hold positions in the civil service on the same terms as men.

Some Russian women greeted these reforms with an outburst of patriotism. Maria Bochkareva, already famous as a woman warrior, formed a military unit that she called the Women's Battalion of Death. With the support of the Provisional Government, this group of about 2000 women was sent to the front to shame the men who at this point were deserting their country's failing war effort in droves. Male soldiers who were sick of war threatened and insulted the women, and 20 were lynched.

Meanwhile the Bolsheviks mobilized working-class women to oppose both the war itself and the Provisional Government that insisted on continuing it. On October 25, 1917, the Bolsheviks attacked the Provisional Government, which met at the Winter Palace in Petrograd. In the ensuing armed conflict, women fought on both sides: the Bolshevik attackers included many female fighters, and Bochkareva's battalion defended the Palace. When the Provisional Government fell and the Bolsheviks seized power, most feminist leaders—who belonged to the movement that the Bolsheviks scornfully termed "bourgeois"—were forced into exile. The future belonged to the Bolsheviks and their very different notions of women's rights and duties.

Let us return to our original question: Did the war contribute to the emancipation of women? Many historians have concluded that though it changed some aspects of women's status, the war preserved gender hierarchies: in all areas, women remained subordinate to men. The French historian Françoise Thébaud argues that the war actually brought an increased separation between women and men which she calls "the triumph of sexual division."[32] But however temporarily, women broke down many of the barriers that had traditionally defined the female sphere. Some did work that had previously been reserved for men; some enjoyed certain male prerogatives, such as personal independence and control of family income; some shared the hardships of the battle front; some took on important roles in government; some gained new rights and benefits. Above all, women had gained a new sense of membership in the national states to which they had contributed so much labor, blood, and treasure. In future years, too, the price of citizenship for women would be participation in men's hostilities, fears, and hatreds.

2
Women as Citizens in the Inter-war Democracies

At the war's end, many women as well as men hoped for peace and harmony, in the family as well as in the state. A popular symbol of peace was the woman who, forsaking her wartime job and mannish clothing, was now once again the domestic wife and nurturing mother. Amid the revelry that marked the signing of the Armistice, the British suffragist Catherine Gasquoine Hartley deplored the behavior of the "screaming girls" who greeted the returning soldiers. "In one group a woman was carrying a baby, and a tiny child dragged at the hand of another girl, crying drearily, and no one noticed. . . . Surely this squandering of Woman's gift, this failure of herself, must cease now that peace has come." [1] But many women contested this one-sided view of women's destiny. Among them was the flamboyant British activist Dora Russell. "In actual fact, a woman is as capable as a man of combining love of a mate, parenthood, and physical and intellectual work," she wrote in 1925. "If we cannot have children and remain intelligent human beings . . . then indeed our emancipation is a mockery." [2]

This chapter will focus on the European nations that lived under democratic governments during the inter-war era. This category will not include all nations that called themselves democracies. At the war's end, many new nations—including Poland, Hungary, Czechoslovakia, and Yugoslavia—were created in Eastern Europe in lands that had once belonged to the Russian and Austrian Empire. Though these nations initially adopted democratic constitutions, only one of them—Czechoslovakia—actually created a functioning democracy. In the others, democracy proved so unstable that it soon gave way to some form of authoritarian rule. In Greece and Portugal, likewise, post-war democracies failed. These nations will be included in the chapter on authoritarian and totalitarian regimes. The German state known as the Weimar Republic, though it too ultimately fell, was sufficiently stable during the years of its existence (1918–1933) to be included among the European democracies; the totalitarian Nazi regime, which came to power in 1933, will be discussed in the next chapter.

We will define a "democracy" as a state with a representative government where citizens enjoyed the basic civil rights that empowered them to form organizations and political parties, to oppose their governments' policies, to express a variety of opinions and ideas, and to make a wide range of personal choices. In some of the inter-war democracies—such as Britain, Germany, the Netherlands, the Scandinavian countries, the Spanish Republic, and Czechoslovakia—women gained the right to vote; in others, such as France, Switzerland, and Belgium, they failed to gain this right during the inter-war years. Nonetheless, with or without suffrage, women in all the countries to be discussed here exercised many other rights of citizenship—the right to organize, to express themselves on a wide range of issues, and to work for many kinds of social and political change. With or without suffrage, women were increasingly active in the public arena.

This chapter will look at the women of the inter-war democracies as politicians, social reformers, workers, housewives, mothers, and as the creators and consumers of culture. In all of these areas, women confronted conflicting and discordant definitions of femininity. An anti-feminist backlash which aimed to reverse the gains made by women not only in wartime but in the entire previous century called on women to leave politics and paid labor to men and to return to home and motherhood. Opposed to this conservative vision was the aggressively emancipated and disturbingly androgynous image of the modern woman, or the "flapper," as she was often known. Many women of this era attempted to find a middle ground between these two extremes by searching for ways to reconcile maternal and family commitments with new aspirations to career success, political activism, and individual autonomy.

Good wifehood and good motherhood: women in home and family

In 1917, the British socialist Wilma Meikle warned that the return of peace would also bring back "the Great Domestic Cant of Good Wifehood and Good Motherhood."[3] The German legal expert Camilla Jellinek observed in 1921 that "sometimes you hear people say very frankly that women should stick with their natural function, having children, and everything else is superfluous and harmful."[4] But though the cult of home and family flourished during the inter-war era, it brought no return to the past. On the contrary, inter-war views of marriage, sexuality, housework, and child-rearing were self-consciously modern and based on new developments in psychology, technology, and medicine.

The domestic culture of the inter-war era was marked by wartime trauma. Soldiers at the front had often envied civilians, including their own wives, lovers, and mothers, whose life they imagined as easy and safe. They were often suspicious about what the women might have been up to during their men's absence. And many men wondered whether women, once accustomed to independence, would return willingly to motherhood and domesticity. In the closing days of the war, women's organizations in many countries renewed their campaigns for suffrage, some of which were successful. Some pessimistic observers feared the outbreak of a "sex war" which might abolish all distinctions of gender.

Alarmed by this sinister prospect, policy-makers advocated marriage as a means of re-domesticating the female war worker, of re-socializing the

traumatized veteran, and of replacing lost population. Governments ostentatiously promoted marriage and the family. The new constitution of the Weimar
Republic provided that "marriage is the foundation of family life and of the
preservation and increase of the nation, and stands under the protection of the
constitution."[5] The constitution of the Irish Republic likewise affirmed in 1937
that "the State recognizes the Family as the natural primary and fundamental
unit group of society, and as a moral institution possessing inalienable and
imprescriptible rights."[6]

In some countries, woman voters supported a long-standing feminist goal:
the equality of husband and wife in the marital relationship. In the 1920s, all
the Scandinavian countries enacted laws that provided for almost complete legal
equality between spouses. But the modernization of marriage did not always
promote individual liberty; on the contrary, the Scandinavian laws strengthened
the power of the state by prohibiting marriage to individuals afflicted with
hereditary diseases, and even requiring some such people to be sterilized. In
France in 1938, the national legislature passed a bill that gave wives the capacity
to control their own financial affairs (such as contracts and bank accounts), to
apply for passports and to take examinations without the permission of their
husbands, and to testify in court. But it left the power to make decisions about
children to husbands. In Britain, wives had controlled their property since the
1880s, and were given equal rights of guardianship over their children in 1925.
Although the new constitutions of Germany and Czechoslovakia granted equal
rights to husbands and wives, conservative public opinion blocked any change
in the laws governing marriage.

With or without legal change, however, culture reconfigured the marital
relationship. Nineteenth-century ideas about marriage had emphasized moral
and religious duties. By contrast, the culture of the inter-war era set the tone for
the rest of the twentieth century by stressing love, romance, and companionship.
A growing body of advice literature, reinforced by countless films, novels, and
women's magazines, affirmed the emotional and sexual satisfaction of both
spouses as the chief criterion for a successful marriage. To be sure, this new
version of the marriage relationship was not egalitarian, for it allotted needs
chiefly to the husband and responsibilities chiefly to the wife. In addition to
caring for her home and children, the wife was also responsible for maintaining
a relationship which was now idealized as a life-long love affair. Advice literature
warned women that neglecting their appearance might have fatal consequences,
and urged them to do everything possible to preserve their youthful good
looks. In addition, the wife was urged to share her husband's interests in sports,
movies, and politics. And, most importantly, she must respect him as the head
of the family. Male supremacy now received a new psychological justification as
the basis for harmonious family life. If the marriage failed, psychological theories
often blamed the wife, whose desire for emancipation might have impaired her
adjustment to the feminine role.

This model of ideal marriage was far from the experience of most
married women, whose hard-working lives left them little time to cultivate
beauty and recreational interests. Nonetheless, by the 1930s a rise in the
marriage rate and a decline in the age at first marriage for both sexes indicated

that marriage had indeed become more popular, and perhaps also more rewarding. Increased life expectancy meant that spouses could anticipate a longer time together; a decrease in the average number of children per family freed energy for the marital relationship; and men and women now shared recreational activities. The British pub, once an all-male sanctuary, opened its doors to couples during this era; and new media such as the movies and the radio were enjoyed by families together. And the new, psychologically oriented discourse on marriage had its advantages for women, for they too could claim what the British feminist Dora Russell called "the right to be happy."[7] Divorce rates, still very low by contemporary standards, rose during this era.

The inter-war era's glorification of heterosexuality carried a disturbing corollary: a new stigma on same-sex relationships, particularly those of women. In the nineteenth century women had considerable freedom to form loving, same-sex attachments. Laws against homosexual conduct applied only to men. Most people did not assume that intimate relationships between women were sexual, and women who could afford to set up their own households often lived with female partners for many years or even their entire adult lives without any loss of respectability. But in the 1920s, new research into human sexuality established that women as well as men sometimes felt sexual desire for members of their own sex. The researchers, who shared their culture's concern for marital and familial stability, portrayed these women as disturbed, sick, and dangerous. The results of this scientific inquiry, which became known as sexology, had a considerable influence on public attitudes. Paradoxically, the new stereotype portrayed the lesbian as both monstrously repulsive and irresistibly seductive. Moralists and legislators warned that if allowed to associate with "normal" women, lesbians might well seduce them and alienate them from men, marriage, and child-bearing. Many called for the dismissal of women suspected of this evil tendency from jobs, such as teaching and social work, that brought them into contact with young girls. And psychologists attributed women's emotional problems, particularly those that arose in heterosexual relationships, to hidden lesbian tendencies. The influential psychoanalyst Wilhelm Stekel charged the lesbian with rejecting femininity and aspiring to be what she never could be—a man. "She wishes to dominate and is afraid to submit.... She plays the "she-man," trying to imitate the habits, qualities, dress...and even the shortcomings of men, smoking, drinking, fighting, and the like. She hates motherhood, she despises nursing, is afraid of giving birth, of labor pains, and she tries to suppress her monthly period."[8]

Even in this hostile atmosphere, many women formed lasting and stable same-sex partnerships. Among the most famous of these couples—Helene Lange and Gertrud Bäumer, and Lida Gustava Heymann and Anita Augspurg—were prominent German feminists. Their relationships were based both on personal compatibility and on common political and professional interests. When Lange, then both the editor of Germany's best-known feminist periodical, *Die Frau*, and a leading figure in several organizations, became ill, the much younger Bäumer cared for her and took over much of the work. Bäumer later became prominent both as a feminist and as a politician. The two women lived together from 1899 until Lange's death in 1930.[9] In the memoir that they wrote together, Augspurg and Heymann spoke both of their common efforts on behalf of women's rights and pacifism and of their delight in each other's company: "not only in our view of the world and our struggle for truth and freedom, but also in every aspect of daily life . . . we were in perfect harmony."[10] The couple, who met in 1896, bought themselves a country estate in Bavaria, on which they employed only female labor. They left this beautiful home in 1933, when the Nazi seizure of power forced them into exile in Switzerland. They lived together until both died in 1943. Women such as these did not regard themselves as members of an oppressed minority, but rather as a pioneering elite who were engaged in creating a new way of life for women who aspired both to personal happiness and to professional self-realization.

Like marriage and sexuality, housework too became the subject of scientific analysis. In the nineteenth century, every family that aspired to respectability had employed at least one servant. But as the supply of servants decreased in the inter-war era, engineers and designers promoted a new style of kitchen that replaced human labor with that of machines powered by electricity. Labor-saving kitchens were installed not only in the homes of the wealthy, but also in the public housing projects that were designed for working-class families. Well-lighted, technologically advanced, and hygienic, these kitchens resembled the era's modern factories on a small scale. And housework, traditionally regarded as a menial form of labor fit only for servants, was reconfigured as a skilled craft in which even an educated woman might find pleasure and fulfillment. To be sure, this modern domestic technology was available to only a small minority of inter-war housewives, and did not reach the majority of households until the 1960s.

Though some feminists may have resented this attempt to glamorize housework, many women's organizations supported it enthusiastically. Religious organizations, such as the French Feminine Civic and Social Union (*Union féminine civique et sociale*) urged married women to return to hearth and home. Large secular housewives' associations, such as the German National Union of Housewives' Associations, or the Danish Housewives' Federation, argued likewise that there was no better job for a modern, emancipated woman than full-time domesticity and motherhood. Because housewives were now expected to meet higher standards of hygiene and comfort, the introduction of labor-saving devices had the effect of increasing rather than reducing the time women spent on housework. Nonetheless, this modern version of the domestic role was popular. The number of married women who worked outside the home—which varied widely from about 30 percent in France to about 9 percent in Sweden and 10 percent in the Netherlands around 1930—declined in many countries during the 1920s.

Inter-war culture portrayed child-rearing as the married woman's most important responsibility. The long-term trend toward lowered birth rates and smaller family size transformed both the theory and the practice of motherhood. In the nineteenth century, the populations of all European countries except France had rapidly increased. But starting in the last decades of the nineteenth century, the birthrates of many Western European countries began to decline—a trend that was probably due to both material and cultural changes.

Families who lived by agriculture had benefited from their children's labor, but in cities large families could be an economic liability rather than an advantage. Legal reforms that made education compulsory and restricted child labor made childhood longer and child-rearing more expensive. Attitudes toward children changed to emphasize their unique individuality and their need for nurture and protection. All these changes produced a widespread tendency—which by the inter-war era had spread from the wealthy middle classes to the working class—to limit the number of children in order to give each child the opportunity to develop his or her potential. Between 1890 and 1933, birthrates per thousand population were cut in half: in Britain the rate declined from 30.2 to 14.4; in Germany from 35.7 to 15.7; in Norway from 30.4 to 14.7; in Sweden from 28 to 13.[11]

As in the pre-war era, governments were perturbed by falling birth rates, which they considered a threat to economic vitality and military readiness. Not only the number, but also the health and fitness—often referred to as the "quality"—of the next generation became a central public concern. As we have seen, during the First World War many governments increased their investment in medical services and other forms of assistance to infants and children. In the inter-war era, these efforts were crowned with success, for rates of infant mortality declined by more than 50 percent: in Germany from 199 deaths per thousand live births in 1901 to 68 in 1933; in France from 142 in 1901 to 66 in 1938; in the Netherlands from 149 in 1901 to 66 in 1938. Partly for this reason, many child-rearing experts shifted their emphasis from the physical health to the psychological well-being of children.

In the large body of advice literature produced by these experts, several approaches to child-rearing competed for the mother's attention. In the English-speaking world, the most influential of these was behaviorism, a psychology that was pioneered by the American child psychologist John Watson and was popularized in countless parents' manuals. Watson exhorted the mother to recognize that "almost nothing is given in heredity and practically the whole course of development of the child is due to the way I raise it."[12] He claimed that the personality was almost entirely shaped by a process of conditioning that began at birth—a process for which mothers were exclusively responsible. Watson reproached mothers for spoiling their children and insisted on rigid feeding schedules and stern discipline. Too much maternal affection, he warned, would create a self-indulgent individual who would be incapable of success in later life.

Psychoanalysis was a way of understanding the human personality that had originated before the war and first became popular among the educated public in the inter-war era. Its founder, Sigmund Freud, believed that the infant's behavior was motivated by innate subconscious drives, including chiefly the Oedipus complex: the male child's sexual desire for his mother and resulting jealousy of his father. Though his theory was different from Watson's, Freud's practical conclusion was much the same: that the mother (when not guided by experts) was a danger to her children. Too much maternal affection could prevent the child from overcoming the fatal attraction to the mother and trans-ferring his sexual interest to a more appropriate object—a process that Freud considered necessary to adult mental health. Another psychoanalytic approach to child-rearing that gained popularity, particularly on the European continent, was that of Alfred Adler, a former disciple of Freud. Adler rejected Freud's emphasis on sexual drives and identified self-assertion and the need to belong to a community as the motive forces of human behavior. But he warned that these drives too could be thwarted by an over-attentive mother or father, whose over-indulgent or anxious behavior could burden the child with an "inferiority complex."

To what degree did these theories influence mothers' behavior? Certainly, economic and social conditions encouraged individualized child-rearing. As average family size decreased, mothers had more time to watch carefully over each child's growth. Improvements in housing and the availability (for the first time) of paid vacations and family holidays encouraged parent–child interaction. And rising educational expectations and school attendance also signaled an increasingly child-centered culture. But parental behavior also varied by class. Some middle-class mothers tried hard to follow the rigid feeding schedules and other methods prescribed by the experts. For lower-class mothers, whose housing arrangements permitted little privacy, this was just too difficult—a crying baby disrupted the entire household.

Traditionally, parents had assumed that children were sexually innocent and had firmly discouraged childish curiosity about sexuality and reproduction. In the inter-war era, however, many psychologists argued that children's interest in sex was natural and that keeping them in ignorance could cause grave psychological problems that might distort their adult personalities. Sex education manuals advised parents on how to deal with an often-difficult responsibility. The British birth control reformer Marie Stopes, whose *Mother, How Was I Born?* was among the most popular of these manuals, advised parents to start their teaching early, when the child was too young to feel embarrassment, and to stress the positive side of sexuality. Questions should be answered "truly, and if possible beautifully." If properly instructed, the child would find this story "thrilling, and also solemn." [13] The French health crusader Germaine Montreuil-Straus and the Swedish birth control advocate Elise Ottesen-Jensen also advised parents to acquaint their children with the facts of life. However, other educators disagreed, fearing that early sex education would encourage immoral behavior.

Psychologists often reinforced this era's anti-feminist backlash by questioning women's abilities, even to raise their own children. But many women were also trained in psychology, and while some proved diligent disciples of their male teachers, others challenged them. Freud's disciple Karen Horney attributed maternal over-investment in children not to innate female weakness, but rather to the lack of other, more constructive outlets for the mothers' energy. Alva Myrdal, a Swedish social reformer who was trained as a teacher, likewise claimed that women whose opportunities for education and professional work had been cut off made poor mothers. The system of pre-school education that the Italian physician Maria Montessori had developed in the pre-war era became popular among inter-war feminists. Montessori insisted that the home was actually an unsuitable environment for children, whose creativity was frustrated by the need to respect their parents' prize possessions. Montessori's nursery schools, which she called "Children's Houses" (*Case dei Bambini*) offered a child-friendly environment where children could learn independently. Feminist reformers of the era approved of the Montessori schools not only for their educational philosophy, but also because they made it possible for mothers to spend some hours away from their children. These feminists asserted that mothers deserved to have lives of their own, and that the mother who was able to pursue her own interests was likely to allow her children the independence that they needed to develop into self-reliant adults. But the campaigns waged by some educators and activists to found public nursery schools gained little support from governments. Official policies encouraged mothers to stay at home—an attitude that was encouraged by the economic crises of this era.

"The ordinary right to paid work": women in education and the workforce

At the war's end, the British feminist Helena Swanwick feared that the cry of "back to the home" would be raised "whether the women have a home or not."[14] Ignoring the increase in the number of widowed or single women that had resulted from the deaths of so many men, governments and private companies ruthlessly dismissed women from their wartime jobs. But many women continued to work for a living. For some, paid work was a necessity, for the war had left many widows and shattered many women's hopes of marriage. For others, it was a choice—an opportunity to live independently, to follow a chosen vocation, or to benefit society. Amid the many economic crises of the inter-war era, women workers often faced unemployment, discrimination, and hostility.

Before the war, the largest segment of the female (as of the male) labor force in most countries had worked in agriculture, and the migration of both women and men from the countryside to the city was the greatest change in employment patterns of the inter-war era. Rural women's traditional way of life became ever more difficult to sustain. Where agriculture was modernized, small family farms were supplanted by large commercial enterprises that offered few opportunities to women. Where the family farm survived, the many women who had lost their husbands in the war found it impossible to run these farms independently. As young men migrated to the cities in search of better opportunities in industry, young women who remained in the countryside had little hope of finding marriage partners.

Landowning women attempted to preserve rural society and their own privileged position by founding organizations such as the German Association of Rural Housewives. In Britain, the Women's Institutes provided educational programs and various forms of assistance to farm women. But despite all attempts to keep them in the countryside, the majority of rural women coveted the higher wages and easier life of city dwellers. In France, the percentage of the female labor force that worked in agriculture dropped from 46 percent in 1921 to 40 percent in 1936; in Germany from 43 percent in 1925 to 38 percent in 1939.[15]

Traditionally, rural women migrating to the city had sought work in domestic service. But this, too, was a declining occupation. During the war, many women had left domestic service for factory and clerical jobs. After the war, most refused to go back to this kind of work, which they detested for its low pay, long hours, and demeaning conditions. Wealthy women complained that servants were hard to get, and some women's organizations (e.g., the German housewives' associations) tried to channel girls into service by mandating a year of domestic-science training for elementary school girls. But overall demand for domestic workers decreased, for many middle-class families had been impoverished by the war and the subsequent inflation and economic turmoil, and could no longer afford them.

Young working-class women usually preferred industrial to domestic work. Since the nineteenth century, women's industrial work had been confined to a few branches, mainly in the textile and garment industries—industries that declined in the inter-war era. But the production of chemical, electrical, paper, and many other products expanded. The manufacture of these products, often by assembly-line techniques, demanded precision, patience, and a tolerance for monotony—qualities that were associated with women workers. Many women were employed in these branches, at wage rates that were 20–50 percent less than those of men doing similar jobs. By reducing the muscle-power required for work, mechanization encouraged the hiring of women. For example, a German factory that in the pre-war years had needed 96 workers to assemble bicycle chains employed 6 women, aided by machines, to do the same task in the 1920s.

Male workers felt little solidarity with the women whom they perceived as a threat to their jobs and wages. To be sure, some male trade unions supported gender equality in principle. For example, some French unions supported women's rights, though others who still followed the nineteenth-century socialist theorist P.-J. Proudhon called on married women workers to return to the home. The programs of German labor unions that supported the Social Democratic Party demanded equal pay for equal work. In practice, however, most male union leaders claimed that women were less productive than men and thus deserved lower pay. Although many women joined labor unions, few became leaders—a difficulty that was due not just to the resistance of their male colleagues but to busy lives divided between work, children, and housework.

Nonetheless, women industrial workers made some important gains. In 1919 the International Labor Organization, an agency of the League of Nations, sponsored an International Congress of Working Women in Washington DC, which attracted trade-union women from many countries. These delegates passed a resolution calling for improved working conditions—including paid vacations and an 8-hour day—for all workers, women and men. They also advocated a compulsory maternity leave for all employed pregnant women and mothers, extending from six weeks before to six weeks after the birth and supported by insurance funding and free medical care. Maternity leaves of some kind were already required in many European countries, and the number of nations that provided benefits for at least 6 weeks rose from 12 in 1919 to 22 in 1931. But the leave was inadequately supported, for insurance funds (where they existed) usually paid only about half of the woman's already low wage. And the extra expense to employers acted as a deterrent to the hiring of women of child-bearing age.

White-collar work—including office work, retail sales, and clerical jobs in the post office and telephone and telegraph services—was the only area of female employment that expanded conspicuously in the inter-war era. White-collar work was cleaner, more dignified, and slightly better paid than domestic or industrial work. Like the industrial jobs performed by women, office work required a high degree of accuracy, tolerance of boredom, and willingness to take orders. During this era, lower-level clerical jobs rapidly lost their earlier male stereotype and were redefined as quintessentially female occupations, for which women were often qualified as much by their youth and beauty as by their skills. But men jealously guarded the higher-paying and more authoritative posts in the corporation, agency, or business for themselves, leaving women only with dead-end jobs that they were expected to leave when they married. The image of the flighty and frivolous office worker was ubiquitous in the popular media. This was highly convenient for employers, who were able to keep this large group of employees at entry-level salaries without being obliged to promote them.

An elite among women aspired to professional work, and to the independent livelihood, high status, dignity, and personal satisfaction that it promised. Access to professional work and to the academic training that it required was a traditional demand of the feminist movement to which the circumstances of the inter-war era gave a new urgency. In the nineteenth century, the daughters of the comfortable classes could often afford to pursue their interests in social reform, education, public health, or other acceptably female concerns on a volunteer basis, or with a nominal salary. But the effects of war, inflation, and post-war tax laws that reduced high incomes put an end to the security enjoyed by the upper classes and compelled the younger generation to compete for paying jobs. Moreover, many upper-class families were no longer able to assure their daughters of a suitable marriage. For example, Simone de Beauvoir—a young French woman who later became a famed author and social activist—was informed by her father that because of the family's wartime financial setbacks he could not provide the dowry that would enable her and her sister to marry within their social class, and that they would have to enter a profession.

De Beauvoir, who had always dreaded the prospect of marriage, responded to these doleful tidings with pleasure. She soon entered the University of Paris, where she passed the difficult final examination, the *Agrégation*, in 1928 at the age of 21.[16] The number of female university students, small in the pre-war era, increased in the 1920s. In 1924, French secondary schools for girls introduced curricula leading to the baccalaureate degree, which qualified successful students for university studies. And many young French women took advantage of this opportunity. In the 1920s, 17 percent of all French university students were women, and women were just under half of all students in the Paris Faculty of Letters, although they were under 8 percent of the university's law students. In Germany, the number of girls' university-preparatory schools increased, and a small group of girls were able to pass the *Abitur*, an examination that was required for university entrance. About 10 percent of all German university students in the 1920s were women. In Finland, female students constituted about a third of all those enrolled. British women were less likely than their continental counterparts to gain either secondary school or university degrees. Britain's elite universities remained male bastions. Though the universities of Oxford and Cambridge included some women's colleges, these lacked the financial resources that the well-endowed men's colleges could command. And whereas Oxford finally consented in 1920 to award university degrees to its female students, Cambridge held out until 1947. In all European countries, women who wished to work as teachers, nurses, or social workers were able to bypass universities and to qualify for their jobs by attending specialized training colleges and practical courses.

When these newly minted professionals entered the job market, their problems were even greater than those that had faced their pre-war role models. To be sure, some forms of gender discrimination were legally abolished in the war's aftermath. In Britain, the Professional Disqualification (removal) Act theoretically removed legal restrictions on women's opportunities. In Germany, new laws admitted women to areas from which they had formerly been barred, such as law and university teaching. In Germany, Sweden, Finland, and many other countries, women were given the right to equal employment opportunity in all civil service jobs, some of which required professional training. But these legal reforms availed little against the determined resistance of male professionals, who through their powerful unions, organizations, and networks did all they could to eliminate female competition for desirable positions.

Although the number of practicing female physicians increased, most were forced to enter private practice because hospitals refused to appoint them. Female university professors were rare (except in the British women's colleges); and female lawyers faced such formidable barriers to establishing a practice that most chose to work for women's organizations. Even in the so-called "helping" professions, earlier considered a distinctively female domain, women were crowded out by men. In Germany, women were 82 percent of all social workers in 1925, but by 1933 held only 67 percent of these positions. In both Germany and Britain, women's share of public-school teaching positions slightly decreased between 1920 and 1930.

The post-war backlash of the 1920s was followed by the Depression and its catastrophic consequences: rising male unemployment and explosive social conflict. Governments and labor leaders deflected men's anger toward the soft target provided by the working woman. Right-wing organizations, including some led by women, blamed employed women for the plight of unemployed breadwinners and their desperate families. Single women suspected of lesbian tendencies were often particularly vulnerable to discrimination and dismissal. In the 1920s, the German Josefine Erkens had reformed three municipal police departments by recruiting female police officers to work with women offenders, especially prostitutes. In 1930, when she held a responsible position in the police department of Hamburg, the suicide of two of her female subordinates (who were known to be close companions) provided her male colleagues with a pretext to accuse Erkens herself of having a lesbian relationship to one or both of the women. As newspapers and magazines used the sensational case to warn against appointing women to leadership positions, Erkens was forced to resign in 1933.[17]

Although aimed at all women, however, this hateful propaganda made the married working women into the greatest villain by accusing her not only of displacing a man, but also of neglecting her domestic responsibilities. Often, the working wife was caricatured as an evil vamp who sacrificed her children's welfare and her husband's masculine pride to her own taste for luxury and high living.

The married women workers who were in the most jeopardy occupied a fairly small range of positions, chiefly civil service jobs that because they usually carried the rights to lifetime tenure plus health insurance and pension benefits were considered very desirable, particularly in times of high unemployment. Even in countries where constitutions guaranteed equal access to the civil service, national and local governments passed laws limiting women's access to these privileged positions. For example, German law required female (but not male) teachers and post office workers to resign when they married and to accept a one-time payment in lieu of their pension rights. In Britain, local governments usually refused to hire married women, and a national policy passed in 1921 barred all married women from the civil service. And in Czechoslovakia, where only a few thousand women held civil service positions, the married woman with a government job nonetheless often took the blame for the crisis that had plunged so many families into poverty. Many national parliaments debated laws that required "double earners," or women civil servants whose husbands also had government jobs, to resign.

Feminist organizations, often allied with women's trade unions, valiantly defended the right of women, whether single or married, to work for a living. The Open Door Council, first founded in Britain in 1926, expanded in 1929 into the Open Door International for the Economic Emancipation of the Woman Worker. Its leader was a British pacifist and former suffrage activist, Crystal Macmillan. "Our aim is to secure an equality of status, liberty, and opportunity between men and women to enjoy the ordinary human right to paid work," stated this group's charter, which was adopted in 1929, "and to ensure that a woman shall not be denied this right, or restricted in its exercise, by reason of sex, marriage, parenthood, or childbirth."[18] Because the Open Door Council opposed all restrictions on women's work, even those designed to protect pregnant women and new mothers, it did not gain the support of the majority of feminists.

But even those who favored some protection for women workers protested wholesale dismissals on the basis of marital status alone. If the objective was to distribute work and opportunities fairly, objected the Czech feminist Mila Grimmichová, then why not also require men who had an additional source of income from land or inheritance to give up their employment?[19] In Germany, where a law requiring female "double earners" to resign was introduced into the Reichstag in 1932, the League of German Feminist Associations (*Bund Deutscher Frauenvereine*) declared that women, like men, had the right to choose the way of life that suited their talents and inclinations. "Our nation is not well served when capable workers are replaced by those who are less capable. And it is an injustice to working women not to recognize that they regard their profession not only as a means of financial support, but of giving meaning to life by the expression of their talents."[20]

In the turbulent atmosphere of the Depression years, these efforts often failed. When deserted by their socialist and trade-union allies, German feminists were forced to give up their struggle against their country's "double earner" law. In Czechoslovakia, a rightist government that took power after 1938 issued an order dismissing all married women from government jobs. In Ireland, the constitution of 1937 stated that "the state shall...endeavor to ensure that mothers shall not be obligated by economic necessity to engage in labor to the neglect of their duties in the home," and forbade the hiring or retention of married women in the civil service.[21]

However, in Belgium, the Netherlands, and Sweden, trade unions and feminist groups resisted this assault on the workplace rights of women. In Norway and Denmark, socialist women's groups persuaded the male leadership of their parties to declare solidarity with women protesting arbitrary dismissals on the basis of marital status. The most successful resistance came from women politicians and feminists in Sweden. Sweden, which was governed by a coalition of the Agrarian and Social Democratic Parties, was more stable than many other countries, and its economic crisis was less desperate. The Swedish unemployment rate in 1932 was 22 percent, compared to 43 percent in turbulent Germany. Even in this relatively favorable environment, however, opposition to "double earners" was strong; 13 parliamentary initiatives called for their dismissal between 1925 and 1931. A group of prominent intellectuals and parliamentarians succeeded not only in reversing this trend but in creating a more positive view of the married woman worker.

Alva Reimer Myrdal, who later became the best-known Swedish woman of her generation, had married the sociologist Gunnar Myrdal in 1922. After her marriage she continued her studies in the field of child psychology and worked as an educator, author, and social reformer. But the arrival of three children plunged her into a severe conflict between her commitments to maternity and to her professional interests. To find solutions to this conflict became the major purpose of her life and work. Along with Kerstin Hesselgren and Elisabeth Tamm, both members of an independent feminist group, Alva Myrdal joined a governmental Committee on the Work of Married Women in 1934. These women and their allies avoided confrontational tactics and adroitly manipulated current political concerns to address the rights and needs of women. In 1934, the Myrdals had jointly published a book entitled *Crisis in the Population Question*, which warned that the prevailing trend toward low rates of marriage and small families threatened the Swedish nation with military weakness, economic shrinkage, and cultural decay. Alva Myrdal contended that "double earner" laws hastened this trend, for young couples often needed the wages of both partners to get married and have children. She argued that the way to build population was not by discriminating against mothers, but on the contrary by assisting them by providing social services such as subsidized housing, child-care centers, and insurance benefits. In 1938, Sweden passed a law that prohibited the firing of women due to marital status or motherhood.

Though they declined in numbers and influence in the 1930s, feminist organizations developed new directions. In the pre-war era, only a minority of feminist theorists had claimed a right to combine marriage and full-time paid work. Many had agreed with the influential Ellen Key that full-time work was a waste of energies that could be more profitably absorbed by motherhood. But in the inter-war years, feminists defended married women from forced dismissal by asserting that the combination of marriage and career was an option that any woman should have the right to choose. Noting the combined effects of lengthening life spans and smaller families, some suggested that women might pursue familial and career interests in sequence. Doctor Houdré-Boursin, author of a popular French advice manual for mothers, counseled that children should be raised at home until the age of three or four, but "but when they start school, and the mother has free time during the day, then why not contribute her skills to society?"[22] This notion of a new female "life plan" combining career and motherhood would become important to the feminist movements of the late twentieth century.

"I do not believe in sexes or classes": women in politics

In countries where women had won the right to vote—Britain, the Scandinavian countries, Germany, the Netherlands, Czechoslovakia, and Spain—women appeared for the first time in legislative assemblies. Suffragists had expected that, when elected to office, women would unite across party lines to advance the rights and well-being of their sex. But female parliamentarians did not consider themselves first and foremost as "women," but rather as politicians who, like their male counterparts, supported a wide variety of political parties and positions. In the short run, therefore, women's entrance into electoral politics did more to disrupt than to strengthen feminism and gender solidarity.

In national parliaments, women gained only a token presence. German women were the most successful in national elections: in 1919, 49 women (or 9.6 percent of the total) sat in the National Assembly that met to formulate the constitution of the Weimar Republic. In subsequent elections their numbers decreased. Very few German women gained high governmental positions—the liberal feminist Gertrud Bäumer, who as an official of the Ministry of the Interior made policy on youth and education, was the most prominent. In Britain, women never constituted more than 2.4 percent of all members of parliament, and only one—Margaret Bondfield, who served as Secretary of Labor from 1929 until 1931—held a cabinet position. Despite the early enfranchisement of women in Scandinavia, very few served in parliaments during the inter-war years; in the 1920s only one, the Social Democrat Kerstin Hesselgren, was elected to the upper chamber of the Swedish Parliament (or *Riksdag*). The first woman outside the Soviet Union to be appointed to a ministerial post was Nina Bang, a socialist who served in Denmark's national parliament, the *Landsting*, from 1915 until 1928 and as Minister of Education from 1924 to 1926.

Female politicians, even those who were feminists at heart, did not wish to be seen as man-hating radicals, and many publicly rejected feminism. For example, as Minister of Education in Denmark Nina Bang supported the Social Democratic Party's opposition to feminism as a movement that distracted working-class women from the class struggle. Often, female politicians projected a traditional, domestic image. The forceful Nancy Astor, a member of the Conservative Party, claimed that she was only filling in for her husband when she gained the seat in the House of Commons that he had vacated when elevated to the House of Lords, and showed no sympathy for feminism. "I do not stand before you as a sex candidate. I do not believe in sexes or classes," she told voters. [23]

In some countries, female politicians disagreed even on the desirability of woman suffrage. In Spain, a revolution unseated the monarchy and initiated the Second Republic in 1931. Though Spanish women (apart from a few heads of families) had no right to vote, they were allowed to stand for public office, and three women were elected to a Constituent Assembly that was charged with writing a constitution for the new state. These women represented different parties: Clara Campeamor Rodriguez came from the Radical Party; Victoria Kent Siano, the Radical Socialist Party; and Margarita Nelken (a German national who could not take her seat until she became a Spanish citizen), the Socialist Party. In October of 1931, all three joined the debate on a constitutional provision that granted women the right to vote. While Campeamor favored woman suffrage, Kent Siano argued against it, claiming that women were not yet ready to exercise rights of citizenship and that their conservative voting patterns might endanger the survival of the Republic. Despite these objections, Spanish women received the right to vote in 1931.

In Switzerland, by contrast, attempts to gain the right to vote for women failed. The Swiss Association for Woman Suffrage renewed its campaign in 1918, a year when an upsurge of radical political activity threatened the stability of this very conservative country. The association (however accidental) of woman suffrage with revolution was a major setback. But Swiss suffragists kept up their struggle. In 1928, they seized the opportunity provided by a popular exhibition of women's work in Bern to stage a parade in which the most conspicuous float featured a huge cardboard snail labeled "the progress of woman suffrage in Switzerland." In the same year, a coalition of feminist and other progressive organizations circulated a petition demanding votes for women, and gained 250,000 signatures. But the national legislature nonetheless refused to act on this petition, and after 1930 a rightward trend discouraged any renewal of the suffrage campaign.

Even in countries where they were still barred from electoral politics, women greatly increased their visibility in public life. French women, whose campaign for woman suffrage had failed, nonetheless played a conspicuous role in political parties. In 1936 the Popular Front, a government composed of several left-wing political parties, recognized women's importance by appointing three to ministerial positions. Suzanne Lacore became under-secretary for child welfare; Cécile Brunschvicq under-secretary for education; and Irène Joliot-Curie under-secretary for scientific research. These women did not have a long time in office, for the Popular Front government fell in 1936.

Women found avenues for political self-expression through organizational work, journalism, and community activism. By far the largest women's organizations supported religious causes. Since the nineteenth century, both the Catholic and the Protestant churches had tried to compensate for the declining participation of lay men by encouraging women to take an active, though still subordinate, role in congregations and religious organizations. In the Catholic countries, church-sponsored women's organizations recruited members in numbers that dwarfed those of the dwindling secular feminist groups. In France, Catholic women's organizations claimed a membership of 2 million women by 1937, when the feminist National Council of French Women had only 300,000 members. The Catholic organizations favored some policies that benefited women, such as grants to large families and charitable services to poor mothers and children. But they opposed the reform of marriage laws, the distribution of birth control, the expansion of women's educational and work opportunities, and welfare benefits for the children of unmarried parents. Protestant women's groups such as the German Protestant Women's Association developed a similar social and political agenda.

In the secular political arena, right-wing women mobilized in huge numbers to support their men. In Spain, the democratic Republic of 1931 was soon threatened by a powerful right-wing opposition that was led by a fascist party, the Falange. Pilar Primo de Rivera was the sister of General José Antonio Primo de Rivera, a member of the military junta who led the Falange. She organized a female auxiliary called the Women's Section, or Sección Femenina, which soon had half a million members. Pilar Primo de Rivera proclaimed that the duty of women to the nation was to "form families ... in which they foster all that is traditional."[24] When the Falange destroyed the Republic and established the right-wing dictatorship of Francisco Franco, the Women's Section became the regime's official women's organization.

Though far less numerous than these conservatives, some women continued to identify themselves as feminists and to work for progress toward gender equality. Inter-war feminist reformers were highly pragmatic. Confrontational strategies, even had they preferred them, would have been futile amid the anti-feminist backlash that pervaded even the most progressive nations. But this political climate also offered opportunities. Among the most important policy objectives of inter-war governments was to build up military strength by encouraging marriage, high birthrates, and the rearing of a healthy and numerous younger generation. Therefore, many governments were ready and willing to enact measures to promote the well-being of mothers, children, and families. The task facing female reformers was to channel this support to families in ways that would also enhance the liberties and rights of women.

Eleanor Rathbone, a British politician who was a Member of Parliament from the Labor Party and also a leader of Britain's chief feminist organization, the National Union of Societies for Equal Citizenship, led one of the most visible of these campaigns. While serving as a social worker during the war years,

Rathbone had observed that the wives and children of servicemen benefited greatly from the dependency allowances given out by the government, and recommended the continuance of these payments in peacetime. In the 1920s, she and her political allies devised a scheme that she called first the "Endowment of Motherhood" and subsequently "Family Allowances." Rathbone claimed that motherhood was a service to the state that deserved a financial reward. After all, why should such an arduous and responsible task as motherhood be the only job that was unpaid? Therefore, she called on the state to provide a cash subsidy to all mothers of children under the age of five. Rathbone insisted that the payments must go directly to mothers, who she said were more likely than fathers to spend the money on their children. Though she regarded motherhood as a profession in itself, Rathbone did not intend to keep mothers out of the labor market—on the contrary, she emphasized that a mother should be free to spend the money on child-care services if she preferred to work outside the home.

Rathbone's proposals sparked a bitter debate among two factions within the British feminist movement. The group to which she herself belonged—which called itself the "New Feminists"—acknowledged gender difference, celebrated the distinctive gifts and values of women, and supported the remuneration of motherhood as a vital and undervalued contribution to society. But others, who split off to form the "Six Point Group," rejected the "family allowance" scheme, claiming that to define women primarily as mothers encouraged gender discrimination. Male-dominated labor unions also strenuously objected to the scheme on the grounds that it would justify wage inequality. Thus the implementation of "family allowances" in Britain would wait until after the Second World War.

However, governmental support for child-bearing and child-rearing gained greater support in France, where the legislature passed a complex program of family allowances in 1939. This program did not fulfill all the hopes of French feminists, who had argued since 1900 that governmental allowances should be payable to mothers. The French law made the father the recipient of most family subsidies though it also allotted a special subsidy to mothers who did not work outside the home.

A much more controversial political issue concerned access to contraceptive technology and to abortion. Wartime casualties and the resulting shortage of men had raised anxieties over falling birth rates and dwindling military strength to a hysterical pitch. Some countries passed laws that were intended to prevent access to any form of family limitation. In France a law of 1920—called by its opponents the "abominable law" (*loi scélérate*)—punished all those who distributed contraceptives, performed or sought abortions, or advocated these practices. Legislatures enacted similar laws in Belgium and Ireland. Opposition to contraception and abortion was reinforced in these Catholic countries by the Papal encyclical *Casti Conubii*, which Pius XI promulgated in 1930. The continuance of low birthrates in these countries showed that legal and religious prohibitions could not prevent women and couples from limiting their families.

In some Protestant countries, by contrast, birth control gained increased public acceptance. Marie Stopes, an energetic and charismatic reformer whose fame rested on her best-selling book, *Married Love* (1918), opened the first British birth control clinic in London in 1922. Stopes claimed that contraception was a means both to marital bliss and to "racial progress," or the improvement of population quality by enabling sick or defective people to avoid breeding. Both the National Union of Societies for Equal Citizenship (NUSEC), Britain's main national feminist organization, and the Socialist Workers' Birth Control Group, likewise asserted every woman's right to use contraception. In 1930 a Labour government directed public medical centers to provide birth control advice to married women.

Germany provided a still more receptive climate for the birth control crusade. Several German organizations distributed contraceptives and set up marriage counseling centers that provided advice on family planning. In 1930, German communists launched a noisy and radical campaign for the complete abolition of all laws against abortion. The campaign failed, and all German organizations that favored birth control and sex reform were forced to disband when the Nazis gained power in 1933.

The birth control movement gained some of its greatest successes in Scandinavia. The Norwegian physician Katti Anker-Møller visited Stopes' London clinic in 1922 and set up a similar facility in Oslo in 1924. Progressive Norwegians who belonged to social democratic parties and labor unions urged their governments not only to legalize the distribution of contraceptives but to subsidize clinics for working-class people who could not afford private physicians. By 1937 birth control clinics operated in 14 Norwegian cities with the support of municipal authorities, and by 1939 with that of the national government as well. Although a group of socialist women under the leadership of Thit Jensen campaigned for public birth control clinics in Denmark, the government refused its support, citing fears of population decline.

In Sweden, the socialist educator Elise Ottesen-Jensen advocated birth control, abortion rights, and sex education in public schools, and eventually founded an organization known as the National Society for Sexual Education in 1934. Ottesen-Jensen had close ties to a group of feminist parliamentarians and reformers, including Kerstin Hesselgren and Alva Myrdal. Despite concerns about falling birth rates, these women contended that banning birth control was not the right way to encourage population growth. Rather, they urged their government to enable those who truly wanted children to raise them by providing various forms of support for families. The legislative package passed by the Swedish parliament in 1938 allotted governmental funding to family planning clinics, permitted some therapeutic abortions, and provided many forms of support for families: loans for newly married couples, subsidized housing, and medical services.

Although the anti-feminist backlash of the inter-war years frustrated feminists, it could not keep women out of politics. With or without the rights to vote and to hold public office, women mobilized—often massively—to promote a wide variety of causes and parties. Disappointing the hopes of pre-war suffragists, women did not vote as a bloc, and most did not give priority to feminist issues. Partly for this reason, discrimination persisted in old and new forms, and gender equality remained a far-off goal. Yet precisely because their political behavior defied all stereotypes, including that of "feminist," the female politicians and activists of this era established a place for women in public life. Women, in fact, were citizens, whose political allegiances and passions were as diverse and unpredictable as those of men. Whatever their views on gender issues, most political leaders recognized women as a formidable political force and competed to gain their support.

"The most discussed animal in the universe": women and culture

In 1928, Virginia Woolf noted that woman was "the most discussed animal in the universe."[25] Indeed, gender was a prominent, even obsessive, theme of inter-war culture. Songs, novels, films, plays, works of visual art, and advertising reveled in images of women that were by turns hostile, disturbing, and alluring. Although print and visual media were male-dominated, women also played an increasingly active role both as producers and as consumers of culture.

Among all popular images, that of the "new woman" was the most sensational. She was usually a single young woman who, for various reasons, rejected marriage, motherhood, and domesticity and lived independently, often supporting herself by a job or career. This figure, whose fictional existence hardly reflected the conditions of most single women's lives, was less realistic than symbolic. She often embodied the various vices—frivolity, rootlessness, decadence—that artists and writers considered typical of the modern era. But though dangerous, she was fascinating. Often, she appeared as a "vamp": a sinister seductress whose voracious and freewheeling sexuality, often tinged with sadism and perversion, threatened to trap and destroy her victims.

Queen of the vamps was Monique, the heroine of *La Garçonne* (*The Bachelor Girl*), by the French novelist and sex reformer Victor Margueritte. An instant publishing sensation in 1922, the novel sold a million copies by the end of its first decade in print, and was translated into many languages.[26] Monique was an androgynous figure: a self-supporting "bachelor girl" who imitated the ways of life and moral standards of male bachelors. But a life of partying and promiscuity brought her no satisfaction. After an abortion, Monique found herself unable to conceive, and reflected sadly that "she had won nothing beside her freedom. Her work? What good was it, if it only fed her loneliness? . . . If no child was to be given to her, what was there left?"[27]

Films—among them one based on *La Garçonne*—also featured the vamp. In Germany, a center of the film industry, a popular plot recounted the fatal attraction of a gullible man to an alluring but unscrupulous woman. In *The Blue Angel*, directed by Josef von Sternberg, Marlene Dietrich played a nightclub singer who seduced a respectable, middle-aged teacher and then destroyed him by her cruelty and infidelity. The promiscuous Lulu, the heroine of *Pandora's Box*, drove her husband to suicide on their wedding night. These films often expressed anger at their wayward heroines by concluding with their violent deaths. However, these films were very popular among women, who may have regarded the female protagonists positively. After all, the vamp was a forceful woman who resisted male domination, domesticity, and dependence.

Dietrich, whose performance in *The Blue Angel* made her a star, often cultivated an androgynous image by combining a masculine top hat with sexy mesh stockings and high heels. In the 1930s, she acted with strength and independence by vocally opposing the Nazis and leaving Germany to make a new start in Hollywood.

Other writers, many of them female, portrayed women as tragic figures caught between traditional subservience and lonely emancipation. Among the characters created by the German novelist, Vicki Baum was a housewife who committed suicide in order to escape from her boring and loveless existence. The British author Katherine Mansfield depicted a young mother who was so traumatized by the experience of forced child-bearing that she could not love her baby: "She was broken, made weak, her courage was gone through child-bearing. And what made it doubly hard to bear was, she did not love her children.... No, it was as though a cold breath had chilled her through and through on each of those awful journeys; she had no warmth left to give them." [28] Some novelists created stronger and more optimistic female figures. In *Honourable Estate*, a novel by the British feminist Vera Brittain, the heroine Ruth was a happy mother and successful career woman. "Don't you see that it is just because I am better qualified than your mother and still able to go on with my work that I care for the twins so much?" Ruth remarked to her husband. [29] But few works of literature presented marriage and motherhood in such a positive light.

Novelists pictured single life as even more dreary than marriage. Unlike the glamorous "bachelor girl," single women were usually portrayed as economically insecure and emotionally unfulfilled. The protagonist of Christa Brück's *The Lives of Typists* (*Schicksale hinter Schreibmaschinen*) complained that "I earn 110 marks now and I don't have to be cold or go hungry any more. Instead, poverty has crept inside me." [30] And when single characters ventured into heterosexual relationships, they usually became pregnant—a plot device that enabled authors to comment on the controversial themes of abortion and unwed motherhood. In a novel by the German Irmgard Keun, the pregnant heroine talked back to a recalcitrant physician. "Listen, doctor, it is the height of absurdity to make a woman give birth to a child that she cannot feed. But it is even more immoral and absurd to force a woman to give birth to a child that she does not want." [31]

Virginia Woolf, the greatest woman novelist of her generation, charged that certain subjects were still off limits to the woman writer, who must hesitate to speak honestly "about the body, about the passions.... Men, reason told her, would be shocked." [32] And among these taboo subjects was that of single-sex relationships. Authors who openly portrayed homosexual relationships risked censorship or other penalties. Even in Germany, where the liberal Weimar constitution prohibited censorship on political grounds, obscenity laws limited the sale and display of material dealing with gay and lesbian life. In this repressive atmosphere, lesbian authors aimed chiefly to refute damaging stereotypes and to assert lesbians' right to love. In Anna Elisabeth Weihrauch's novel *The Scorpion*, the protagonist Myra distinguished her own high-minded love for a woman from the promiscuous relationships in which she claimed most homosexuals engaged.

The most famous British lesbian novel was Radclyffe Hall's *The Well of Loneliness*, published in 1928. The author attributed the sexual preferences of her protagonist—a woman named Stephen—to a hereditary condition that had produced a man in a woman's body. Stephen pleaded that despite her abnormal inclinations she was capable of a faithful and honorable love and was entitled to tolerance, even to respect. When the book appeared, journalists attacked it; police forces raided bookstores that sold it; and its publisher was convicted of violating obscenity laws. British lesbians, who were accustomed to being let alone, were shocked by this display of hostility.[33] But Hall was also defended by many prominent intellectuals and received thousands of letters of sympathy.

Works that dealt with androgyny and same-sex attraction more obliquely not only escaped censorship, but became popular. The heroine of Virginia Woolf's *Orlando* lived from the Elizabethan age until the 1920s. This fantastic plot permitted Woolf to comment playfully on the history of gender relationships throughout the modern age. Having begun life as a man, Orlando miraculously changed his sex halfway through the novel and became a woman. But whatever his/her sex, Orlando (who was modeled on Woolf's lover Vita Sackville-West) was a lusty and joyous figure who loved both men and women, engaged in both male and female pursuits, and challenged all conventional notions of gender. The era's fascination with androgyny was exploited by the advertising industry, which used the image of slim-hipped and broad-shouldered women dressed in mannish attire to sell a wide range of products.

The anti-feminist backlash of the inter-war era could not turn back the clock. Indeed, by its very virulence it expressed an uncomfortable awareness that the old gender order was declining. These years saw the further erosion of the nineteenth-century ideology of "separate spheres." Though women's role was still domestic, the home was no longer separated from the world of work, commerce, and politics. Indeed, the family—its material existence, reproductive patterns, stability—was a public concern, and many of the era's political controversies centered on it. Despite their limited success in electoral politics, women made a place for themselves in the public sphere. Working women faced discrimination, but the effort to expel them from labor forces failed—indeed, the defense of women's right to work, and to combine paid work and motherhood, laid the foundation for the massive transformation of the labor force that would occur in the second half of the twentieth century.

3

Women in the Authoritarian and Totalitarian States of the Inter-war Years

Vladimir Ilyich Ulyanov (better known as Lenin), the leader of the revolution that brought his party, the Bolsheviks (later called Communists), to power in Russia in 1917, had always had strong opinions on the "woman question." "Women are crushed by their domestic drudgery," he proclaimed in 1918, "and only socialism can relieve them of this drudgery." In the new socialist society created by the Russian Revolution, he promised that women would be able to become "fully free and emancipated."[1] Adolf Hitler, the head of the National Socialist (Nazi) Party that took power in Germany in 1933, had a very different view; he declared in 1934 that a woman's world must be limited to "her husband, her family, her children, her home."[2] Certainly these statements reflected broader differences in the ideologies of Soviet communism and German Nazism. However, Lenin and Hitler shared one underlying assumption: that the state and its ruling party defined the status and shaped the lives of women. Democratic governments had promoted norms of female conduct, but had allowed some space for individual preferences. Dictatorships enforced conformity.

The regimes that this chapter describes fall into two categories: authoritarian and totalitarian. These regimes arose when democracy failed to take root in many European countries after the First World War. Though they seized power in different ways, all offered strong and undivided leadership as a solution to the chaos and social conflict that attended the collapse of unstable parliamentary systems. All these governments were dictatorships that vested power in a ruling party and its leader, and denied their citizens rights to freedom of expression and assembly, personal privacy, political dissent, and many other liberties. Nonetheless, their aims and methods differed. Authoritarian regimes such as those that arose in Eastern and Southern Europe were conservative and generally aimed to preserve an existing social order: an established church, a class system, a set of national customs and traditions. Totalitarian regimes—and only Germany, the Soviet Union, and Italy fall into this category—aimed at radical change. Often showing open contempt for traditional norms and customs, these regimes mobilized their populations to pursue the utopian outcomes that their ideologies promised: a "classless society" in the Soviet Union; racially based empires in Germany and Italy. This chapter will look at the status and the everyday lives of women under the communist system of the Soviet Union, the conservative authoritarian regimes of Portugal, Poland, Hungary, Romania, Yugoslavia, and Latvia, and the Fascist and Nazi regimes in Italy and Germany.

By contrast to the women of the democracies, who despite their disadvantages had considerable freedom to organize and to work for social change, women who lived under these dictatorships had little choice but to conform to coercive policies that often regulated their entire lives, including their most intimate and private affairs. Despite their ideological differences, all of the regimes to be discussed here had all-male leadership structures, permitted women little or no say about governmental policies, and sanctioned male supremacy in public and private life. But this does not mean that the women of these states can be seen only as oppressed and silenced victims of male tyranny. On the contrary, the ruling parties realized that the support of women was essential to their continued existence, and all of them offered advancement to women who zealously promoted the state's ideology and embodied its feminine ideal. A female elite occupied conspicuous positions in organizations, the professions, and culture, and a large number of women benefited from the privileges that were allotted on the basis of racial or national identity or party membership. We shall see that these women shared responsibility with men for the many forms of injustice and persecution suffered by members of less privileged groups, including many women.

Workers and mothers: women in the Soviet Union

The policies of the Soviet Union, which was founded as a result of the Russian Revolution of 1917, originated in the utopian visions of nineteenth-century socialist thinkers. These theorists—whether Utopian or Marxist—dreamed of a new social order that would abolish capitalism, reorganize work, distribute material resources fairly, provide social services and education, and put an end to oppression and exploitation. But where did women fit into this utopia? Friedrich Engels, a companion and collaborator of Karl Marx, linked marriage as practiced in Western civilization (to which he referred as "bourgeois marriage") to the capitalist system. According to Engels, bourgeois marriage had little to do with love: it was just a way for men to exercise property rights over women and to ensure the orderly transmission of property from one genera-tion to the next. Because women's oppression arose from capitalism, only the overthrow of capitalism by a socialist revolution would emancipate them. In the socialist society, women would work for a living and would not need to marry for financial support. Spouses would have equal legal status in the marital relationship, divorce would be easy, and the state would assume many of the family's traditional functions, including most crucially the raising of children. Love would not die out under socialism—on the contrary, it would flourish as a bond between free and equal partners.

Alexandra Kollontai, an author and socialist organizer who became the leading female theorist of the new Soviet state, developed Engels' theory in a feminist direction. The socialist revolution, she promised, would not only end gender inequality, but eventually—as the state took over child-rearing and communal households replaced nuclear families—would abolish marriage, leaving both men and women free to find personal happiness in whichever relationships they chose. In her own way, Kollontai was certainly a feminist. But she denounced feminist organizations—which she claimed served only the interests of the capitalist class—and admonished working-class women to work with their male comrades to hasten the end of capitalism and build socialism.

In principle, male Bolshevik leaders were also feminists. Both Lenin and Trotsky expressed a sincere loathing of the domestic slavery in which so many working-class women passed their lives. Nonetheless, the Bolsheviks gave a lower priority to women's issues than other socialist groups, and their support was rooted in pragmatism rather than conviction. They tolerated radicals such as Kollontai chiefly in order to compete with organized women's movements—some of which advocated alliances among women across class boundaries—for the allegiance of working-class women. Moreover, the important role of women in the urban food riots that resulted in the overthrow of the Tsar in 1917 had demonstrated how effective women's political activism could be.

The Bolsheviks aimed to use, to direct, and to control women's political energies. When they assumed dictatorial power in 1917, they banned feminist and other independent women's groups along with all other non-Party organizations. Nonetheless, they insisted that women must participate along with men in the building of the new society. Under Kollontai's leadership, a Party-controlled "Women's Department" (*Zhenotdel*) dealt with issues of concern to women and organized them to work toward the goals set by the Party.

Once in power, the Bolsheviks faced the task of ruling a vast country where the devastation caused by the First World War was continued by a bloody and chaotic civil war. During the first years of the new Soviet state, from 1917 until 1922, the combined impact of war and revolution caused the breakdown of economic life, the disruption of families and communities, the emptying-out of cities, and catastrophic loss of life due to violence, famine, and privation.

This was not an auspicious time to launch a utopia. But Soviet propaganda nonetheless boasted that the new state had solved the "woman question." The Family Code of October 18, 1918, made marriage a civil contract, gave both spouses equal rights in the marriage relationship and as parents, allowed divorce at the request of either partner, and abolished alimony except for spouses who were disabled. This measure was probably motivated less by concern for gender equality than by a more important Bolshevik agenda—the destruction of the Orthodox Church, which had controlled marriage and family relationships. Another set of laws, which opened many educational and professional opportunities to women, served a practical purpose: the mobilization of female labor to rebuild a war-ravaged country. And in 1920, the Soviet Union became the first Western state to legalize abortion. Amid chaotic conditions where family ties were fragile, rape and violence ubiquitous, and contraceptives unavailable, many women had resorted to abortions, most of which had been carried out in unsanitary conditions that caused injury and death. The Soviet decree called abortion an evil that was due to the "difficult economic conditions of the present," and specified that it must be carried out in hospitals and by physicians.[3]

During the first years of the Soviet state, the women of the *Zhenotdel* worked energetically to turn ideology into reality. But they had little power to put their recommendations into effect. Appointed as Commissar for Social Welfare in 1918, Kollontai called on her fellow citizens to abolish the patriarchal family and to replace it with communal living arrangements, dining halls, laundry facilities, and child-care centers. As a first step toward these utopian goals, she established a maternity hospital, which she grandiosely named the Palace of Motherhood. In a country where the majority of people still held traditional values, such experiments aroused chiefly suspicion, and the Palace was burned down by people who alleged that by admitting unmarried mothers the hospital encouraged immorality and prostitution. Kollontai resigned in 1918, and was appointed as her country's Ambassador to Norway—a prestigious position that disguised her real loss of power and influence. And her model orphanages and child-care centers were never constructed. The many thousands of homeless and orphaned children who roamed city streets were placed in institutions that lacked basic necessities such as food and heat or in foster homes where they were valued chiefly as laborers.[4]

Zhenotdel delegates, who worked through periodic all-Soviet Women's Congresses or committees of women workers, doggedly promoted the upgrading of women's vocational skills, the advancement of women in the Party and the government, the replacement of the nuclear family by communal households, and cultural changes that would realize the official ideals of gender equality in daily life. The *Zhenotdel* even penetrated the Muslim regions of the Soviet Union, where women activists worked to enforce laws that prohibited such customs as the bride price, polygamy, and veiling.[5]

However, despite the favorable responses of many women, these efforts were unsuccessful. From 1922 until 1926, the government launched the so-called New Economic Policy—a policy that was designed to promote recovery by relaxing state regulation of the economy and allowing some profit-making enterprises. Under this new economic regime, no funds were forthcoming for the day-care centers and other social services that the government had promised. Many women were unemployed, and those who did work were consigned to unskilled and low-paying jobs and had little time or enthusiasm for political involvement. And though it enlisted an intellectual and professional elite, the revolution had done little to change the attitudes of the majority of people, who still held to traditions of male supremacy. Measures designed to help women often actually worsened their plight. The new marriage legislation inspired some local officials to declare that marriage was abolished and women were now public property, sexually available to all Party comrades—a notion that was condemned by Party leaders, but widely put into practice.[6]

The loosening of marriage ties produced no utopia of free love and personal fulfillment. On the contrary, the chief result was the disruption of marriage and an increase in the number of transitory non-marital unions, deserted wives, and abandoned children. Dismayed by these unforeseen consequences, the Party quickly retreated from its earlier enthusiasm for sexual freedom, which its leaders now condemned as "libertinism." In 1926 the Family Code was revised to recognize non-marital unions as common-law marriages, and to require spouses to pay limited alimony and child support in case of divorce or separation. Fathers of children born out of wedlock were obligated to support them—if paternity was uncertain, then several men could be called upon to contribute. Many married women fiercely opposed this latter provision, which threatened the financial security of married women and their children.[7]

In 1928, Joseph Vissarionovich Djugashvili, commonly known as Stalin, consolidated his position as the head of the Party and the state and launched the first of the Five Year Plans that were designed to bring all aspects of the economy under centralized state control. The collectivization of agriculture—whereby the state confiscated privately owned farms and incorporated them into large, state-owned collectives—was justified on grounds of efficiency. Its motivation, however, was chiefly political. Stalin classified property-owners (whom he called *kulaks*, or rich peasants) as enemies of the regime and declared that they must be "liquidated as a class." "Collectivization" was an atrocity of genocidal proportions. Millions who resisted the state's confiscation of their property were condemned to execution, exile, or imprisonment in the regime's infamous labor camps. Many more died of hunger in a famine that was due in part to the government's intentional confiscation of food supplies. Among those resisting collectivization were many women, who refused to give up their crops and livestock and to cooperate in the dispossession of their neighbors and the "socialization" of equipment. The Party took this as a pretext to abolish the *Zhenotdel* and to bring the unruly political energies of women more firmly under state control.[8]

During the Stalinist era, a totalitarian regime of repression, regimentation, and terror eradicated the last traces of revolutionary utopianism. Stalin based his view of women less on ideology than on a brutal pragmatism. First and foremost, they were a massive reserve labor force, and thus an important resource in a nation whose male population had been reduced by war. The goal of the Five Year Plans was the rapid and massive growth of heavy industry, and women were called into the labor force in record numbers. This was often not a matter of choice: inflation, a decline in men's wages, and the massive displacement of rural populations forced many women to seek employment in order to support their families. Most of these women did rough, laborious, unskilled work.[9]

Because women were such an important segment of the labor force, the government made an effort to upgrade their skills and qualifications. Factory-based training programs required women to participate. Women's educational levels also rose: according to official statistics the number of girls in primary schools rose from 2.7 million in 1924 to 8.2 million in 1932; universities were required to fill quotas of women students; and the number of women in professions such as engineering, teaching, and medicine increased rapidly. Certainly some women benefited from these opportunities. But they were not available to all; members of families that were classified as kulaks or suspected of political disloyalty were barred from higher education. Though the network of social services expanded, it was far from sufficient to meet the needs of working women, whose burdens now included both a job and housework that was made more difficult by shortages of decent housing and of all consumer goods.

In order to ensure complete compliance with its directives, the state tightened its control of the family as well as the workforce. In the mid-1930s, official policy-makers once again revised laws relating to the family, gender relations, and reproduction. As the Party newspaper *Pravda* declared, "so-called 'free love' and all disorderly sex life ... have nothing to do with either socialist principles or the ethics and practices of Soviet citizens." [10] Parents were now responsible for any crimes—including political offenses—committed by their children. Divorce became expensive and complicated, and family stability became a widely publicized norm. And, alarmed by the falling birth rates since 1917, the government abolished most legal abortions in 1936, allowing abortion only when the life or health of the mother was in danger. Even in the repressive atmosphere of the Stalinist era, many people protested openly against the cruelty of this law. "I consider that the projected law is premature, because the housing problem in our towns is a painful one," wrote one woman to the newspaper *Isvestiya*. "If the draft included an article assuring married couples who are expecting a baby of a room—that would be a different matter." [11] The government also allotted financial subsidies to large families. As birth rates rose, women's participation in educational programs (apart from higher education) declined, and they were once again relegated to unskilled jobs. [12]

In 1938, Stalin suspected that his associates were plotting against him and launched the "Great Terror"—a massive purge of the Communist Party, the army, the universities, and every other institution of Soviet society. People who were identified—often by their neighbors or co-workers—as enemies of the regime were arrested, tortured until they confessed to their alleged "crimes," and then executed or sent to the massive network of labor camps that was known as the "Gulag." The total number of people who were executed or imprisoned is uncertain—estimates for the year 1938 range from 2.5 to 18 million. Women were a minority of victims, constituting about 8 percent of the population of the Gulag by 1940, and 20 percent by 1955 (a trend that probably reflects the increase in women as a percentage of the Soviet population as a whole). In general, women's political activities were less important to the state than those of men. [13]

Among the women who were arrested were many members of the small female elite. Evgenia Semyonovna Ginzburg, a university instructor and a loyal communist, was arrested in 1937 and accused of associating with a group that supported Stalin's rival, Trotsky. Having endured months of coercive interrogation, torture, and solitary confinement, she spent 18 years shuttling among the huge and expanding network of labor camps that made up the "Gulag." These camps were not designed to kill their inmates, but many died of cold, hunger, disease, or mistreatment. In the Kolyma camp in Siberia, Ginzburg was assigned to a labor brigade:

> I only remember the ferocious wind, the forty-degree frost, the appalling weight of the pick, and the wild, irregular thumping of one's heart. . . . Back in the camp,

we received our longed-for piece of bread and soup, and were allowed half an hour in which to huddle around the stove ... After we had toiled again with our picks and spades until late in the evening, Senka (the overseer) would come ... and abuse us for not doing more. ... Finally, a night's rest, full of nightmares, and the dreaded banging of a hammer on an iron rail, which was the signal for a new day to begin.[14]

Ginzburg was released in 1956, shortly after Stalin's death in 1953.

According to such observers of Stalinism as Hannah Arendt and George Orwell, totalitarianism isolated the individual by destroying every personal relationship that might provide refuge from the unlimited power of the state. Indeed, Party propaganda exalted the state over the family. Schools and youth organizations exhorted children to imitate a boy named Pavlik Morozov, who had denounced his own father to the police for hoarding grain and was subsequently murdered by his angry neighbors. Nonetheless, the Great Terror did not destroy family loyalties. In fact, memoirs of that period report that families still discussed politics openly in the privacy of their homes, and that children seldom reported on their parents. Governmental propaganda urged wives of suspected men to divorce them, but in fact most of these women displayed great determination to find out what had happened to their husbands and to provide whatever help they could. And the fact that the family members of prisoners were usually not arrested themselves suggests that, despite its official ideology, the regime was cautious about penalizing family loyalty. Presumably, Soviet leaders feared that too much disruption of family ties might imperil the social discipline upon which the survival of the state depended.[15]

Authoritarian states

The authoritarian states of eastern and southern Europe—Poland, Hungary, Romania, Croatia, Latvia, and Portugal will be the examples considered here—boasted that they were different from the Soviet Union. In these countries, right-wing regimes denounced communism as the destroyer of religion, the family, and morality, and upheld traditional values, including those of the patriarchal family. But these governments' practice often contradicted their rhetoric. They too, mobilized women—sometimes by politicizing the home and its domestic and reproductive activities, and sometimes by encouraging women to leave the home and to join government-sponsored organizations.

All of the countries to be discussed here adopted democratic constitutions after the First World War, some of which gave women the right to vote and run for office. When these democratic governments proved too weak to survive the economic instability and political turbulence of the post-war years, right-wing groups assumed power and established one-party, dictatorial regimes. The unstable Portuguese Republic was overthrown by a general, Oliveira Salazar, in 1926. Salazar created what he called a "new state," based on Catholic religion and fascist ideology. In 1931, this state accorded the right to vote to a very limited group of women—those who had completed secondary education—and allowed women's organizations to continue their activities, although under very restrictive conditions. Under Josef Pilsudski, the dictator who ruled Poland from 1924 until his death in 1935, Polish women continued to exercise the political rights that they had gained in 1918. Literate Hungarian women, who were granted the right to vote after the First World War, continued to exercise that right under the dictatorial regime of Miklos Horthy after 1919. In Latvia, the right to vote that was accorded to women by the nation's initial democratic constitution was maintained by the regime of Karlis Ulmanis. But in Romania and Yugoslavia, also ruled by conservative and authoritarian governments, women did not gain the right to vote during the inter-war era.[16]

Quite unlike totalitarian regimes, which often aggressively overrode traditions in order to transform their societies, authoritarian regimes were conservative, basing their authority upon established institutions such as churches and aristocracies and upon long-standing national customs. Portugal's constitution was based on the Papal encyclical (a statement that the Pope sends to all Catholic congregations) *Casti Connubii*, which called on the Catholic faithful to condemn divorce and birth control and upheld male supremacy in the home. The constitution made the husband the head of the family, gave him control over its financial affairs and the education of the children, and restricted the right of couples who had celebrated a Catholic wedding to divorce.[17]

Authoritarian regimes urged women to spurn the false attractions of feminism—which they associated with communism, the decadent culture of the Western democracies, or unpopular minorities such as the Jews—and to return to their true vocation for domesticity and motherhood. Despite the flowery rhetoric that justified it, this view of women's role was basically pragmatic and driven more by economics than by ideology. Unlike the Soviet Union, where the fast pace of economic development created a need for female labor, all other European countries experienced economic crises that culminated in the Great Depression of the 1930s. Sending women back to the home was a strategy to reduce male unemployment and the social disruption that jobless men often caused. Women's organizations cooperated fully in spreading their governments' message. According to the Yugoslav Women's Association—an organization that was dominated by women of Serbian nationality—women were naturally gifted for domesticity and privileged to be financially supported by men.[18] Moreover, feminism, smoking, and drinking were harmful trends that had undermined feminine morality and national strength. The Council of Latvian Women's Organizations not only campaigned for women's rights, but also admonished women to return to domesticity, which it claimed was a traditional part of Latvian culture.[19] Similarly, the Orthodox National Society of Romanian Women promoted a view of the family that was inspired by the norms of the Orthodox Church. The more modern and forward-looking Reunion of Romanian Women urged women to base their claims to equality on their role as mothers and nurturers, rather than on the interests that they shared with men.[20]

The familial ideologies developed by these organizations served their governments' political, religious, and ethnic agendas. In Portugal, an organization knows as the Mothers' Association for National Education aimed to create a "new man" and a "new woman" to be citizens of the new Portuguese state. The organization's leaders urged women to join in a campaign to arrest the decline of the family—which was declared to be "in crisis"—and to prepare girls for their future maternal, domestic, and social duties. Portugal rewarded its female citizens in official Mothers' Day celebrations and awards to mothers of numerous families.[21] In Poland, women's organizations mobilized house-wives to defend the Christian religion through a boycott of Jewish businesses as well as through their votes: "every vote," stated a pamphlet of 1919, was an "arrow aimed against Jews and enemies of Poland."[22] The Yugoslav Women's Union also politicized the domestic sphere by admonishing wives to encourage their husbands to "work for the nation and wipe out the enemies."[23] Likewise, Croatian women—members of a nation that constituted a minority within the Serb-dominated Yugoslav state—urged housewives and mothers to rear their children to respect Croatian national culture and traditions.

Despite their official disapproval of feminism, authoritarian regimes prized the support of women, and especially of the female elite who possessed valu-able skills and educational attainments or occupied influential social posi-tions. Educated women often assumed conspicuous public roles. In Poland, Pilsudski encouraged women to serve in the national parliament, or *Sejm*. Elite Portuguese women were also highly visible as leaders of state-sponsored women's organizations such as the Portuguese Female Youth Organization (*Mocidade Portuguesa Feminina*). These leaders, many of whom were qual-ified professionals, cultivated a feminine but highly public image as volun-teers in kindergartens, youth centers, and medical services and as educators of young children and girls. Some cautiously supported feminist goals. Maria Joana Mendez-Leal, the head of the Portuguese Female Youth Organization, advoc-ated what she called "integral education," which cultivated not only domestic skills, but also physical, literary, and artistic knowledge among the daughters of the country's elite.[24] Female parliamentary deputies in Poland advocated legislation aimed at improving the status of illegitimate children and of women workers.

Educated women were often willing to support any political agenda that promised them opportunities. Hungary's territorial losses in the First World War had increased the proportion of Jews to Christians in the population and stirred up endemic anti-Semitic prejudice. In 1920, Parliament began debating a bill that would have barred women from universities in order to make room for veterans and for refugees from the territories that Hungary had lost as a result of the recent war. University administrators temporarily closed some faculties to women. But some far-right parties shifted the focus of the debate, claiming that restrictions should be placed on the enrollment of Jews rather than women. The National Association of Hungarian Women did not hesitate to appeal to anti-Semitism in order to create opportunities for its predominantly Christian members. When a new law limited the enrollment of Jews to 6 percent, but set no quota for women, Claire Tormay, the head of the National Association, supported the law "not in order to oppress the alien race, but in order to promote our own race, because we think it would be insane and suicidal on the part of the nation not to want to recruit its intelligentsia from among its own native race."[25] And in fact, the feminists' political strategy was successful: most university faculties were reopened to women in 1925 and in 1926 the Minister of Education supported their admission to the medical faculties. Thereafter, the National Association of Hungarian Women adopted an aggressively anti-Semitic stance, barring Jews from membership and admonishing supporters to vote only for Christian candidates.

In 1926, the Romanian national women's organization Astra created a group called the "Feminine and Biopolitical Subsection" which promoted eugenics, a popular science that aimed to improve the genetic quality of populations through planned breeding. Its highly educated leaders used eugenic theories to argue against "miscegenation," or interbreeding among ethnic groups, and especially between Romanians and Hungarians (an unpopular minority in Romania). They denounced Hungarian women as devious, malicious, and intent on trapping Romanian men.[26]

By comparison to totalitarian governments such as those of Germany, Italy, and the Soviet Union, authoritarian regimes had a very limited impact on the lives of women. These governments solicited the support of elite and educated women, and even allowed some to play public roles—roles that a few women eagerly accepted. But the majority of women took little interest in politics and continued in their traditional ways of life.

Right-wing totalitarianism: Germany and Italy

At first glance, the totalitarian states of Germany and Italy might seem to have had much in common with the right-wing dictatorships discussed earlier. Adolf Hitler and Benito Mussolini claimed to be the saviors of Western civilization from the menace of communism, especially as practiced in the Soviet Union. Both dictators included female emancipation among the false ideals promoted by a system that they alleged had destroyed the unity of the family, the virtue of women, and the authority of religion. Officially, the German Nazis and the Italian Fascists supported a traditional feminine ideal centered on domesticity and motherhood. But their actual policies toward women had more in common with those of the Soviet Union than with those of the authoritarian dictatorships. Though they might pay lip service to traditional values, both Hitler and Mussolini in fact aspired to overturn them and to transform gender roles and the family in accordance with their political ideologies.

Benito Mussolini was the head of the Italian Fascist Party which ruled Italy from 1922 until it was overthrown in 1943. Mussolini was a misogynist who claimed that women were born to "keep house, bear children, and plant horns"(in folklore, horns grew on the heads of husbands whose wives were unfaithful).[27] However, he was also an opportunist who adapted his program to the prevailing political climate. While rising to power, he appealed to progressive social groups who were impatient with Italy's conservative social mores. Among these were female writers, political activists, and intellectuals, to whom he promised not only the right to vote—for which women in Italy as elsewhere campaigned in the years after the First World War—but also legal and cultural changes in the family. But after he was appointed as Prime Minster in 1922, Mussolini soon came to terms with the conservative elements of Italian society—including business, industry, the Catholic Church, and the traditional, commercial, and landowning elites—that he had originally scorned. Aspiring to respectability, Mussolini abandoned his flirtation with feminism, and endorsed many traditionally patriarchal attitudes. In 1925, he proposed giving the vote only to a small number of women, and in 1926 he made the issue moot by calling a halt to all elections. Thenceforth, women—like most of their male fellow citizens—would have no real political power in Fascist Italy, which became a one-party state under Mussolini's dictatorial rule. However, this does not mean that they were excluded from politics—on the contrary, Mussolini mobilized women as well as men to serve party and state.[28]

Mussolini defined totalitarianism in a memorable phrase: "all within the state, nothing outside the state, nothing against the state." However, the Italian dictatorship was always too weak and disorganized to put this ideal into practice. Although the regime abolished all socialist and communist women's organizations, it allowed some middle-class organizations to exist until the late 1930s. As a result of the Fascist regime's Concordat (agreement) with the Catholic Church, Catholic associations, including women's groups, continued and attracted large numbers of participants.[29]

The large secular organizations created by women of the Fascist Party urged their members to break with traditional norms of conduct and to become modern women who combined "virile daring and exquisite femininity."[30] During the first years of the regime, some male Party leaders opposed the political mobilization of women. However, amid the economic crisis of the Depression, the regime remembered how useful women's volunteer work could be. The Women's Fascist Organization (*Fasci Femmenili*), founded in 1919, greatly expanded its membership among middle-class women, who accepted a new political rationale for a traditional role—providing charitable services to poor women and children. Elite women enthusiastically accepted their leader's call to be active "outside the narrow confines of the family circle."[31]

Though they proclaimed that national identity trumped all social and occupational differences, the Party's organizations accentuated class inequality. Women who worked in industry were organized into the Section of Workers and Laboring Women (*Sezione operaie e lavoratrice*), founded in 1938, which offered some training in work skills and support in applying for state benefits. Another group, the Rural Housewives (*Massaie rurale*), provided educational programs and services to farm women. The Italian Girls (*Piccole italiane*) and the Fascist Youth (*Giovane fasciste*) were the female counterparts of the male youth groups. By 1939, this organizing effort had taken on massive proportions, and about 3,180,000 women and girls were active in a Party-sponsored group.[32]

Mussolini insisted that the labor of women outside the home was damaging to both family and state—an opinion that he summed up in the slogan "*Le donne a casa!*" ("Women back to the home!"). As in other Western states, the Depression of 1930—a crisis that was easier to blame on women who had taken jobs from breadwinners than on the complicated workings of the economy— reinforced this anti-feminist agenda. Unlike such nations as Germany and the United States, which created government-sponsored work projects for the male unemployed, the Italian government addressed this problem chiefly through discriminatory measures aimed at reducing women's participation in the labor force. In 1934, a law limited the employment of women in certain trades; in 1938, another law set a quota of 10 percent on the female workforce in certain desirable white-collar jobs in governmental and private offices. Legislation also barred all women from night shifts and young women from work defined as "dangerous" and "unhealthy." These measures limited women's access to elite jobs in business, government, and industry, but had little effect on the majority of women workers who continued to work in domestic service, agriculture, or other low-level occupations. In 1938, under the influence of its German ally, Italy enacted laws that excluded Jews from public schools and universities and from jobs in the civil service and limited their right to own and manage businesses. Along with their men, Jewish women and girls suffered many forms of discrimination.[33]

The campaign to exclude women from employment also served another end—an increase in Italy's lagging birth rates. Mussolini's grandiose visions of imperial expansion depended on population increase—"I tell you that the most fundamental, essential element in the political, and therefore economic and moral, influence of a nation lies in its demographic strength," he proclaimed in 1927.[34] He insisted that Italy's population of 40 million must increase to 60 million by the middle of the twentieth century. How a country where most people already lived in poverty could feed so many extra mouths was a question that the dictator did not answer. The burden of reproductive labor fell mostly on women. New legislation stiffened penalties for abortion, banned the distribution of birth-control devices, and forbade sex education in schools. After 1938, racial laws prohibited marriages between Jews and Christians.

Along with these harsh prohibitions went measures that purported to show official concern for the welfare of mothers. A new government department, the National Agency for Mothers and Children (*Opera Nazionale Maternità e Infanzia*, or ONMI) offered services that included the provision of children's clothing, soup kitchens, and nurseries to poor mothers and children. A large number of their clients were children born out of wedlock—in some areas, one-third of all children fell into this category. Even Mussolini himself had two children by his partner, Rachele Guidi, before he made their union official in 1925. The leaders of ONMI championed the right of unmarried women to sue the fathers of their children for financial support. But the continuing power of the Catholic Church doomed this campaign to failure, and the new law obligated the state rather than fathers to support the children of unmarried parents. Along with material assistance, ONMI offered education in modern methods of infant care and child-rearing. Although Italy's rate of infant mortality declined by about 20 percent between 1922 and 1940, it still exceeded that of more prosperous countries such as France and Germany.[35]

Fascist policy-makers assumed that fathers made the decision to bear children, and awarded most government benefits to male heads of household. Along with a tax on bachelors—who were denounced as unpatriotic "deserters" of the demographic battle—the regime provided financial benefits to fathers according to the number of their dependents. However, the allowances did not greatly increase the resources at the disposal of most families, for they compensated for reductions in the income of many male industrial workers, whose working hours were shortened in 1936. Only middle-class families received generous insurance benefits as well as housing, recreational opportunities, sick leave, and other advantages.

Thus while extolling the family as a sacred and private realm, the Italian state in fact regulated even its most intimate functions. But in Italy, the state's control of private life had definite limits. Although the Catholic Church approved of the regime's natalist measures, such as the ban on birth control provision, abortion, and sex education, it prohibited governmental restrictions on child-bearing. Partly for this reason, Italy never adopted the eugenic policies—including compulsory sterilization and eugenic abortion—that were enacted not only by Nazi Germany, but by many other Western countries as well.

Adolf Hitler, the leader of the National Socialist (Nazi) Party which seized dictatorial power in Germany in 1933, scorned feminism as a subversive doctrine invented by such enemies of the state as liberals, communists, and Jews. "The slogan, 'emancipation of women' was invented by Jewish intellectuals and its content was formed by the same spirit," he proclaimed in 1933. "We do not consider it correct for the woman to interfere in the world of the man, in his main sphere. We consider it natural if these two worlds remain distinct." [36] This and similar utterances by Hitler and other leaders give the impression that the Nazis held a traditional, even conservative view of gender relations that stressed motherhood, domesticity, and feminine characteristics.[37] But in fact Nazi ideology and practice gave gender no consistent meaning, but rather defined it along with another human attribute called "race"—a lethally inexact concept that classified individuals on the basis of ethnic, religious, national, medical, or political characteristics.

After their seizure of power in 1933, the Nazis moved decisively to organize women. In 1933, most secular women's organizations, including all feminist and many civic and charitable groups were abolished, and their members integrated into an umbrella organization called the German Women's Enterprise (*Deutsches Frauenwerk*, or DFW). Church-sponsored groups were temporarily allowed to continue, but were abolished in 1938. The National Socialist Women's Association (*Nationalsozialistische Frauenschaft*, or NSF), originally designed to recruit a female Nazi elite, became a mass organization of 2.3 million members. The League of German Girls (*Bund deutscher Mädel*) included children and teenagers. But as the term "German" in their titles implied, these organizations did not include all women and girls, but excluded those of undesirable religious, ethnic, or political background.[38] Among these undesirables were Jews, those suspected of political disloyalty, and members of ethnic minorities such as the Sinti and Roma (commonly known as Gypsies).

Gertrud Scholtz-Klink, the head of the National Socialist Women's Association, flaunted the title of "leader of German women." However, neither she nor any other woman had any real decision-making power within the Nazi state, which was controlled by an all-male clique around Hitler. Herself the mother of 11 children, Scholz-Klink appealed to "the mothers of the nation...to join voluntarily in the chain of helping hands and to create a relationship of unbreakable trust among German women."[39] Nazi women's organizations defined their mission as the education of women to fulfill their responsibilities to the National Socialist State. The prime duty of the female citizen was to bear the healthy children who would ensure the future of their nation.

A National Mothers' Service (*Reichsmutterdienst*) set up "mother schools" that trained young women in household management, maternal health, and child-care. Another agency, entitled National Economy/Domestic Economy (*Hauswirtschaft/Volkswirtschaft*) offered courses in home economics, cooking, decorating, and sanitation. Carried by periodicals, brochures, and radio programs, the Party's educational message penetrated even remote rural areas. Though still portrayed as a private sphere, the home was politicized. Courses on domestic science urged the patriotic housewife to conserve food and other resources and to adapt her menus to wartime food shortages. Practical tips on child-care were combined with theoretical lessons on eugenics and racial "science" and reminders to heed the laws of heredity when choosing a life partner.

Certainly these programs were popular: By 1944, about 5 million girls and women had attended lessons on child-rearing, and about 1 million had taken cooking courses. But to what extent were these women drawn to the political, as distinct from the merely practical content of these courses? As the historian Jill Stephenson has remarked, the Nazis had less success in organizing women than men. Partly, this was because they gave women much lower priority. However, the loyalty of many women to churches and religious organization probably made them less receptive to the highly secular National Socialist ideology. Of course, Jewish women and those of other stigmatized minorities were excluded from Nazi organizations and educational offerings.[40]

In their view of women's employment, the Nazis differed little at first from most other regimes of the 1930s. As we have seen, both dictatorial and democratic governments responded to the Great Depression by urging women to give up their employment and to return to their "natural" role as wives, mothers, and homemakers. And some of the discriminatory measures enacted by the Nazis— such as "double earner" laws that forced women in civil service jobs to resign when they married—had their counterparts in other countries. Like the Italian Fascists, the Nazis set quotas upon the number of women who were admitted to universities, and forbade women to practice law or become judges—professions in which Nazis believed women would show too much compassion and sentimentality. Employment policies did not affect all women equally. A law of 1933 barred all persons of Jewish descent from all civil service jobs, exempting only veterans or the sons of veterans. Jewish women who worked in the civil service were thus more likely to lose their jobs than Jewish men. But their suffering was not due to gender, but rather due to racial discrimination.

These policies had little permanent effect on the female labor market. Although female employment figures were low during the period from 1933 to 1936, this was due more to the Depression than to the government's legal edicts. And, like those of other countries, German employment policies responded flexibly to changing circumstances. In 1936, when a massive rearmament program and the renewal of the military draft created a labor shortage rather than surplus, prohibitions on female employment were eased, and female labor-market participation rose. However, most "German" women showed no great enthusiasm for paid work, and employment figures never rose to the level of the late 1920s. Perhaps these women obeyed their leader's exhortation to stay home and have babies, or perhaps they found the available jobs unattractive.[41]

Opportunities for trained professional women—such as teachers, nurses, and social workers—improved as war approached. As of 1936, the quota on women in universities was removed, and female enrollment in fields such as science and medicine increased. At the same time the academic and professional opportunities available to educated Jewish women—who before the Nazi takeover had achieved conspicuous success in many fields—were steadily cut back by discriminatory legislation. The lucky ones were able to emigrate and to use their professional skills to support themselves and their families in exile.

Like most European governments of this era, the Nazis were obsessively worried about the falling birth rates that seemed to threaten military readiness and cultural vitality. In order to encourage marriage and child-bearing, the Nazi government offered "Marriage Loans" to newly married couples (of course, only those of acceptable racial and political background) who needed financial assistance in setting up housekeeping. When this measure was passed in 1933, it required the wife to give up her job—a provision that was later eliminated when full employment was reached and labor shortages threatened. For each child that the couple bore, a portion of the loan was forgiven. In 1936, the government also allotted monthly allowances to families who had five or more children, and later this number was reduced to three. Despite propaganda that extolled German motherhood, these measures actually benefited chiefly fathers, to whom the allowances were normally remitted.[42]

Racially and politically qualified mothers received some government-supported services, such as medical care and subsidized holidays in "recuperation homes," where they could recover from illness or exhaustion. And unmarried mothers, too, received some subsidized services. However, most mothers were eligible only for honors that carried no financial reward. The government awarded medals to mothers of large families—gold to those with eight or more children, silver to those with six or seven, and bronze to those with four or five. And the Nazis celebrated Mothers' Day with pompous ceremonies that exalted the mother who was ready to sacrifice her son for the Fatherland. Though the honor accorded to motherhood was empty, the penalties for refusing it were real. The Nazis banned the sale and distribution of contraceptives and stiffened punishments for most abortions—indeed, in wartime, the death penalty was enforced on those who sought or carried out an abortion.

Some have assumed that Nazi reproductive policies created a "mother-cult," which extolled motherhood as the natural vocation and destiny of all women. But this was far from the truth. In fact, the regime defined parenthood not as a right or a duty but as a privilege accorded to the racial elite and denied to those who were outside it. In 1933, a "Law for the Prevention of Hereditary Disease" required the compulsory sterilization of persons afflicted with a wide range of conditions that the medical science of the era classified as hereditary. In itself, this policy was not distinctive to the Nazis—in fact compulsory sterilization was legalized in many American states and in several European countries during the 1920s and 1930s. What was unique was the systematic and ruthless way in which the Nazi regime carried out this program, which by 1943 had claimed about 300,000 victims. Though some of these belonged to racial or ethnic minority groups, most were members of the "German" population—an elite group whose genetic quality the policy aimed to improve by preventing "inferior" elements from reproducing. Both men and women were sterilized, but because the female procedure was much more invasive, more women died. As another measure toward the goal of racial purification, the Nazis legalized abortion according to the "eugenic" indication—that is, in order to prevent the birth of a sick or handicapped child—while continuing to prohibit it under any other circumstances. Prisoners in concentration camps and forced laborers often suffered sterilization and coerced abortions.[43]

Whatever the suffering of "German" women, that of their Jewish fellow citizens was incomparably worse. All of the services, subsidies, and awards given to mothers and families were awarded according to racial criteria that excluded Jews as well as other persecuted minorities. While "German" families received assistance, Jewish families faced destitution. Anti-Semitic measures deprived increasing numbers of Jewish breadwinners of their employment. By 1939, Jews in Germany were no longer permitted to practice professions, to own businesses, to patronize most shops (except during restricted hours), to attend public schools and universities, and to use parks and public facilities. Moreover, as a result of the 1938 pogrom—called *Kristallnacht*, or Night of the Broken Glass, because the show windows of so many Jewish shops were broken—some Jewish men found themselves prisoners in concentration camps.

Though Jewish women were less likely than male Jews to be arrested or beaten, they carried a heavy burden. As wives of unemployed or imprisoned husbands, they often had to find a way to support their families. Forced to break out of traditional gender roles, women who had spent their lives as housewives and mothers now became the protectors of their men, who were at greater risk of violence and imprisonment. As mothers, they witnessed the suffering of their children, who were excluded from schools and vocational opportunities and exposed to persecution and violence.

In general, Jewish women were more willing to consider emigration than their husbands, who were often reluctant to give up their businesses, professional activities, and social connections to face an uncertain future in a strange land. Many women took the lead in making the arrangements and securing the documentation that would enable their families to emigrate. However, opportunities to settle in other countries were hard to find, particularly for older people. Some parents tried to save their children from persecution and disadvantage by sending them to other countries, knowing that they would probably never see them again. Women were more likely than men to stay in Germany in order to care for elderly or handicapped relatives who were not able to emigrate.[44]

Unlike the Jews, a group of more than half a million who included prominent figures in business, the professions, and the arts, the Sinti and Roma were a marginal element of Germany's population. Numbering only about 26,000, they were for the most part poor and illiterate, and partly for this reason much less is known about their fate. However, we know that Gypsy women endured many of the same hardships as their Jewish fellow citizens. Gypsies, too, were regarded as an inferior race, and excluded from some benefits that were provided to "Germans." Gypsies as well as Jews were forbidden by the Nuremberg Laws of 1935 to intermarry with "Germans." Because Gypsy men had high rates of unemployment, many were labeled "asocial" or "work-shy"—designations that could lead to imprisonment in a jail or a concentration camp. Like Jewish women, Gypsy women became the protectors of their men, and often petitioned persistently for their release. Some traveled to Berlin in order to confront the authorities in person; others badgered police officials, who often complained of the nuisance. Gypsies who could not read or speak German and did not conform to the majority culture were often labeled mentally retarded or habitual criminals and subjected to compulsory sterilization.[45]

The history of women under National Socialism is a controversial subject for historians, who often ask whether they should be regarded chiefly as victims or as perpetrators of Nazi crimes. Certainly, the Third Reich was a patriarchal society in which women as a group occupied a subordinate position and wielded no real power. We are therefore tempted to regard them as victims of a ruthlessly sexist, cruel, and exploitative form of male supremacy. However, a closer look at the historical record shows that there was no group of women to whom we might apply such a generalization. In the Third Reich, race (as the regime defined it) always took precedence over gender as a determinant of individual status.

Although Jewish and Gypsy women were certainly victims, this was not chiefly due to their gender—on the contrary, they fully shared the suffering of their men. And although some "German" women might be victimized because of their gender, their racial identity also placed them in the role of perpetrator with regard to women (and men) of other racial groups. To be sure, women had no significant role in creating the policies that mandated exclusion and persecution. But they bore some responsibility for condoning, supporting, and enforcing these policies. Some female physicians, nurses, and social workers played an essential role in compulsory sterilizations: they identified the victims, filled out the necessary forms, and performed the procedures. Some female teachers condoned or encouraged the persecution of Jewish pupils and female business owners often refused to serve Jewish customers. Leaders of women's organizations encouraged loyalty to the regime, taught its doctrines to large groups of women, and exercised social pressure on dissenters. Housewives and mothers sometimes abandoned their Jewish friends and turned a blind eye to the suffering of their neighbors. The fact that these women were following laws made by men does not relieve them of responsibility for their actions.

Women who opposed the Nazis often suffered imprisonment, exile, and even death. To name only one example, Emmy Freundlich was an Austrian socialist who in 1921 became the president of an international organization based in England, the Women's Cooperative Guild. After Hitler's seized power in neighboring Germany, Freundlich led demonstrations against Nazism and militarism in Vienna. In 1934, when she was arrested by the authoritarian Austrian government, her English colleagues used their influence to secure her release. She soon returned to Vienna but was forced to flee again in 1939, after Austria came under Nazi rule.[46]

In the early years of the twentieth century, the leaders of woman suffrage and other feminist organizations had aspired to an ideal of citizenship that combined integration and emancipation. They declared their patriotic loyalty to the national state and their determination to work alongside their male fellow citizens. But they also demanded the liberties that male citizens enjoyed, and looked forward to a happier future when both men and women would be free to live according to their preferences and convictions. Many feminists assumed that these two goals would naturally go together, and that women's admission to the rights of citizenship would be a giant step toward freedom, democracy, and social justice for all. The rise of authoritarian and totalitarian states discredited this optimistic vision. Women were, indeed, recognized as citizens of these states and integrated—though at a subordinate level—into public life. But the result was not the broadening of women's rights and liberties but rather an increase in their subservience. To be sure, the governments might urge women to leave the home and to take on new roles—as worker, as Party member, as professional. But beside these images were others—of the nurturing mother, the submissive wife, the thrifty homemaker. Only one message was consistent—that women must serve the state in any way that it might demand.

4

Women in the Second World War

The Second World War was in many ways a continuation of the First, fueled by old grievances and waged over familiar battlefields to a conclusion that the earlier conflict had foreshadowed. But in other ways—and especially as it affected gender relations—this was a new kind of war. Throughout the history of the West, warfare had been a quintessentially masculine occupation, in which women had been involved only at the margins. The First World War, both the culmination and the end of this traditional form of warfare, had separated the sexes by sending men to the battlefields and leaving most women at home. Though women played an important role as civilian workers, the war's casualties were almost exclusively male, and commemorative art and literature focused on the soldier as hero and victim. The Second World War broke down the distinction between the home and the battlefield. More civilians than soldiers died, and both men and women were involved as combatants, as workers, and as the perpetrators and victims of violence, atrocity, and genocide.

Like all momentous episodes in history, the Second World War is the center of historical debates, and no aspect of it is more controversial than its effect on gender relations. Some historians have downplayed its significance. Looking at the war's immediate effects, Penny Summerfield concluded that it "did not cause profound changes, defined in relation to equality or difference, to women as a category."[1] However, seen in the longer chronological context of the twentieth century as a whole, the war marked an essential stage in gender relations. In the wartime emergency, long-term changes in the status of women—such as the movement of wives and mothers into full-time employment and into traditionally male jobs—gained in visibility and social acceptance. And these were trends that would continue to transform the home and the workplace in the latter half of the twentieth century. This chapter will look at women in the military, on the "home front," as Holocaust victims and perpetrators, and as members of resistance movements.

Women on the battlefield

During the Second World War, many women volunteered for or were drafted into military service. However, most governments were reluctant to deploy these women in combat. Their reluctance arose less from an objective estimate of women's abilities than from ancient and powerful taboos that defined men as the fighters and women (along with land, possessions, and honor) among the things men fought for—prize assets to be defended or spoils to be seized. During the Second World War, these taboos remained in force. But although the majority of military women worked in non-combatant roles, some—and many more than in the First World War—also fought alongside men.

The extent to which belligerent nations used women in combat depended chiefly on their manpower needs. For example, the American Army Chief of Staff George C. Marshall was convinced that women were fit for some kinds of combat, and recruited members of the WAAC (Women's Auxiliary Army Corps, later Women's Army Corps) to staff a mixed unit that operated two composite anti-aircraft gun batteries and the accompanying searchlight unit. But although their commanding general, Edward W. Timberlake, praised their performance highly, Marshall put an end to the experiment, fearing to offend public opinion, which continued to oppose the use of women in combat. Having plenty of men to draw on, the U.S. Army preferred to keep women in administrative and medical positions.

The situation of Britain, then under constant attack by German bombers, was far more vulnerable. Desperate for manpower, Prime Minister Winston Churchill responded enthusiastically to the suggestion that women might help to defend the homeland in order to free up men for overseas combat. Over the course of the war, 125,000 British women were drafted into military service by the National Service Act, and 430,000 more volunteered. General Frederick Pile recruited members of the women's Auxiliary Territorial Service to serve in a mixed anti-aircraft unit, and by September of 1943, over 56,000 women belonged to such units. Churchill wrote to the Secretary of State for War that the "complex against women being involved in any kind of lethal work" must be overcome.[2] On November 21, 1941, a mixed unit shot down its first German plane.

British public opinion responded with discomfort to the unaccustomed spectacle of women in combat. The sight of men and women working and living together gave rise to lurid fears of sexual immorality. For this reason, middle-aged men (who were presumably less likely to be led astray by young women) were assigned to the units at first, but the two age-groups did not work together well. With men their own age, however, the woman formed good relationships that for the most part were not sexual, but comradely. These working relationships were vital to unit cohesion. "Loyalty means loyalty in a mixed battery, and 'devotion to duty' has a more definite meaning than it has had.... Isn't a woman's devotion more sincere and lasting than a man's?" commented a battery commander who had initially rejected the notion of commanding a mixed unit.[3] The women themselves were proud of their service: "we always seemed to be smarter than the rest of the service," recalled one, and had "acted accordingly."[4]

Though they served at home rather than overseas, the women were in harm's way. Enemy pilots often fired on anti-aircraft units, and especially on the searchlights that were tended by women. When Private J. Caveney, the first woman to be killed by enemy fire, was hit by a bomb splinter, another woman soldier replaced her "so promptly that firing was not interrupted."[5] In all, 389 British women were killed or wounded in action throughout the war. The American general Dwight D. Eisenhower was so impressed with the British women's service that he changed his mind about women in combat: "Until my experience in London, I had been opposed to the use of women in uniform. But in Great Britain I had seen them perform so magnificently in various positions, including service with anti-aircraft batteries, that I had been converted."[6]

However new it might seem, the deployment of these women was also limited by many traditional attitudes. To expose women to the risk of death—a risk they shared with all British women who lived in cities that were constantly targeted by enemy bombers—was acceptable to public opinion. But expose them to the risk of capture, which carried with it the possibility of rape, was unacceptable. Therefore, British women's combat service was limited to the defense of their homeland. And although they participated fully in almost all the duties assigned to their units, there was one that they were not allowed to perform. Women aimed and adjusted guns, but were never allowed to fire them. "We have learned to do every job in camp except fire the guns—and I bet we could do that if we were allowed," protested one woman.[7]

Of course, only a small group of British military women went into actual combat. Most performed a wide range of non-combat functions. As the work-force shortage grew more acute, the range of jobs open to women increased to include not only nursing and secretarial work, but also carpentry, telegraphy, electrical work, and many other stereotypically masculine trades. Women in the WRENS flew transport planes. The women themselves were proud of their service. "I wanted to be in on the fight," recalled one young volunteer.[8]

The British public expressed its ambivalence about women in uniform by denying them the praise that was lavished on their male counterparts. The female—but not the male—soldier gained a reputation for sexual promiscuity. A young woman who joined the WAAF (Women's Auxiliary Air Force) heard that it was popularly known as "the groundsheet for the army."[9] Although male soldiers were issued condoms to protect them from venereal disease, women were not supplied with contraceptive devices to protect them from pregnancy.[10]

The Germans were much more reluctant than the British to mobilize their women to serve in the war effort—a policy that they feared would damage the morale of armed forces and civilians alike. When the government finally ordered a female draft in 1944, the chaotic atmosphere of a country under invasion made the order impossible to enforce. However, between 65,000 and 100,000 uniformed female volunteers served in anti-aircraft units, though as in Britain they were forbidden to fire guns. Some women—including the famous Hanna Reitsch—served as test pilots, but were not deployed in combat. Though they promised to remain feminine and never to become "rough warriors," these women were proud of their performance and their good working relationships with their male comrades. Nonetheless, the public expressed its distaste for female soldiers by giving them the condescending name of "lightning girls" (*Blitzmädchen*). Military leaders overcame their stubborn resistance to training women in the use of weapons only in remote border areas, where armed women defended their homes against Soviet invaders. German women volunteers also served in many other capacities: as nurses, administrators, accountants, and laboratory workers. In 1945 Hitler created a women's military division, but this was chiefly a symbolic gesture to shame the male soldiers who were deserting their units in large numbers.[11]

Finland, which was an ally of Germany, already had a strong tradition of female auxiliary service. In Finland's war of independence against Russia in 1917 and the ensuing civil war, a militia called the Civil Guard (*Suoljeluskunta*) played a prominent role. The women's volunteer corps that supported the Civil Guard called itself the "Lottas"—a name that they derived from a patriotic poem that celebrated the valiant Lotta Svärd, who had followed her soldier husband to war. The mission of the organization was to defend "creed, home, and fatherland" by fundraising, manufacturing medical supplies and clothing, and working as cooks and nurses for their country's armed forces. The uniformed Lottas organized courses for their members in skills such as nursing, first aid, air surveillance, and signal training. By the year 1939, when the Second World War began, their membership numbered 130,000 and increased to 173,000 by 1943. During the Winter War, in which Finland resisted a Soviet invasion in 1939–1940, Lottas worked in hospitals, clothing factories, field post offices, and air-surveillance posts, and continued those services in the Continuation War that followed. Lottas were classified as non-combatants, and few carried weapons. But 145 volunteer Lottas worked in an anti-aircraft unit that defended Helsinki, and were trained in the use of both searchlights and rifles.[12]

Of all belligerent countries, the Soviet Union made by far the most extensive use of female fighters. Reeling under the shock of the massive German invasion in 1941, the Soviet Union needed to mobilize all of its resources. And its totalitarian government, which exercised tight control over all expressions of public opinion, was indifferent to its citizens' reaction to the use of women in the military. At first, military women performed the female-stereotyped jobs of cook, laundress, or nurse—jobs that often placed them on the front lines and in harm's way. Nurses came under fire when they rescued wounded men, whom they often carried on their backs or dragged to safety. In fact, casualties among women medical personnel working with military units were second only to those of the soldiers themselves.

However, from the first days of the war women also carried and used weapons. In a conflict that was not confined to the battlefield but also targeted civilians, female militias took up machine guns to defend cities such as Kiev and Odessa. Like the women soldiers of Britain, Germany, and Finland, Soviet women served in anti-aircraft units, but unlike these counterparts they also fired guns. Women also joined the partisan bands that harassed German troops throughout the countryside. By 1942, the Central Committee of the Communist Party began to recruit women into the armed forces, and by the end of the war about a million women—close to 8 percent of all combatants—had borne arms.[13]

The classic personality traits of the warrior—daring, aggression, *esprit de corps*, and a willingness to take risks—came as naturally to some women as they did to some men. Before the war, the daredevil aviatrix Marina Raskova had made a name for herself by flying from the western to the eastern boundaries of the Soviet Union, thus breaking a world record for female pilots. For this exploit, she received the medal of a Hero of the Soviet Union. In 1941, she used her prestige to persuade Stalin to authorize three all-woman regiments of flyers, whose recruitment and training she supervised. In addition to women pilots, these units included female mechanics, armament fitters, and other personnel. The only aircraft available to these women were obsolete bi-planes that weighed less than a ton, could carry only two bombs, and were made chiefly of wood and fabric so that they easily caught fire. Parachutes were not available until 1944. In these rickety and dangerous planes, the women flew more than 24,000 bombing missions and dropped a total of 23,000 tons of bombs.

Particularly in nighttime bombing missions over the German front lines, these women aviators were highly effective. Lieutenant Galina Pavlovna Brok-Beltsova recalled that most of the women pilots were about 20 years old, and if they survived until 23 they were termed the "old ladies."[14] For months, one regiment flew 15–18 missions a night. Beltsova recounted how, night after night, she and her comrades destroyed the barracks of the German soldiers, who ran out in their underwear cursing the "night witches (*Nachthexen*)."[15] Women pilots earned 23 "Hero of the Soviet Union" medals and many other honors.

One might expect that these women who had displayed so much patriotism and martial valor would have been widely admired. But sadly, they received chiefly insults. In the Soviet armed forces, many women faced sexual harassment and rape. Among the general public, aversion to the very notion of a woman fighter expressed itself through negative and sexualized stereotypes. Women who had sexual relationships with men at the front were called by the demeaning name of "campaign wife." No similar epithet was applied to the men who engaged in these liaisons. So widely were military women suspected of being nothing more than prostitutes that many feared to appear in public in their uniforms. Official propaganda lionized the male soldier and cast women in the reassuringly familiar roles of faithful wives, devoted mothers, and suffering victims of German atrocities.[16]

The insulting treatment that women soldiers in all countries encountered showed that many people found the sight of a woman in arms profoundly disturbing. But however seemingly incongruous, the deployment of women in combat was fully in the logic of modern warfare, in which the use of mechanized weapons often required more intelligence and skill than physical strength. It was also consistent with modern women's own aspirations to share both the opportunities and the responsibilities of men—aspirations that some fulfilled through military service. In the years following the Second World War, public attitudes toward women in the armed forces changed, slowly but surely, from opposition to acceptance.

Women in civilian life

During the First World War, the term "home front" was commonly used to refer to civilian participation in the war effort. The term acknowledged the contribution of civilians while at the same time emphasizing the distance between home and battlefield. Though this term was still used during the Second World War, it lost much of its original meaning. Because victory depended as much on destroying the enemy's factories, railroads, and cities as on military success, traditional restraints on the treatment of non-combatants disappeared. In many belligerent countries, civilians no longer lived in safety, but in fact were deliberately targeted. In this war more than ever before, women as well as men were exposed to terror, violence, and death.[17]

During the depression that had immediately preceded the war, attitudes toward married women in paid work were overwhelmingly negative and most governments—both democratic and totalitarian—declared their intention to keep them out of the workforce. Even in the Soviet Union, governmental propaganda of the 1930s had often extolled the housewife and mother. But these norms were highly flexible and could be modified instantly when wartime conditions called for female labor. All belligerent nations mobilized women for work in war-related branches of the economy, but the extent and success of these efforts differed from country to country.

When war began in 1939, the British government called on women to volunteer but at first avoided any form of compulsion. In fact, as many industries that had employed large number of women shifted to war production, female unemployment actually increased. But by 1941 Ernest Bevin, the British Minister of Labour, called upon all women aged 19–40 to register their occupations with their local Employment Exchanges and to be available for compulsory labor if necessary. By 1942, the upper age limit was raised to 45 and by 1943 to 50. In the same year, the Employment of Women Order provided that single women between the ages of 20 and 30 could be employed only through these Exchanges, which directed them into war-related jobs, and by 1943 this group was enlarged to include those up to the age of 40. Therefore, many women were subject to a form of military service, and many others volunteered.

The participation of women in war-related industries increased dramatically. The number of women engineers rose from 97,000 in 1939 to 602,000 in 1943, and the percentage of women in such formally all-male branches as the electrical and chemical industries, transport, electrical work, and shipbuilding climbed from 14 percent in 1939 to 34 percent in 1943.[18] The percentage of all females 14–59 in the workforce, which in 1934 had stood at 34.2, had reached 44.5 percent by 1943. Educated women were directed into white-collar jobs, a category that also grew considerably.[19]

But although some assumptions about women's work had changed, others had remained much the same. British feminists insisted that the women workers must receive pay that was equal to that of the men they replaced. Labor unions that wished to preserve their male members' high wages against cheap female competition supported this demand. However, employers found many ways to get around it. Workers who did a job that had "commonly" been done by women before the war—even in cases where they were replacing men—were held not to deserve a raise to the male wage level. Similarly, a process called "dilution" allotted a lower wage to many women workers because they were supposedly less productive and in need of more supervision than the men they replaced. In 1943, women in the Rolls Royce plant at Hillington objected to receiving a "women's wage" for exactly the same work for which the men they had replaced had received a "male wage," but even a week-long strike did not get them a pay raise. In general, women war workers worked for 50–70 percent of the male wage.[20]

In theory, Germany already had a system of conscription that could have provided the basis for the efficient mobilization of women. In 1939 a year's "labor service" for young women in agriculture or domestic work was made compulsory. When the war began, some government officials were strongly in favor of conscripting women into war-related industries, but others advised against it. Hitler himself was exceedingly reluctant to subject women (of course, only those of the elite "German" nationality) to any form of compulsion—a reluctance that was dictated by both ideological principle and public-relations strategy. Nazi ideology admonished woman citizens to produce and care for large families, and Hitler and his advisors feared that the drafting of women might make them more reluctant to have children. Remembering the collapse of civilian and military morale at the end of the First World War, they were also afraid to enact any measure that might cause discontent among the fighting forces or their families. As a result, it was not until 1943 that a Law for the Defense of the Reich required the conscription of all women between the ages of 17 and 45 for labor, with exemptions for those who were pregnant or had one child under six or two or more under 14 years of age.

Though reluctant to conscript women, the German government urged patriotic women to enter war jobs voluntarily. This effort seems to have failed, for the rate of female participation in the German labor force rose by only about 1 percent during the period from 1939 until 1943. Why did this totalitarian state have so much less success in harnessing the labor of women than democratic countries such as Britain and the United States? In part, it was because of the Nazi state's inefficiency—several agencies competed to organize women workers and the campaign was never well coordinated, allowing many women to escape conscription. Governmental propaganda urged women to volunteer, but the message did not address them as individuals, but as faithful wives and mothers working to support their men. By contrast to American propaganda in which a muscular "Rosie the Riveter" affirmed that "we can do it!" German propaganda stressed chiefly sacrifice and submission to a government that in the later years of the war was fast losing its credibility.[21]

For whatever reason, the Nazi government did not succeed in finding enough German women to replace the men who were called into the armed forces. It therefore recruited foreigners (both men and women) from areas under German occupation. Some of these were volunteers but most were forced laborers who had been kidnapped from their countries of origin and were often imprisoned under atrocious conditions. The growing population of the concentration camps, ghettos, and extermination camps—including Auschwitz, which provided labor for the chemical firm I.G. Farben—also worked for the German war effort.[22]

In countries that were allied with Germany and under German occupation, women were also mobilized for wartime work. But due to these regimes' ideological opposition to the waged work of married women, this mobilization was relatively slow and ineffective. In France, the Vichy regime—a wartime government that collaborated with the German conquerors—began to reverse policies that limited married women's labor in 1942, but mobilized all women aged 18 to 45 only in 1944, when the war was almost over. Some young, unmarried French women volunteered or were forced to do war-related work in Germany. Mussolini's Italy, where policies designed to keep women out of the workforce had been in force since the 1920s, suddenly reversed these policies in 1940, and the participation of women in industrial jobs and in public administration increased.[23]

In the Soviet Union there was no room for individual choice or preference, and no need for artful propaganda to lure women into the workforce. The need to defend the homeland was only too apparent, and though Stalin's brutal regime was not popular, people rallied to it in this time of crisis. The entire population was mobilized, and there was little difference between civilian and military service. A law passed in December, 1941, decreed that anyone who was absent without leave from a war-related job was liable to five to eight years in prison, and by 1943 workers on railways, telegraph services, and water transportation were made subject to similar regulations. Women worked at all jobs, including mining, railroad work, and heavy industry. In the effort to transfer industrial facilities to the east away from the war zone, women worked 12- to 14-hour shifts in freezing weather, sometimes sheltered only by tents or caves. "I did not want to go back home," wrote a woman who worked at gathering firewood. "I was cold and hungry, but it was for the front, for victory."[24]

Soviet women also took over the responsibility of feeding the country. By 1945, 91.7 percent of the agricultural workforce was female. Farm workers were chiefly older women and mothers of small children, for young and childless women were placed in factories or in the armed forces. Because most tractors, horses, and other equipment had been requisitioned by the armed forces, farm work was backbreaking, and many women pulled their own plows. Still worse were the conditions endured by the inmates in the huge network of forced-labor camps, whose labor was also used to support the war effort.[25]

In all of the belligerent countries except the Soviet Union, where Stalin's massive program of industrialization had already brought both married and single women into the labor market in the 1930s, wartime demands for labor changed the composition of the female workforce. Since the Industrial Revolution had removed most paid work from the home to a factory or other workplace, the full-time woman wage worker had typically been young and single. But now, women who were or had been married entered the workforce in large numbers.[26]

Child-care, formerly needed by only a small minority of women workers, now became a much more widespread concern. The German government prided itself on providing child-care. Women's organizations opened "harvest kindergartens" for the children of farm workers, and the Labor Service also sent young girls into families to help care for children. By 1944, 32,000 German day nurseries enrolled 1,200,000 children.[27] The Soviet Union, which had developed a network of day nurseries in the 1930s, expanded its capacity to care for 1,500,000 children by 1945.[28] By contrast the government of Britain was more hesitant to offend public opinion, which still disapproved of the employment of married women, by encouraging mothers to work outside the home. The Ministries of Health and of Labor cooperated to assist local governments in setting up nurseries where they were needed. But their hours were often insufficient to accommodate industrial shifts and their capacity was inadequate—only about 25 percent of the children who needed day-care could be cared for.[29]

Women adjusted to this extra labor while also enduring overwhelming stress. Families were separated as men went off to war. In France, which had surrendered shortly after the German invasion of 1940, the loss of life was considerably less than in the First World War, but many men were taken prisoners and remained in captivity for the duration of the war. Their wives received a small government allowance, but most still had to find work to survive. Under the terms of the surrender the French government was committed to supply Germany with food, machinery, coal, and other kinds of equipment. Because of the resulting shortages, finding food and fuel was often difficult, and malnutrition weakened adults and stunted the growth of children. In Britain, some foodstuffs were also rationed, and a major complaint of married women who worked was that due to long shifts they had no opportunity to shop for such food as was available. Employers objected that these women often left work without permission to shop.

But the hardships of women in Western Europe were as nothing compared to those that their counterparts in the Soviet Union were forced to undergo. Not surprisingly, the agricultural output that was produced by the few women left in the countryside was inadequate to meet the needs of the workforce. Most wartime workers lacked adequate nutrition and sufficient clothing—only those who worked in heavy industry received sufficient rations to stay healthy. During the three-year siege of Leningrad, the city's government tried to distribute rations fairly (of course, making exceptions for privileged Party officials). Still, about a million people died, mostly from malnutrition and hunger-related diseases. A mother named Elena Kovicheva took her baby to a pediatric clinic for a three and one-half ounce daily ration of soy milk, but this was not enough and Kovicheva watched helplessly as the child weakened and died.[30]

Hunger, shortages, and family separation are of course common wartime hardships. But this war's impact on civilian populations brought some new hardships as well. During the First World War, children had suffered from cold and hunger, but they had shared this suffering with their mothers. During the Second World War, governments that feared widespread loss of life from bombing raids evacuated civilians from cities to safer areas. In Germany, mothers and children were usually evacuated together, but British children were often sent to live with foster families while their mothers stayed behind in the cities— a policy that inflicted great misery on mothers and children alike. In Britain, the psychiatrists Anna Freud, Dorothy Burlingame, and John Bowlby saw the devastating impact of this experience upon young evacuees' mental health, and concluded that of all the misfortunes that could befall children in wartime, separation from their mothers was the most traumatic. This new appreciation of the importance of the mother–child bond would exert an important influence on post-war psychological theories and family formation.[31]

Even in these catastrophic conditions, women struggled to maintain a minimum of sociability and family cohesion and to find some relief from anxiety and overwork. Religious services, family gatherings, and cultural events such as plays and concerts provided consolation and a reminder of better days. But as in the First World War, women who sought recreation met with disapproval. Everywhere, the separation of married couples raised the disconcerting prospect of wives' infidelity, marital breakdown, and sexual promiscuity. In France, the Vichy government promoted a domestic and conservative ideal of femininity and cracked down on sexual immorality. In France and Germany, abortion became a crime against "state security" that was punishable by death. In Britain, the sight of women sitting alone in pubs reinforced a general fear of moral and family breakdown. In fact, these fears were exaggerated; though births to unmarried British women increased during wartime, this was due less to any change in sexual behavior than to the postponement of many marriages due to the men's absence on military service.[32]

Among the many forms of suffering to which civilians were subject, the worst was the bombing raids that destroyed cities and killed many hundreds of thousands. From September of 1940 until May of 1941, the German Air Force (*Luftwaffe*) bombed Britain, first aiming chiefly at military targets but then shifting its focus to cities, with the purpose of terrifying and demoralizing civilians. In London, people sought shelter in subway stations and in their own homes. A woman named Kathleen Brockington recalled that her family often took refuge under their sturdy dining room table. But when the house took a direct hit, she had no time to get under the table: "There was a tremendous bang and I ducked. All the windows came in and a couple of walls . . . and there was incredible smoke everywhere." In her neighborhood, she reported that about 50 houses were damaged, though no one died.[33] In all, about 40,500 people died in London during the eight months of the "Blitz," and the majority were women and children. About 70,000 women served as firefighters in London during the bombing raids.

Allied air forces retaliated by bombing German cities, also purposely targeting civilians. A woman in Duisburg recalled that, at the sound of the air-raid siren, "My sister and I put our babies into their carriages and ran with my father to the bunker. Many phosphorus bombs were dropped and everywhere houses were in flames. . . . Finally, I took my baby out of the carriage and ran on with him in my arms. By the time we reached the bunker, bombs were falling on all sides. I was completely exhausted and said I could never go through this again."[34] On February 13, 1945, the bombing of Dresden created a firestorm, in which the setting of many large fires at once heated the air above them and created a burning wind that destroyed everything in its path. Margaret Dreyer, one of the few survivors, remembered a woman carrying a baby. "She runs, she falls, and the child flies in an arc into the fire."[35] According to some estimates, 40,000 people died in Dresden in that one night.

Women and the Holocaust

The war aims of the Nazis can be summed up in the phrase "race and space." They aimed to defeat their enemies, to dominate Europe, and to make room for expansion of the German people into the vast territory of the Soviet Union. The racial "cleansing" of this space was an integral part of this plan. Hitler had declared that the Jews were the eternal enemies of the German people. In 1939, he had accused the Jews of starting the war and of other crimes, and vowed to annihilate them. Though in 1939 the Nazis may as yet have had no specific plan for achieving this end, they certainly aimed to rid the German Empire of its Jewish population in one way or another. The Second World War, and particularly the invasion of the Soviet Union in 1941, provided the context in which this fantasy could become reality.

Victims of the genocide that we now call the Holocaust included people of all ages, many nationalities, all social classes, many ethnic groups and, of course, both sexes. Why, then, does this story belong in a history of women and gender? Many historians claim that any reference to gender differences among Holocaust victims is inappropriate, and even profanes the memory of the dead and their common suffering. But others have insisted that gender issues are central to our understanding of the Holocaust and of other genocide. For what exactly differentiates genocide, a crime distinctive to the twentieth century, from the other episodes of massacre that have occurred throughout history? The main difference is in the scope and purpose of the killing. The goal of conventional military actions is to destroy the enemy's will and ability to fight, and thus they focus on combatants who are chiefly men—if women and children are killed, it is as a result of combat and its repercussions. But genocide aims to wipe an entire people off the face of the earth, and therefore makes no distinction of age, gender, or military status. In fact women, upon whose reproductive power the future of any population depends, are often specifically targeted.[36]

The first act of genocide committed by the Nazi state was the so-called "euthanasia" program, directed against the ill and handicapped. "Euthanasia"—which usually means a merciful, and sometimes a chosen death—was a euphemism for the murder of many thousands of people whom Hitler and his advisors considered a drain on the nation's resources. During the years from 1939 to 1941, the government ordered hospitals, nursing homes, and asylums for the mentally ill to identify patients that they considered incurable. Medical personnel then transported these patients to fake clinics which were actually killing centers equipped with gas chambers and crematoria. Of these 70,000 victims, an unknown percentage were girls and women. Among them was Helene Melanie Lebel, a native of Vienna who at the age of 19 began to show symptoms of schizophrenia. In 1936, she suffered a mental breakdown and was placed in a psychiatric hospital. After the Germans annexed Austria in 1938, Lebel was confined in the hospital and not allowed to come home on leave even though her health had improved. In 1940, her parents received the information that she had been transferred to another hospital. In fact, Lebel was taken to a converted prison in Germany, where she was murdered in a gas chamber designed to look like a shower room.[37] In 1941, the "euthanasia" program was temporarily put on hold in Germany due to popular protests led by some prominent religious leaders, but the killing of the sick and handicapped continued in territories under German occupation.

When the Nazis invaded Poland, they cleared wide areas of their population in order to make room for German settlement. Driven from their villages, Jews were confined in enclosed sections of large cities called "ghettos," which were created throughout German-occupied Eastern Europe. The Jews of the ghettos, who performed forced labor for the German armed forces, died by the thousand from hunger and disease. The transition from persecution to genocide occurred sometime during the summer of 1941, when Germany invaded the Soviet Union. Special police squads euphemistically called "Special Action Groups" (*Einsatzgruppen*) followed close behind the front. In an action that was officially defined as a police measure against partisans and communist functionaries, these groups engaged in a series of mass outdoor shootings in which a total of about 2 million people—most of whom were Jewish civilians—were murdered. At first, these squads seemed unsure of their orders: some included women and children in their operations, and some did not. But by the end of the summer, they regularly killed women and children along with men.

The transition to total genocide was one that Heinrich Himmler, head of the SS (*Schutzstaffeln*, or political police), admitted had been difficult. "We came to the question: what about the women and children?" reflected Himmler, who took the lead in planning the extermination of the European Jews and other groups. "I did not regard myself as justified in exterminating the men ... while letting avengers in the shape of the children ... grow up. The difficult decision had to be made to make this people disappear from the earth." [38] The change in the method of killing from outdoor shootings to gas chambers began with the construction of the first extermination camp in Belzec, Poland, in the fall of 1940. Killing centers such as Belzec, Sobibor, Treblinka, Auschwitz, and Maidanek (the latter two were also labor camps) provided more efficient, cheaper and "cleaner" way of killing women and children—a task that even the most hardened killers sometimes found upsetting. During the years 1942–1944, millions of Jews from all over German-occupied Europe were transported to these and other camps. Among the other inmates were Gypsies (Sinti and Roma), male homosexuals, prisoners of war, political dissidents, Jehovah's Witnesses, and criminals.

Gender difference shaped not only the perpetrators' choice of victims, but also their fate. This is not to say that one gender suffered more than the other (for who can measure suffering?) but merely to point out, in the words of the historian Mary Felstiner, that "along the stations toward extinction ... each gender lived its own journey." [39] Although reliable statistics are lacking, it is likely that among Jews in Western Europe, especially Germany and Austria, more women were deported to death camps than men. Young people were more likely to emigrate, and women made up a disproportionate number of the elderly. In addition, women often remained to care for elderly relatives who could not emigrate, and thus exposed themselves to danger. The German Jewish physician Lucie Adelsberger declined the offer of a faculty position at Harvard in 1933 in order to stay with her paralyzed mother, who could not have obtained an exit visa. At one point, she considered ending her mother's suffering by euthanasia, but decided against it. "I, who had spent her whole life struggling to save each and every human life, was I supposed to kill my mother, the person most dear to me in all the world?" Adelsberger was deported to Auschwitz, and was among the few who survived to tell her story.[40] Among German and Austrian homosexuals, gender had a decisive influence, for only male homosexual actions were defined as criminal, and therefore only males were imprisoned specifically for these offences. Women known or thought to be lesbians might sometimes come under suspicion as non-conformists, and were therefore vulnerable to arrest and imprisonment.

Among the large Jewish populations confined in the ghettos of Eastern Europe some traditional gender roles and behaviors changed, but others persisted. The Nazi authorities appointed Jewish community leaders to positions of authority in the so-called "Jewish Councils," which were responsible for enforcing German policies in the ghettos. With only one exception, all of these leaders were men.[41] Women's employment patterns differed. In the Lodz ghetto, anyone who did not work was classified by the German administration as "superfluous," and thus subject to deportation and death. Almost all women worked and by 1944, 60 percent of the ghetto's labor force was female. In the Warsaw Ghetto, however, work was scarce, and many women and men were unemployed.

Whether or not they worked outside the home, women took on the major responsibility for providing for their families, and sometimes for other people who were desperately in need. Food rations for ghetto dwellers were sometimes as low as 300 calories per day. In order to supplement this inadequate diet, women resorted to trade, barter, and smuggling. Traditional female knowledge of hygiene and food preparation helped families to survive. Many women deprived themselves of food in order to feed their husbands and children. David Sierakowiak, an inhabitant of the Lodz ghetto, wrote in his diary that before she boarded the train to Auschwitz, his mother admitted that "she had given her life by lending and giving away provisions, but she admitted it with such a bitter smile that I could see that she didn't regret her conduct at all." [42] But despite their reputation for self-sacrifice, women (probably due to their lower average calorie requirement and other biological advantages) often survived longer under these conditions than men. In 1942, for example, 7172 female inhabitants and 12,084 male inhabitants of the Lodz ghetto died, probably mostly from hunger and hunger-related illnesses. Women's advantage was only short-term, for in 1944 all remaining inhabitants were deported to their death.[43]

The Nazis believed firmly in sex segregation, and organized almost all their institutions accordingly. Concentration camps were no exception. There were many different kinds of camps: labor camps in which inmates were forced to work under conditions that were often fatal; death camps (Belzec, Treblinka, Sobibor) where almost all inmates were killed upon arrival; and camps such as Auschwitz and Maidanek which served the dual purpose of industrial production and of mass extermination. In all of these, most Jewish inmates were separated by sex upon arrival, and remained separate throughout their imprisonment. Sometimes, the mere fact of being a woman, and especially a mother, was fatal. On the arrival ramp at Auschwitz, camp physicians ordered small children to accompany their mothers, and both mothers and children went immediately to the gas chambers. The fathers might be spared for a while if they were fit for work. Both male and female prisoners were forced to strip naked, their hair was shaved, and they were issued camp clothing. This procedure was often more traumatic for women because it was carried out under the brutal gaze of men. Similarly, the consequences of starvation and overwork—which caused the cessation of menstrual periods—inflicted a distinctive form of psychological suffering on women, who feared the total loss of their fertility.

Women who were pregnant faced the prospect that both they and their babies would be killed. Many opted for secret abortions, which were carried out by fellow prisoners with medical training. The Hungarian gynecologist Gisella Perl, who was deported to Auschwitz in 1944, recalled how she would often kill babies who were born alive in order to save the mothers. "I took the warm little body in my hands, kissed the smooth face . . . then strangled him and buried his body under a mountain of corpses waiting to be cremated."[44]

In order to reconstruct women's everyday life in the camps, we must depend upon the written and oral testimony of survivors. And these are often difficult to interpret, for survivors may not have been typical prisoners—after all, most prisoners died—and, like any other narrators, they selected the events that they chose to recount. Women's memoirs often differ in tone and emphasis from those of men. Whereas famous male memoirists such as the Italian Primo Levi emphasize the individual's struggle to survive, women stress solidarity, friendship, and mutual aid.[45] Lucie Adelsberger tells us about the two orphaned girls whom she mothered and who formed her camp "family."[46] Ruth Kluger and Judith Magyar Isaacson, both of whom were imprisoned along with their mothers, attribute their survival partly to the support that came from family relationships (though these were often problematic as well).[47] Charlotte Delbo, a French resistance fighter who was sent to Auschwitz, remembered her friend Lulu, who when Delbo had collapsed into tears on a work detail shielded her from the sight of the overseer (or *kapo*). "Now I no longer know why I am crying when Lulu suddenly pulls me: 'That's enough now! Back to work! Here she comes!' She says it so kindly that I am not ashamed of having cried. It's as though I had wept against my mother's breast."[48]

The feminist scholar Joan Ringelheim asks whether these memories were shaped by real differences in experience or rather by the narrators' own culturally influenced attitudes, which stereotyped men as competitive strivers and women as compassionate nurturers.[49] The image of women prisoners as typically more kind and compassionate than man may well be false. Women as well as men took advantage of the opportunities that the camp system offered to gain advantages for themselves at the expense of others.

But among women as among men, there were also a few heroes. To give only one example: Friedl Dicker Brandeis (1898–1944) was a painter from Prague who in 1942 was deported to Terezin, a ghetto where conditions were slightly better than in many other concentration camps. Brandeis taught an art class as part of an educational program organized for the many children who were imprisoned along with their parents. She searched tirelessly for scrap paper, pencils, paint, and other materials that were scarce or unavailable. Neither Brandeis nor the children lived much longer—all of them were deported to Auschwitz in 1944—but the children's pictures, which were accidentally preserved, testify to the strength of the human potential for creativity even amid hunger, suffering, and death.

The Nazis also claimed that Gypsies (Sinti and Roma) were genetically inferior and prone to "asocial" behavior (i.e., conduct that did not conform to the norms of the dominant culture). Many Gypsy men and women were among the victims of the mass shootings on the Soviet front in 1941, and many others were imprisoned in ghettos and concentration camps. However, others were able to escape death because in practice the Nazi authorities targeted chiefly Gypsies who led a traditional nomadic life, while settled (so-called "socially adjusted" Gypsies) often survived. And when they deported Gypsies to camps, the authorities probably originally intended to remove this unpopular minority from Germany rather than specifically to murder them.[50]

The treatment of Gypsy camp inmates sometimes differed from that of Jews. In Auschwitz, about 23,000 Gypsies were confined in a "family camp," where women were allowed to remain with their husbands in family groups, to wear their own clothes, and to let their hair grow back after the initial shaving. They were not subject to work assignments. However, their diet and shelter were so inadequate that many died of diseases such as typhus, dysentery, and scabies. Marie Sidi Stojka was an Austrian gypsy who was deported to Auschwitz with her six children. "I watched over my children as best I could in that terrible place," she reported, "but my youngest son died of typhus."[51] Often raped and sexually molested by guards, some Gypsy women prisoners tried to survive through prostitution.

The chief physician of the Auschwitz Gypsy camp, Dr. Josef Mengele, often chose Gypsies as subjects for atrocious medical experiments of which most died. Another physician who worked at Auschwitz, Dr. Carl Clauberg, used Gypsy women as subjects for his research on sterilization. His experiments, conducted without anesthesia, included injecting a corrosive liquid into the uterus of women inmates—a method by which he claimed that he could sterilize 1000 women a day.[52] Meanwhile, starting in 1943, some inmates of the Gypsy "family camp" were killed in gas chambers, and others who were capable of working were transferred to other camps. In August of 1944, the remaining Gypsy inmates were killed. In all about 20,000 Gypsies died in Auschwitz. The reason why they were killed is not certain—perhaps the purpose was to make room in the camp for new shipments of Jews. The total number of Gypsies killed in the Holocaust cannot be reliably known, but estimates range from 90,000 to about 200,000 (out of about 800,000 Gypsies in Europe).[53]

Jehovah's Witnesses, often called the "forgotten Holocaust victims," were also among the inmates of the Nazi concentration camp system. Most German Witnesses, who belonged to the majority "German" ethnic group, were persecuted not on racial, but on religious grounds, because their faith forbade them to perform military service and to perform patriotic rituals, and because they refused to obey laws against proselytizing and distributing literature. The Nazis did not intend to exterminate them, but merely to break their resistance, and those who promised to renounce their faith were released. Nonetheless, most Witnesses remained in the camps, where their solidarity helped many to survive. Magdalena Kusserow, born in 1924, was arrested and confined in juvenile prisons until she was 18, when she "was told that I could go home if I signed a statement repudiating my faith. But I refused." Kusserow was sent to the women's concentration camp at Ravensbrück, where her mother and sister soon joined her. "With God's help, we Jehovah's Witnesses stuck together." [54]

Women not only suffered as victims, but also acted as perpetrators. Of the thousands, even millions of people who shared the responsibility for the crimes of the Nazis, many were women. To be sure, women played no role in making the decisions or giving the orders that set the genocide in motion. But, chiefly in their roles as workers or professionals, women were nonetheless deeply involved in carrying out those orders. As social workers, women did the paperwork that consigned victims to compulsory sterilization or euthanasia; as nurses, they helped to carry out these procedures; as clerks and secretaries, they kept records of them.

About 10 percent of concentration camp guards were women. Trained at Ravensbrück, for most of its existence the only concentration camp designed specifically for women, these guards supervised the women's divisions of many camps. With the exception of jobs that required carrying a gun or patrolling the camp's outer perimeter, women guards had the same duties as their male colleagues. Guards were chiefly single, working-class women, some of whom had been conscripted for labor and chose this job because it offered food, clothing, and lodging. Not surprisingly, male guards had a low opinion of these women, whom they accused of being "soft" and emotional. But according to the testimony of survivors, the women guards at Ravensbrück and its neighboring camp of Uckermark behaved very brutally. They beat prisoners with police batons and pistol butts, kicked them with their heavy boots, set attack dogs loose on them, and drove them with whips. [55]

Among the physicians who were tried in 1945 at Nuremberg was one woman, Dr. Hertha Oberheuser, who had operated on prisoners at Ravensbrück. Oberheuser tried to appeal to gender stereotypes by testifying that she had only been an assistant to her male superiors and had known nothing of the consequences of these procedures—medical experiments that often resulted in death or permanent disability. "My position was that of an assistant physician," she testified. "I had no choice, and I did not know anything about it." She was sentenced to 20 years in prison, of which she served seven. [56]

These stories show us how gender identity intersects with other characteristics to define the destiny and life stories of individuals. In the racist Nazi empire, ethnicity or nationality ranked far above gender in importance. Jewish women suffered along with their men; women of the "German" elite, and those of other privileged ethnicities, were implicated in the crimes of their nations. But within these categories, gender difference shaped both experience itself and the ways in which it was interpreted. Perpetrators, victims, and bystanders suffered and acted not only as members of their ethnic groups, but also as women and men.

Women in resistance movements

Though at the outset, resistance to the seemingly invincible German armed forces seemed hopeless, when the German war effort suffered reverses, resistance movements arose in the countries occupied by Germany, in Germany itself, and in the concentration camps. By the end of the war, resisters in some countries had built formidable military forces and political movements that would claim a leading role in post-war governments. Women, who were the majority of the civilian populations of Nazi-occupied territories, played an important role as resisters.

Some female resisters took advantage of female biological and gender identity and the possibilities that it offered. Bronka Klibanska, a Polish Jew, took the dangerous step of escaping from the ghetto and living on the "Aryan side" (the non-Jewish area) of her native city of Bialystok, while acting as a courier for a Jewish resistance movement. Less identifiable as Jews than Jewish men, who were circumcised, women were much more likely to succeed in living under cover. "I wasn't afraid," Klibanska recollected, "I was determined, determined to do something to take revenge for what the Germans were doing to our people. And that gave me strength." [57] Another Jewish resister who "passed" took advantage of her blond hair and blue eyes to flirt with German soldiers and obtain necessary information. [58] Many resisters took advantage of the fact that women attracted less attention than men. Miep Gies of Amsterdam smuggled supplies to the hiding-place of her friends, the Frank family, and retrieved the diary that Anne Frank left behind when she was deported with her family. Italian nuns concealed hundreds of Jewish children in convents, knowing that police forces would be hesitant to search for them there.

Many women resisters consciously took on the typically female role of professional helper or community activist. In Nazi-occupied France, Jewish and non-Jewish charities, many run by women, helped to rescue and hide Jewish children. Two social workers, Mila Racine and Marianne Cohn, were arrested and executed as they smuggled Jewish children into Switzerland. [59] Dutch nurses rescued Jewish children from the places where their families were detained before deportation, and placed these children with Dutch foster families. Magda Trocmé, a French pastor's wife, declared that her concern for another woman motivated her to start the remarkable effort through which she and her husband made the French town of Chambon sur Lignon a refuge for hundreds of Jewish refugees: "A poor woman came to my house one night, and she asked to come in. She said immediately that she was a German Jew, that she was running away, that she wanted to have shelter.... And I said 'Come in.' And so it started." [60]

Women were more likely to give personal than political reasons for their courageous actions. As an Italian woman who hid Jewish refugees commented, "I said 'let me save this one; he's a mother's son, just like mine,' my hope being that somebody would treat my own with the same care." [61] The Polish Irena Sendler, who worked for an organization called the Council for Aid to the Jews

(*Zegota*) to smuggle children out of the Warsaw ghetto, was inspired by her family background: "All my life, I had Jewish friends.... My family taught me that what matters is whether people are honest or dishonest, not what religion they belong to."[62]

When women aspired to a more masculine role by joining a partisan band or a military unit, they usually encountered resistance. To be sure, women were useful assistants: they provided supplies, passed messages, smuggled weapons (sometimes in baby carriages), and used their extensive network of friends to gain valuable information. But in part as compensation for the humiliation of defeat and occupation, resistance movements cultivated a highly masculine image. Women were seldom allowed to occupy leadership posts or to bear arms, and often came under pressure to form a sexual relationship with a male leader in order to be accepted into a group.

But there were a few women who played conspicuous roles as leaders. Among these was Berty Albrecht (1893–1943), a French Jew who trained as a nurse and during the inter-war years became well known as a sexual reformer, an advocate of reproductive rights, and a factory inspector. In 1940, she took advantage of this latter position to hide escaping prisoners. Along with her colleague Henri Frénay, she helped to edit *Combat*, the secret journal of the French Resistance. At the same time, she worked to aid the families of imprisoned resistance fighters and to establish liaisons among resistance groups. Arrested in 1942 by the authorities of Vichy France, she simulated insanity and was transferred to an asylum, from which she managed to escape. She refused to take refuge in England, continued her work, and was arrested again, this time by German occupation forces, and interrogated under torture. She committed suicide in prison in 1943.[63]

Though a new kind of conflict, the Second World War concluded in a sadly traditional way. Many fighting forces celebrated their victory and the humiliation of their enemies by taking women as spoils of war. Advancing into Germany, Soviet soldiers wreaked their vengeance on the destroyers of their homeland by raping German women. About 2 million women were raped, many repeatedly. About 10 million Germans—mostly women and children—fled westward from the Soviet advance in the winter of 1945. Many of these refugees died on their way. In Western European countries that were liberated from Nazi occupation, the men who had fought in resistance movements took out their anger against the Germans by humiliating, tormenting, and sometimes killing or imprisoning the women whom they suspected of having had sexual relations with German soldiers. Men avenged the humiliation of defeat and occupation by signaling that they were once again in control of "their" women.[64]

Did the Second World War mark a major turning point in the history of women and gender relations? Some historians assert that wartime changes in the lives of women, though striking, were also temporary. At the war's end, women who had served in the military were not only demobilized, but sometimes shamed for their unfeminine behavior. Those who had replaced men in the labor force were often dismissed to make way for returning veterans. These were policies that the majority of women accepted and even approved. The suffering, deprivation, and grief of wartime produced massive nostalgia for what most people considered "normal" life, in which women returned to the home and men to their traditional position as family breadwinners.

But these were short-term effects. In the longer term, the war marked an essential stage in a long-term process of change. This process was marked chiefly by the decline of the ideology of "separate spheres" and the integration of men and women in many aspects of economic and cultural life. In many ways, wartime conditions created new forms of gender solidarity. For women could not be accused, as during the previous war, of living safe civilian lives while men fought and died. On the contrary, men and women often fought, suffered, and died together. The Second World War also destroyed some of the regimes— Fascist Italy, Nazi Germany, and many authoritarian governments—that had most aggressively promoted male supremacy and female subordination. The war did not directly cause social changes such as the movement of women into previously male-identified jobs and of married women into the workforce, for these trends had begun much earlier. But because women's labor was so obviously needed during the wartime emergency, public attitudes toward their workforce participation became much more positive than they had been during the Depression. And these new patterns of female employment would continue, with only a brief reversal, in the post-war era. This development and its effects on families, workplaces, and women's life plans provided the context for the emergence of a new feminist movement in the 1960s.

5

The Best of Both Worlds? Women in Western Europe in the Post-war Era, 1945–1970

Since the publication of Betty Friedan's *The Feminine Mystique*, historians have associated the post-war era (1945–1970) with political conservatism, a revival of domesticity, and a return to traditional gender roles.[1] This was a view that was convenient for the generation of feminists who came of age in the 1970s, for it justified their claim that they alone had liberated women from the tyranny of the "feminine mystique." But a more balanced account of the era calls these claims into question. In the first post-war years, nostalgia for the reassuring traditions of the past was widespread, and conservative governments warned against social experimentation that might threaten their nations' newfound stability and prosperity. Nonetheless, new economic and social forces soon transformed the family, reproductive patterns, gender relations, the workforce, and many other aspects of culture.

In the cultural environment of post-war Western Europe, women received contradictory messages. The family was highly prized. Men returned home from war and captivity; women left or were forced out of their wartime jobs; and an upsurge of marriages and births expressed hope for the future after long years of death, bereavement, and despair. But post-war culture also encouraged individualism, personal ambition, and rising expectations. Educational levels rose; skilled labor was in demand; and advertisers promised happiness and social acceptance to those who could afford the many new products that were now so lavishly available.

We will look at women in post-war Western Europe as they dealt with these contradictory messages in the areas of politics, the family, the workforce, and popular culture. We shall see that the stereotype of the post-war "happy housewife" was far from the complex reality. The domestic ideal soon came into conflict with the many opportunities for employment, education, and self-realization that the newly prosperous societies offered. The result was a new sense of stress, uncertainty, and ambivalence. "At this juncture in our social history women are guided by two apparently conflicting aims," stated the influential social scientists Alva Myrdal and Viola Klein, "on the one hand, they want . . . to develop their personalities to the full. . . . On the other hand, most women want a home and family of their own."[2] Myrdal and others called on women to devise a new life plan that would give them "the best of both worlds." But could women attain this goal simply through their own individual efforts? Or would it require broader social and cultural change? We will conclude the chapter by looking at these questions as they were raised by a new generation of feminist thinkers.

From patriarchy to partnership

The Swiss feminist Iris von Roten remarked in 1958 that women owed the right of suffrage that they had gained in most countries "to the international catastrophe of war," which had forced men to accept them as "something like comrades."[3] In the period following the Second World War, women gained the right to vote in several countries—France, Italy, Belgium—where they had been refused it after the First. In Greece, women gained the right to vote in 1952, though this right meant little under the monarchy that had been established with military backing in that same year. But as in the inter-war era, the granting of woman suffrage was not intended to encourage feminism or any other movement for social change. Male politicians appreciated women's wartime sacrifices—many of the first women elected to the French National Assembly in 1946 had been heroes of the French Resistance—and believed that these patriotic citizens would support conservative values and social stability.

By the 1950s, the only Western European countries that had not given women the right to vote were Portugal, still ruled by a dictatorship, and Switzerland, Europe's oldest democracy (along with its neighboring micro-state, Liechtenstein). In 1945, the lower house of the Swiss Federal Assembly, the National Council, once again debated woman suffrage, which conservatives warned might disrupt households, break up families, and threaten Swiss manhood. "If the woman becomes a parliamentary deputy, she must also attend meetings," warned one anti-suffragist. "And then would her husband have to cook and take care of the children? We can't always get servants!"[4] The majority of the National Council voted favorably on the resolution, but legal authorities objected that its implementation would require a constitutional change. When after another drawn-out process of deliberation the constitutional change passed both houses of the Federal Assembly in 1957, many hoped that Switzerland would finally follow the example set by the rest of Europe and the civilized world. But Switzerland's unique system of direct democracy required this and most other new legislation to pass not only a parliamentary vote, but also a referendum in which all voters participated. The all-male voting public proved more conservative than their parliamentary representatives, and defeated the measure in 1959 by a substantial majority of 69 percent.

Although Switzerland's electoral system was unique in Western Europe, the Swiss voters' conservative attitude was not. In the immediate post-war years, most commentators prophesied confidently that women had no desire to enter the political arena and would make little use of their right to vote. And indeed, even in countries where women voted, their participation and influence in politics declined. In France, 35 women were elected to the National Assembly in 1946, 6.48 percent of the total, and the number of female delegates did not reach that level again for the next 40 years.[5] In the British House of Commons and in the parliaments of the Scandinavian countries, women held only about 5 percent of seats during the 1950s; in the Federal Republic of Germany, their share of delegates to the lower house of the national parliament, the *Bundestag*, was only about 7 percent. The failure of women to increase their representation in the halls of parliament was due partly to the decline of feminist organizations, which during this period lost members, financing, and influence.

Moreover, the political tensions produced by the Cold War created an unfriendly environment for feminism and any other form of solidarity among women. In France and Italy, communist parties attracted large numbers of working-class women. In Italy, the Union of Italian Women (*Unione donne italiane*), and in France the Union of French Women (*Union des femmes françaises*) were huge communist organizations that completely overshadowed both countries' dwindling feminist groups. Led by women, these organizations opposed employment discrimination and called for workplace reforms, publicly financed child-care, and other benefits for working mothers. However, the male leaders of the French and Italian communist parties gave these and other women's issues very low priority. And when forced to compete with conservative parties for votes, the communist parties abandoned whatever was left of their pre-war programs—some of which had promoted birth control, abortion rights, and other controversial issues—and joined enthusiastically in the popular cult of motherhood, family life, and domesticity.

In countries where communism had less influence, democratic socialist parties such as the Labour Party in Britain and the Social Democratic parties in West Germany and Scandinavia claimed to speak for working-class women. These parties, too, emphasized tasks such as repairing wartime damage, building new housing, reviving economic life, and maintaining social stability. Many progressive women chose to support these left-wing parties and hesitated to raise gender issues that might be controversial and divisive.

Feminism was even less popular on the right than on the left. In many Western European countries, including West Germany, France, and Italy, conservative parties developed an ideology termed "Christian Democracy"—a religiously inspired approach to politics that supported a capitalist economy combined with a welfare state that cared for vulnerable members of society. A central focus of these parties' foreign and domestic policies was opposition to communism, which (despite the communists' own disavowal of feminism) Western European conservatives associated with revolutionary notions of female emancipation, familial breakdown, and sexual anarchy. Christian Democrats pictured the ideal woman citizen as a dutiful wife, mother, and church member.

But despite the temporary decline of feminism, the confident prediction that women were tired of emancipation and would want nothing to do with politics proved mistaken. Women who were busy raising children and building families soon revisited a project left unfinished by previous generations of feminists— the reform of marriage and the family. In Britain and Scandinavia, most laws concerning the marital relationship had been modified in the direction of gender equality during the inter-war era. But the laws of other countries still rested on nineteenth-century legal codes that enforced patriarchy. These laws made husbands and fathers the heads of their families and empowered them to choose the family's place of residence, to control most of its financial affairs, to prevent their wives from working for pay, and to make most decisions about the children. Rooted in religious belief, morality and custom, family law had resisted reform for a century and a half.

Beginning in the post-war years, courts and legislators gradually dismantled legal patriarchy. In many countries, this process began with constitutional guarantees of gender equality. In West Germany, the drafting of the new "Basic Law" (or constitution) of 1949 gave rise to a debate on the legal status of women in the *Bundestag* (the lower house of the national parliament). Against heavy opposition from the conservative CDU (Christian-Democratic Union, or *Christlich-demokratische Union*), the socialist deputy Elisabeth Selbert championed a constitutional provision stating that "men and women have equal rights" which became Article 3 of the Basic Law. Selbert herself proclaimed that she was not a feminist, and that the position of women in German society must be based on "their specific character and qualities."[6] But German women, many of whom were busy repairing the country's bombed-out cities and supporting children whose fathers were often dead, missing, or disabled, objected to outmoded stereotypes of submissive femininity. These women expressed their newfound confidence by demanding the repeal of laws that gave fathers exclusive control over decisions affecting children—a campaign that succeeded in 1957. West German law still discriminated against the unmarried mother, who was not accorded full parental rights, and defined women's status in the marital relationship primarily as that of homemaker.[7] West German women did not become fully equal to their husbands in the marital relationship until 1977.

In other countries, too, the abolition of legal patriarchy was a highly controversial process, and therefore beset by delays and setbacks. Nonetheless, the trend toward gender equality was steady. The French Civil Codes still made the man the head of the family, and not until 1965 did French wives gain the right fully to control their own property (though the husband still administered all joint property).[8] French mothers did not gain full parental rights over their children until 1970, and even then fathers controlled their children's financial affairs. In Italy, a new constitution enacted in 1948 guaranteed the equal rights of women. But this provision had few practical results until the 1970s, when Italian women (and men) gained the right to civil divorce and equal parental rights.[9] The end of legal patriarchy was a revolution, though a quiet one, which opened the way to new form of marriage—one that was based on gender equality rather than on male supremacy.

In countries that were still ruled by right-wing dictatorships, legal patriarchy survived longer. In Portugal, marriage laws compelled women to do unpaid domestic work, gave them no control over their property or their children, and allotted only token punishments to husbands who killed wives who were suspected of adultery. In Spain, the right-wing military government of Francisco Franco preserved similar legal traditions and made sixteenth-century religious treatises on female chastity and wifely submission the central texts in girls' schools. Not until the 1980s, after these dictatorships were overthrown, did Spanish and Portuguese wives and mothers improve their legal status.

Rising expectations

To the war-weary peoples of Europe, the long-awaited peace promised a return to an ideal of normality that most people still associated with the family ideal that had become popular in the first half of the twentieth century—the father as breadwinner, the mother as full-time homemaker, and the children as protected dependents. Women, asserted the prestigious West German sociologist Helmut Schelsky, had been "over-emancipated" in wartime, and had discovered that the combination of family and wage labor brought chiefly stress and overwork. Callously overlooking the many German families left without fathers, he stated confidently that German women would surely choose to leave breadwinning to men and retire to the home. But the opposite occurred, for by the end of the post-war era the full-time housewife role had declined in popularity and prestige, and women often combined domesticity, motherhood, and paid work.[10]

At first glance, the nations of Western Europe seemed to provide the ideal environment for home life and child-rearing. Rapid economic growth provided full employment, high wages for male heads of household, and an ample tax base on which to build social services. Governments aimed not only to replace the population lost to low pre-war birth rates and the war itself—France, declared General Charles de Gaulle, who served a brief presidential term in 1945–1946, needed 12 million beautiful babies—but also to promote social stability by providing for the needs of their people. European welfare states varied greatly in their social policies and aims. Scandinavian countries aimed to level class differences by taxing high incomes heavily and using the money to help lower-income people. France, Britain, and West Germany provided many universal entitlements such as pensions and health insurance, but preserved class differences. All provided a wide range of services to mothers, children, and families. Among these were publicly funded health services; "family allowances" that subsidized child-rearing by channeling payments to parents; paid maternity leaves for working mothers; and many other social services.

Certainly, these benefits did a great deal to improve the health of mothers and children, to reduce poverty, and to encourage child-bearing. Unprecedented rates of marriage and family formation temporarily reversed the century's long-term trend toward declining birthrates. In France, live births to women aged 15–49 increased by about a third, from 60 per thousand in 1935 to 82 in 1960; during the same period this birthrate grew in Britain from 54 to 77; in Norway from 55 to 78; in the Netherlands from 77 to 90.[11] The "baby boom" affirmed life and hope after the death and despair of the war years. Improved medical and social services accelerated the downward trend in infant mortality that had begun at the turn of the century. For the first time in history, parents could expect that all of their children would reach adulthood.

However beneficial to families, the welfare state had ambiguous consequences for women, for it was designed not only to assist but also to control them.

In many ways, welfare state policies reinforced the male breadwinner role. In most countries, including France, Italy, Ireland, and West Germany, "family allowances" were usually payable to fathers, except in cases where a mother was the sole breadwinner. Only in Britain and Scandinavia, where feminists since the 1920s had linked state assistance to the empowerment of women, were the subsidies paid directly to mothers. Some labor-market policies were set up in order to induce mothers to leave the workforce: for example, in France and Belgium, mothers (regardless of income) received an extra payment if they withdrew from the labor force.[12]

Some nations' family allowance schemes encouraged large families and population growth by starting payments with the second or (in West Germany) the third child. Such policies left out most single mothers—divorced, widowed, or never married—because, though their households were among the neediest, they seldom had families large enough to qualify. Other benefits—for instance, retirement pensions and health insurance—were linked to employment, thus reducing non-working married women to dependent status and leaving out unemployed single women. In its original form, the welfare state thus reinforced gender inequality by increasing the power of male heads of household.

In many other ways, post-war conditions initially stabilized the male-headed family. In an era of economic growth and full employment, most male workers were able to support their families and few married women who lived with their husbands were compelled to work outside the home for survival. Moreover, the separation, insecurity, and anxiety of the war years heightened the attraction of cozy domesticity. Memories of wartime also shaped parent–child relationships. Dr. John Bowlby, a British psychiatrist, worked with children who had been separated from their mothers by evacuation from bombed-out cities, long-term hospitalization, or other traumatic wartime events. Observing the multiple psychological problems that these children suffered, he concluded that any interruption of a mother's care could have serious consequences for a child's mental health. He warned that children who suffered from "maternal deprivation"—even for short periods of time—might well grow into adults who were incapable of forming healthy relationships and functioning normally.[13]

Bowlby's theory influenced not only child-rearing practices, but also the status of working women. Policies that limited women's labor-market opportunities and encouraged stay-at-home motherhood—adopted chiefly in order to reintegrate returning soldiers—now received an additional, psychological justification. Citing the harmful effects of mothers' work outside the home, governments closed many of the day-care centers that had been opened during the war. Mothers who—by choice or by necessity—left home to work or to pursue other goals met with social disapproval. And constant interaction with their children left many mothers frustrated and starved for adult companionship.

However, Bowlby also sent a more positive message. By contrast to inter-war psychologists who had stressed the danger of spoiling children, he emphasized love, spontaneity, and enjoyment. This was also the message of the American Dr. Benjamin Spock's *Common Sense Book of Baby and Child Care*, which was first published in 1946, went through several editions, and was translated into many European languages. Spock counseled mothers to enjoy their children and to trust their own instincts.[14] The reception of Spock varied among European countries: in West Germany, for example, the permissive child-rearing methods that Spock advocated did not become fashionable until the 1960s.[15]

The post-war family soon disappointed the hopes of the era's conservatives that it would uphold traditional attitudes and behavior. It was quickly transformed by the effects of prosperity and economic expansion. The recovery of post-war economies depended on the manufacture and sale of consumer goods to populations who, after years of depression and war, were in need of almost everything. For the first time, household appliances were available not only to the rich, but to people of average incomes. As of 1962, only 14 percent of West German households possessed a telephone; 36 percent a television set; 24 percent an automobile. Within just 20 years, 64 percent of West German households owned cars, and almost all had vacuum cleaners, television sets, telephones, automatic washing machines, and many other household appliances. The same process occurred, though more slowly, in the poorer countries of Europe. In 1961 only 39 percent of Greek homes had running water and 50 percent, electricity; by 1970 almost all had these amenities. In the same period, the number of Greek households with indoor plumbing had risen from about 12 percent to about 40 percent.[16] And even in Spain, where a dictatorial regime tried hard to head off social change, many middle-class families acquired household appliances during the years from 1950 to 1975.

What was the effect of this consumer culture on the status of women? In some ways, it reinforced their domestic role. According to Betty Friedan's influential analysis, the glossy advertisements showing smiling housewives operating their new machines only glamorized women's traditional duties.[17] Friedan is right that the new technology did not change the household division of labor. Advertising affirmed that housework was women's job by urging men to buy their wives a washing machine rather than help with the washing. Some women reported that so-called "labor-saving" devices did not reduce the time that they spent on housework. Middle-class women's workload may actually have increased, for machines often replaced domestic servants, who became less available during this period. However, for the many working-class women who had always done their own housework, the new technology greatly reduced the time and energy that were required to maintain a home and family.

But the consumer society also had some emancipatory effects, for it did a great deal to raise women's expectations and increase their self-confidence. A long-term process of change that began with the Industrial Revolution had transformed the function of the home from production to consumption. The housewife was now less a worker than a consumer, whose purchasing power provided her family not only with necessities but also with the luxuries and comforts that signaled prosperity and rising expectations. Advertisers competed for her patronage by appealing to her as a discriminating shopper with a taste for convenience and elegance. Despite its manipulative purpose, this message could be empowering, for it implied that women's wishes and desires mattered. Moreover, women felt justified in leaving the home and taking a job in order to raise their families' standard of living by purchasing the new products.

Another trend that transformed families and the lives of women was the availability of effective birth-control techniques. In the area of population policy, the end of the Second World War marked a decisive turning point. During the era from 1870 until 1945, when military strength depended directly on the number of men who could be put into the field, governments obsessed with population numbers had sternly restricted access to contraception and abortion. After 1945, changes in military technology that made numbers less important and the rising birthrates of the "baby boom" alleviated fears of population decline and its consequences. In the post-war era, birth could finally become respectable. Its proponents affirmed the era's cultural values by promising that expanded access to contraception would make marriages happier, families more harmonious, and women better mothers to the children whom they could now freely choose to bear.

In Scandinavia, where the distribution of contraception had been legalized in the inter-war era, and in Britain where it had never been illegal, most opposition to birth control disappeared by the 1960s. British national health insurance began to cover family planning services in 1967. In some other countries, however, there were many obstacles. In France, stern inter-war laws that limited access to contraception and forbade abortion were still on the books and still defended by the Catholic Church and by some secular politicians.

Simone de Beauvoir's widely read book, *The Second Sex*, asserted in 1949 that these laws enslaved women by forcing them to become mothers against their will.[18] One of de Beauvoir's readers, Évelyne Sullerot, was a young French woman who had trained as a teacher and during the 1950s was the full-time mother of three small children. Along with a physician, Marie-Andrée Lagroua Weill-Hallé, and a few other young women, Sullerot founded an agency in 1956 that was at first known as Happy Motherhood (*Maternité Heureuse*) and later changed its name to the French Family Planning Movement (*Mouvement Français pour le Planning Familial*). This organization dispensed contraceptive advice, though at first very cautiously and only to a limited circle of members, and campaigned for legal changes that would make birth control accessible. The distribution of contraceptives was legalized in France in 1967, although it was not until the 1970s that they became freely available through public health facilities.[19]

In Austria in the 1950s, in West Germany and the Netherlands in the 1960s, in Italy in 1971, and in Belgium in 1973, national legislatures took most laws that had limited access to contraceptives off the books. In Spain, Portugal, and Greece, the legalization of birth control would await the 1980s, when dictatorships were overthrown and democracy established in all three countries. In devoutly Catholic Ireland, women had little access to birth control until 1979, when a new feminist movement finally persuaded the national legislature to legalize the sale and importation of contraceptives.[20]

Even more transformative than these legislative changes was the invention and distribution of the contraceptive pill, which came onto the market in some countries in the early 1960s. Of course, the pill was not the first birth-control method, for couples had limited the number of their children for more than a century. But unlike earlier methods, most of which had a high failure rate and required the cooperation of the male partner, the pill was reliable, easy to use, and entirely controlled by women. The pill was the first contraceptive technology that became truly popular—by the 1980s, the majority of reproductive-age women in Western Europe used it.[21] After the peak of the post-war baby boom, birthrates began to decline in the mid-1960s and continued to drop for the rest of the century.

This was indeed an important change. Throughout history, most women had assumed that—with or without their consent—they would become mothers and devote the greater part of their adult lives to pregnancy, lactation, and child-care. But now many felt more free than ever before to plan lives in which motherhood could be chosen, but was not inevitable. And those who chose motherhood—still the vast majority—had time for other pursuits. In the mid-nineteenth century the average woman in Western Europe had five or six children; by the mid-twentieth century she had two, and the time she spent on pregnancy and lactation decreased from about 15 to about 4 years. Moreover, whereas in 1900 the average woman in the more prosperous European countries could expect to live about 50 years, by 1970 her life expectancy had increased to about 74 years. Full-time motherhood consumed only a short period of a lengthening life span.

By legitimating the separation of sexuality from reproduction, the acceptance of family limitation also encouraged tolerance of non-marital forms of sexuality. The 1960s saw a greater openness not only to non-marital heterosexual relationships, but to homosexual relationships as well. In both West Germany and Britain, laws that criminalized male homosexual conduct were repealed during the 1960s. Lesbians—who were not directly affected by the laws—took advantage of the changing culture to form their first associations. In Britain, the first of these organizations was the Minorities Research Group, founded in 1963, which produced a periodical entitled *Arena Three* and provided counseling services. Another organization, known as KENRIC, sponsored social events where lesbians could meet and mingle. These associations set up several local branches.[22]

Women's two roles

Far from retreating to the home as some analysts had predicted, women of the post-war era increased both their participation in and their commitment to paid work. From the beginning of the Industrial Revolution until the 1930s, the typical female worker had been a young, single woman who quit her job when she married and never returned to full-time work. But in the post-war era, an increasing number of women combined marriage with employment. In France between 1954 and 1962, the labor-force participation of married women increased 28 percent, and 53 percent of the female labor force was married in 1968. In Britain, only 10 percent of married women had worked outside the home in 1931, but 30 percent of such women were employed in 1960, and 67 percent by 1980.[23] In Italy, where the decline of agricultural employment actually reduced the number of employed married women in the first two post-war decades, their share of the workforce rose after 1970.

In this prosperous era, most married women did not need to work in order to survive, and many regarded the decision to seek employment as a personal choice that any woman, regardless of marital status, should have the right to make. They demanded the repeal of laws that required the dismissal of women from civil service jobs when they married and empowered husbands to forbid their wives to take up employment. In Britain, the "marriage bar" for teachers, which had been struck down during the war, was never reinstated. German legislators abolished marriage bars and laws that gave husbands control over their wives' employment choices in the 1950s. Even in Spain, which the dictatorship headed by Francisco Franco did its best to insulate from all modern influences, an expanding economy brought women into the workforce. A law of 1961 increased the educational and career opportunities open to Spanish women, though husbands kept the right to forbid their wives to work outside the home.

Why did married women go out to work? Working-class mothers, such as the British women interviewed by the sociologist Pearl Jephcott, usually said that their primary reason was to earn money in order to acquire the consumer goods that would move their families into the middle class.[24] Another important motive was self-realization. Women complained that, once their children went to school, they were bored at home, and they enjoyed the sociability of the workplace. "You get a laugh mixing with the girls," said a British factory worker interviewed by Jephcott.[25] The age structure of the female workforce changed as many women quit work to raise children and then returned to the labor force in their mid-thirties, often continuing to work until retirement.

Women's attitudes toward what came to be called the "double burden" of family and paid work differed by class. Working-class women still regarded themselves chiefly as wives and mothers, were in general not ambitious for advancement, and admitted to worrying about the effect of their employment on their families and households. But middle-class women, particularly professionals who had worked before marriage, often expressed frustration at what they considered the waste of their talents: "I certainly think that it is a pity that so many women, because they want a family, are more or less forced to spend their time doing domestic work when they might be doing something more useful," remarked one such woman to the British researcher Judith Hubback.[26] These women thought of their domestic responsibilities as an obstacle to be overcome, rather than as a primary source of identity.

The employment of married women, traditionally a sign of poverty, was correlated in the post-war years with high income and educational levels. Because many more families than before could afford to keep their children in school until adolescence or early adulthood, educational opportunities expanded. For example, in Sweden about 26 percent of young people 16–19 years of age were full-time students in 1963, but about 33 percent by 1977, and among the group aged 20–24 this figure rose from about 8 percent in 1963 to 12 percent by 1970.[27] Universities faced a crisis of overcrowding as their enrollments ballooned. And women, whose educational opportunities had traditionally lagged behind those of men, now began to close the gap. In West Germany, women constituted 19 percent of university student bodies in 1950, but 42 percent by 1985.[28] Even in conservative Spain, the number of women attending university doubled between 1950 and 1961 (when they constituted 22–24 percent of all university students).[29]

Rising educational qualifications did not eliminate gender stereotyping. University graduates and other professionally trained women were clustered in a few female-identified fields such as teaching, social work, child development, and medical services. But though not so prestigious as male professional skills, these qualifications were nonetheless useful, for they were in demand in the schools, child-care centers, social agencies, recreational facilities, and health-care services that were overwhelmed by the numerous offspring of the "baby boom." Faced with a labor shortage, governments and private employers forgot their earlier opposition to married women's employment and urged qualified women to return to work.

What was the impact of these new conditions upon the status and the self-image of women? This question was addressed by one of the era's most widely read books, which was entitled *Women's Two Roles; Home and Work*, co-authored by the Swedish activist and scholar Alva Myrdal and the British sociologist Viola Klein and first published in 1956. We have already met Myrdal as a social reformer who helped to formulate Sweden's policies on married women's work and family benefits in the 1930s. In 1948, she moved to Geneva with her husband Gunnar Myrdal who had taken a prestigious job with the United Nations. As the wife of a prominent diplomat, she had little time or opportunity to pursue her own interests. According to her daughter, Sissela Bok, "she felt ... buried alive, locked into the superficial role of hostess while shielding a wifely role that had become nothing but a mask." [30] When Alva Myrdal herself was offered a job by the United Nations, she accepted it despite the fact that she had to move away from her family to New York and later to Paris—a decision for which her two daughters, then aged 13 and 15, never entirely forgave her.

According to Myrdal and Klein, the second half of the twentieth century had created new conditions for female existence. In the past, most women had derived their identity primarily from one role, that of wife and mother. Now another role—that of paid worker—had gained equal importance. In the short term, these two roles might seem to conflict, but over the course of a lifetime they could be combined. The authors advised women to live their lives in three phases of about 20 years each: the first devoted to study and career training, the second to full-time child-rearing, and the third to a career or paid job. The end of the second phase, when the children had ceased to be dependent (a point that the authors assumed would come when a woman who had borne children in her twenties was about forty), would probably be marked by an "acute emotional crisis." But retired mother could alleviate her sense of "emptiness and lack of purpose" by returning to her career. Women could have it all—just not all at the same time.[31]

To an extent, this plan was realistic, for many women did, indeed, leave their jobs for a period of several years of child-rearing and then return. But it was very optimistic, for even in the booming post-war economy it was unlikely that a worker could afford to leave her job for such a long period and then expect to re-enter it without a considerable drop in status and income. In fact, mothers who worked outside the home seldom took a break of 20 years—some returned to work when their youngest child entered school, and some never quit at all. Rather than "phasing" employment and motherhood, they combined both in a workweek that sometimes exceeded 90 hours. Although some women—chiefly professionals—took pride in the seamless performance of their double role, many others complained of fatigue, stress, and health problems.

Myrdal and Klein's bright picture of the ambitious career woman took little account of the many forms of discrimination that women in the workplace encountered. To be sure, the laws of some European countries supported the principle of equal pay for equal work. In 1957, six European nations formed the European Common Market, which began with an agreement to lower tariffs and move toward free trade among the member countries. The drafters of the Common Market's founding document, the Treaty of Rome, were concerned that member countries that paid low wages—especially to women, who were always the most underpaid workers—might profit at the expense of countries that mandated higher minimum wage levels. The Treaty of Rome attempted to even out these disparities by ruling that men and women must receive equal pay for equal work. This agreement was followed by others that affirmed women's right to equal treatment in the workplace.[32] The Common Market, later known as the European Union, expanded both its membership and its regulatory authority, and by 1980 had grown to include 9, and by 2000 to 15 member nations.[33]

But in fact, men and women did not usually do the same jobs and therefore these regulations were seldom enforced. In all segments of the labor force, women earned less than men. For example, in 1962 the average earnings of French female factory workers were about 69 percent of those of their male colleagues and French female professionals earned 63 percent of the average male professional income. In the early 1960s, German women's average wage was about 60 percent of the average male wage; by 1984 it had risen to 72 percent.[34] Women were much more likely than men to work part-time—a form of employment that combined low pay with insecurity. Because training and apprenticeship programs were often reserved for men, women had little access to the high-paying positions created by new technologies. And when the post-war boom ended in the recession of the 1970s, women were more vulnerable than men to unemployment.

Feminists such as Myrdal and Klein expected that the women who now played "two roles" would make progress not only toward personal self-realization but toward gender equality. In fact, however, women entered the labor force under conditions that ensured that most would not be able to compete with men. For, though its boundaries had become more porous, the "female sphere" and its attendant gender stereotypes continued to shape women's lives. Women's labor was still deemed different from, and in general less valuable than, that of men, and many bore the "double burden" of paid and domestic work. The living out of the "two roles" produced new tensions, new conflicts, and new problems.

Expanding horizons

The new prosperity brought with it new opportunities for leisure and recreation. Tourism, entertainment, and luxury consumption—previously the pastimes of a minority of rich people—were now available to a much wider segment of the population, which now included groups such as teenagers or young singles. Women, too, were an important market. Advertisements promised them many forms of fulfillment, as wives, mothers, and individuals.

Manufacturers of clothing, cosmetics and beauty products emphasized glamour and femininity. Abandoning the tailored styles of the 1930s and the wartime years, dress designers of the 1950s promoted long skirts, cinched-in waists, and fitted bodices and sweaters. The cosmetics industry declared that true beauty depended on the proper selection and application of makeup, and ads for grooming products promised social success to the users of the right shampoos, home permanents, and deodorants. The female body was sculpted: breasts and buttocks by undergarments; hair by permanent waves; legs by stockings and high-heeled shoes. When the voluptuous 1950s fashions were superseded by the girlish styles of the 1960s, the stick-thin British model Twiggy became the new beauty ideal. All over the Western world, women went on starvation diets to transform their bodies to fit the new fashions.

But advertisements did not simply encourage conformity, but also appealed to individualism. The most ordinary woman, they implied, could re-create herself and her life by making the right choices. Advertisements showed women in luxurious surroundings engaging in rewarding pursuits with a poise and confidence that—or so the ads implied—could be gained by anyone who purchased the right products. Consumer culture undermined religious codes of morality based on self-sacrifice by legitimating the pursuit of pleasure and self-realization. Moreover, the women's magazines in which most of the ads appeared also contained stories that, despite their conventionally romantic or domestic plots, featured women who triumphed over obstacles and gained control over their own lives, often by using their sex appeal to manipulate men.

The movie industry also popularized new ways of being female. The stars of the post-war era were softer and more feminine than the hard-edged, sexy "vamps" of the 1920s. Film plots usually showed the heroine finding the right man and living happily ever after. But films could also send out more subversive messages. In 1956, the French film *And God Created Woman* attracted international attention to its star Brigitte Bardot, who (though 22 years old at the time) played a wayward and sultry teenager. The movie appealed to the public's new taste for leisure and tourism by showing the luscious Bardot frolicking on the beach in a bikini, sunbathing in the nude, and dancing in the bars of a resort town. Obviously, men liked this movie, but so did many young women. Bardot's informal dress, artfully disheveled hair, and casual manners provided an attractive alternative to conventional norms of proper feminine behavior. Parents and teachers denounced her, but teenage girls imitated her. And Bardot's character was not a pliant and available female—on the contrary, she used her sexual appeal to gain her own ends, which included independence of adult authority. Bardot created a female version of the rebellious adolescence portrayed by male stars such as James Dean.

The tourist industry, too, promoted its product through images of freedom and enjoyment. Until the 1930s, most workers never had a paid vacation, and leisure travel had been for the rich. During the 1930s, when vacations became available to a larger segment of the population, travel and resort accommodations were often managed by governments or by political parties (e.g., by the Nazis in Germany and the Popular Front in France). In the 1950s, a paid vacation became part of almost every worker's contract and tourism became widely popular—over 50 percent of French families took a summer vacation in 1974.[35] Post-war tourism was managed by private companies that offered carefree fun in the sun. The French Club Med was a chain of resorts that started out in public ownership but by the 1960s had become a highly successful commercial venture. Located in scenic tropical spots, Club Med emphasized escapism, relaxation, and pleasure, including a permissive sexual atmosphere. Tourism did not explicitly promote gender equality—in fact, it created another kind of exploitative and low-paid employment for women. Nonetheless, it raised the aspirations of some women by providing them with an escape from familial responsibilities. And in Greece and Spain, which became popular tourist destinations, contact with visitors from more prosperous countries broadened the horizons of many women.

The emergence of a new group consisting of teenagers and young adults was among this era's most important trends. In earlier years, most young people had been full-time workers who had contributed their earnings to their parents' household and had kept little to spend on luxuries. Now, young people were more likely to spend their wages or the allowances that they received from their parents on themselves. And industry appealed to this growing market by creating distinctively youthful styles in clothing, music, and entertainment.

As in many other areas, this youth culture set new norms in gender relations. Rejecting the cautious respectability of their parents, young people of both sexes valued pleasure, spontaneity, and self-expression. The riotous response of European young people to American rock stars such as Elvis Presley shocked respectable public opinion. And especially horrifying was the behavior of girls, who forsook dresses for tight sweaters and blue jeans (sometimes with their idol's name painted on the seat), ballroom dancing for the jitterbug, and feminine restraint for raucous enthusiasm.[36] These teenagers were much more likely to have sexual relations before marriage—a loosening of conventional moral standards that the birth control pill made possible. Although male-dominated, youth culture minimized gender differences in many ways. Male and female clothing, hair styles, social mores, and consumer preferences were quite similar, and girls mixed with boys in venues such as movie theaters, rock concerts, bars, and sports events.

Forerunners of feminism

During the post-war era, many commentators assumed that organized feminism had outlived its usefulness. After all, it had already achieved its most important goals, having won for women the rights to vote and to run for office, an improved status in the family, access to higher education and the professions, and expanding job opportunities. And if some forms of inequality remained, surely those that were not due to "natural" and beneficial gender differences would disappear in time. But a few thinkers—most of whom did not identify themselves as feminists, but rather as independent scholars and authors—questioned their era's complacency. They pointed out that progress toward formal equality—that is, equal legal and political status—had not greatly changed most women's lives. Nor had it made much impact on male supremacy in politics, higher education, the workplace, and culture. When women entered these male-dominated realms, it was almost always in a subordinate and gender-stereotyped position. And most women were still required to do the unpaid labor of child-rearing and motherhood. Why, these thinkers inquired, did women accept these disadvantages? And what could they do to overcome them?

A book that did much to shape post-war conceptions of the status of women was *Women's Two Roles*, published by Alva Myrdal and Viola Klein in 1956. As we have already seen, the authors presented women's new life patterns, which often involved a combination of marriage and motherhood with paid work, in a generally positive light. But ten years earlier, the junior author had painted a more problematic picture of this new pattern. A Jewish refugee from Czechoslovakia whose parents both perished in the Holocaust, Viola Klein studied sociology in Britain with her fellow exile Karl Mannheim, and in 1945 published a book entitled *The Feminine Character: History of an Ideology*. Klein noted that although women were rapidly gaining legal equality, culture was slower to change, and that it was "the sphere of emotional and unconscious attitudes which offers the most stubborn resistance to changed material circumstances."[37] The tension between domestic and professional roles was not only practical but psychic. The pressure to act competent and confident at work, and "pretty, sensitive, adaptable ... and if possible, not too intelligent" at home often produced a state of "inner tension and frustration."[38] Klein emphatically rejected the popular view that this conflict was best solved by a return to domesticity, which she compared to slavery. Citing the philosopher Erich Fromm, she urged women to accept their new freedoms and the accompanying risk and uncertainty.

Much the most important feminist work of the early post-war era, and one of the most significant of all time, was Simone de Beauvoir's *The Second Sex* (*Le deuxième sexe*), first published in two volumes in 1949.[39] A well known author and the partner of France's most respected public intellectual, Jean-Paul Sartre, de Beauvoir appeared to be the very model of an emancipated woman—an image that concealed the complex reality of her life. Though she refused to identify herself as a feminist, she acknowledged that much of her life had been shaped by her gender, and used her skills as a scholar and a philosopher to address a highly unconventional question—exactly what was a "woman"?

De Beauvoir asserted that femininity was not innate but acquired: "one is not born, but becomes, a woman."[40] Women were the products of a male-supremacist culture that denied their individuality and valued them only as sexual objects and producers of offspring. In violation of the era's norms of propriety, de Beauvoir frankly described how girls became women through experiences such as menstruation, sexual intercourse, pregnancy, childbirth, domestic life, motherhood, and same-sex relationships. Though of course men also had bodies, she claimed that they were not enslaved to them, but had the opportunity to develop their intellectual capacities. By contrast, women were tied to their sexual and maternal functions.

In a country that still prohibited access both to many forms of contraception and to abortion, and thus denied women control over their fertility, de Beauvoir debunked her era's conventional belief in motherhood as a woman's most fulfilling vocation. Rather, she called it a kind of forced labor which unprepared and unwilling mothers usually performed badly, to the detriment of their children as well as themselves. Women's enslavement was not only physical but cultural, for in a culture that equated masculinity with humanity, women would always be the "other"—a being defined by her deviation from the male norm.

When it was first published, *The Second Sex* set off a storm of protest. In France and in the many countries where the book appeared in translation, commentators of all political tendencies—communist, socialist, conservative—denounced its author as a hysterical harridan bent on undermining all decent values. But the effect was to call attention to the book and, ultimately, to broaden its readership and influence. Almost single-handedly, de Beauvoir called the attention of a younger generation of female intellectuals to the condition of women.[41] By breaking conventional taboos, the book created space for a broader and franker discussion of sexuality, reproduction, and gender relations. And by tracing gender inequality to its roots in culture and psychology, de Beauvoir began a process of inquiry that would later inspire feminist scholars throughout the world.

As the only European democracy where women had not yet won the right to vote, Switzerland in the 1950s seemed trapped in a time warp. Iris von Roten, a lawyer who was married to a member of the national parliament, had given up her practice at the birth of their daughter and turned her efforts to research and writing. The result was *Women in the Playpen* (*Frauen im Laufgitter*), a book that was obviously influenced by de Beauvoir. In a style that was both incisive and entertaining, von Roten demolished the conventional assumption that women lived in a new age of freedom and opportunity. Rather, she insisted that, apart from a few fortunate or privileged individuals, the woman of the 1950s had the same limited options as her great-grandmother. A woman might live as "an exploited drudge" in the workforce, or as "the servant of a household head and his offspring," or a "bored or amused luxury-wife" in the home.[42] Like de Beauvoir, von Roten exposed romantic love as a flowery rationale for domestic slavery, motherhood as a "burden without dignity" (*Bürde ohne Würde*), and women's careers as underpaid and disrespected drudgery.[43] The book appeared in 1958, as a campaign for a constitutional change that would give all Swiss women the vote reached its peak (it failed in 1959). So vitriolic was the response to the book—typesetters refused to produce it, and an anti-suffrage cartoon showed the author as a dominatrix whipping a helpless man—that even some of von Roten's fellow suffragists accused her of discrediting their highly respectable movement. Von Roten gave up feminism and never wrote on women's issues again.

Feminism had always been an international movement, and the new technologies of the post-war era facilitated the movement of people and ideas. In 1963, the American author Betty Friedan published *The Feminine Mystique*, a book that made such a sensational impression in the English-speaking world that it was soon translated into many other languages: it appeared in French in 1964, in Spanish in 1965, in German in 1966.[44] Friedan vividly evoked the unsatisfying life of the American housewife, the victim of what she called the "feminine mystique"—the post-war cult of domesticity that glorified home, family, and the full-time housewife. In Europe, the book debunked a utopian myth of America as the land of wealth, optimism, and especially of female emancipation. The revelation that the American woman was not happy—indeed, often felt like a prisoner in her home, which Friedan called the "comfortable concentration camp"—discredited the pictures of perfect families that adorned the glossy pages of American women's magazines and other publications.

European women, too, recognized what Friedan called the "problem that has no name"—the frustration of women whose energies were stifled by domestic life. Friedan's translator in France was Yvette Roudy, a socialist who would later serve as her country's Minister of Women's Rights. "I recognized them," said Roudy of the women described by Friedan. "I saw them everywhere.... This suffering that comes from living below one's full capacity is not the prerogative of American women.... I witnessed serious crises. I saw suicide attempts and suicides." [45] And the Dutch Joke Smit-Lezingen, the head of an organization called the Men and Women's Society (*Man-Vrouw Matschaapij*), remarked in 1967 in a widely read essay entitled "The Discontent of Women" that domestic life and child-rearing no longer provided sufficient content for an adult life, and urged women to throw off the housewife role and develop new interests outside the home.[46]

Despite progress in many areas, these and other authors insisted that women's lives were still marked by subordination and dependency. Unlike earlier generations of feminists who had targeted chiefly the public sphere of law, politics, and institutions, this generation explored the inner world of the psyche. They suggested that no real change in women's status could be imposed from the outside, through legal or political reforms, but that the process of change must begin within the mind of the individual woman. These authors said much less about changing men, whom they portrayed sometimes as women's oppressors and sometimes as their role models. And they said little about the obstacles that confronted women who wished to change their lives and move toward equality.

Change and continuity

Though it began in the shadow of war and genocide, the post-war era quickly developed a prosperous and dynamic economy and a culture marked by optimism and rising expectations. The family experienced perhaps the greatest transformation in its modern history. Contraceptive methods—for the first time widely legalized and accepted—gave women an increasing measure of control over their fertility. In 1987, when a survey asked Belgian women what they thought was the most important change in the status of women since 1900, 70 percent named the introduction of the contraceptive pill, and only 27 percent, the winning of the right to vote.[47] The new consumer culture glamorized housework but also encouraged an increasing number of married women to combine their domestic responsibilities with paying jobs. By the 1970s, the busy superwoman who combined work and domesticity had superseded the homebound wife as a female role model. Meanwhile, new educational opportunities and the lure of social and geographical mobility weakened the hold of traditional religious and secular ideologies that prescribed obedience, self-sacrifice, and passivity as the virtues of women. Laws that subjected women to the authority of their husbands were abolished or modified in many countries, creating a basis for the evolution of the marriage relationship in the direction of gender equality.

Beneath all these changes, however, ran an undercurrent of continuity. Since the beginning of the twentieth century, the status of women had been shaped by a trend toward the breakdown of the nineteenth-century regime of separate spheres, and the integration of the sexes. In the post-war period, women mingled with men in workplaces, in schools and universities, in recreational activities, and in social life. But, in a world that was still dominated by men and structured to suit their interests and preferences, women could have only a subordinate place. A new generation of theorists asked why, amid so much social change, male supremacy and female subordination still continued. Their insights would be of central importance to the new feminist movement that arose in the 1970s.

6

Too Emancipated? Women in the Soviet Union and Eastern Europe, 1945–1989

Since its founding in 1917 the Soviet Union had presented itself to the world as a utopia of perfect sexual harmony. After 1945, Eastern European states that became Soviet satellites made the same claim. Scornfully denouncing Europe's capitalist countries as bastions of conservatism, the Eastern European communist regimes boasted of their own enlightened policies, which mandated gender equality in the family, in the workplace, in educational institutions, and in politics. In 1978, the East German author Christa Wolf acknowledged that the women of the Eastern Bloc were fortunate in many ways. "Yes, economically and legally we are equal to men, largely independent by virtue of equal educational opportunity and the freedom to make our own decisions about pregnancy and birth, no longer separated from the man of our choice by barriers of class or rank."[1] However, Wolf lamented that even this enlightened system had not fulfilled women's aspirations to be "able to live as a whole person, to make use of all their senses and abilities."[2] Why had communist governments' efforts to raise the status of women not produced better results?

In order to answer this question, we must consider both the specific history and structure of communist states, and the more general economic and social conditions that were common to all post-war societies, both communist and capitalist. On both sides of the Iron Curtain, women's educational level and workforce participation increased (but much more rapidly and coercively in the communist states). In both areas, this was called emancipation, but might more accurately be characterized as a process of gender integration, in which women joined men in workplaces, educational institutions, and—to a more limited extent—in political activities. In both East and West, the integration of women into the world of men caused similar problems, chiefly arising from the difficulties of combining familial and paid work. But while Western women tended to rejoice in their growing independence and prosperity, Eastern women complained of overwork, coercion, and oppression. Many rejected gender equality even as a goal, contending that women had become "too emancipated." In order to understand how women might think themselves "too emancipated," we must look at the gap between the bright promise and dismal reality of communist societies in several areas: politics, the family, the workplace, and culture.

The power of the powerless: women in politics

The communist governments of the Eastern Bloc followed the example of their sponsor and imperial overlord, the Soviet Union, by making women equal citizens who exercised the rights to vote and to hold political office. This change had more impact in some countries than others. Some, such as Czechoslovakia, Hungary, and Poland, had already granted women some political rights, including suffrage, in the inter-war years. But in Albania and the southern and eastern regions of Yugoslavia, women's status in 1945 was still much as it had been under the Ottoman Empire—a Muslim state centered in Istanbul that had ruled these areas from the fourteenth until the early twentieth centuries. Women had no political rights, and were subject in every way to the male heads of their extended families.

Declaring that this dark era of oppression was now at an end, the communist states abolished all legal restrictions on women's political participation. And on the surface, the results were striking. All communist governments sponsored huge women's organizations—for example, the Union of Albanian Women, the Yugoslav Women's Conference, and the Committee of Bulgarian Women— some of which were led by the wives of dictators or other prominent women. In the 1970s, the head of the official Soviet women's organization, the Soviet Women's Committee, was the famous woman cosmonaut (the Russian equivalent of the American "astronaut") Valentina Nikolaevna-Tereschkova. These groups' official mission, ostentatiously publicized in parades, ceremonies, and speeches on International Women's Day (March 8), was to improve the status and enhance the welfare of women and girls. So convincing was the glossy image that these governments sent out to the world that a few Western feminists idealized the Eastern Bloc as a paradise of gender equality. But the reality of what many Eastern Europeans referred to as "really existing socialism" was less impressive than the propaganda.

The Soviet Union and its satellite states claimed to be democracies—a term that was featured in the names of many satellite countries—and had a full range of representative institutions, including national and regional parliaments and elected boards of directors in collective farms and state enterprises. By including a substantial group of women in these bodies, governments appeared to give women a voice in political decision-making. But in fact these were totalitarian states, where only one party exercised power and opposition was forbidden. Elected representatives met chiefly to approve decisions that had already been made by the party leadership and had very little independent power. Real power resided with a small, closed, and ever-shifting group of leaders, to which women were rarely admitted.

Perhaps the only woman who forced her way into the power elite of a communist state through her own efforts, and not by riding the coattails of male relatives, was the Romanian Ana Pauker. Born as Hannah Rabinsohn into an orthodox Jewish family in 1893, Pauker became a communist party member and activist in the 1920s. Between 1940 and 1944, Pauker lived in exile in Moscow, where she became the leader of the Romanian communist community there. She re-entered Romania when Soviet forces occupied it in 1945, and, after the communist seizure of power, became the country's foreign minister. In 1948, Pauker's portrait appeared on the cover of *Time* captioned "The Most Powerful Woman in the World."[3] In Romania and throughout the world, she acquired the reputation of a fanatical Stalinist who would do anything— including denounce her own husband to the police—to carry out her leader's dictates. In fact, as the historian Robert Levy points out, Pauker opposed some Stalinist policies, including the forced collectivization of Romanian agriculture, and we do not know why her husband became a victim of Stalin's purges. But the demonic image that she acquired expressed the fear and hatred that the spectacle of a powerful and ruthless woman evoked.[4] Pauker fell from power when she and her faction were expelled from the Romanian Communist Party in 1952, and she died in 1960.

In the Soviet Union, the only woman to serve at the ministerial level was Ekaterina Furtseva, appointed by the Soviet Premier Nikita Khruschev as Minister of Culture in 1957 and fired four years later, probably because she had criticized him in a telephone conversation. Furtseva was one of only two women who were ever elected as full members of the Party's powerful Politburo, or executive committee. The historian Barbara Alpern Engel estimates that at the end of Khruschev's administration in 1964, women held only about 4 percent of positions that conferred genuine political power.[5] Likewise in communist Czechoslovakia, women constituted only about 7 percent of the Politburo.[6]

Communist dictators who needed women's labor in order to rebuild their countries often posed as enthusiastic champions of gender equality and osten-tatiously promoted women. "It is not fair," proclaimed the Romanian dictator Nicolae Ceauşescu in 1969, "that in enterprises in which ninety percent of the employees are women, all or nearly all the managers and chiefs should be men."[7] In the 1970s, Ceauşescu increased the representation of women on the elite Executive Committee of the Communist Party; whereas in 1969 only 6 percent of the members had been female, by 1984 their share had increased to 20 percent. In 1979, nine female members were promoted to the Party's central executive body, the Political Executive Committee.[8] But it was precisely at this time that real political power shifted away from the Executive Committee toward its inner circle, the Bureau—a body of which Elena Ceauşescu, the wife of the dictator, was the only woman member.

In some countries, the presence even of token women in government marked a real change—the emergence of the first generation of women who exercised any kind of influence outside their own households. In communist Albania, women attended secondary schools and universities for the first time after 1945, and some of these educated woman became a new female political elite. In the 1970s, several Albanian women held ministerial positions, and one, Lenka Cuko, was appointed in 1976 to the Communist Party's Politburo.[9]

Though seldom in leading positions, women were more numerous in local politics, where they often served on the governing bodies of collective farms, cities, social agencies, or regions. Women politicians usually worked in areas that were stereotyped female, such as health, education, social services, or the distribution of consumer goods. These women exercised a limited influence over policies that affected the lives of women and children. Even in these low-level jobs, women's careers typically differed from those of men: the women tended to be less experienced and less qualified, to hold their jobs for shorter periods, and to serve in regions that were far from the capital city.[10] And they took care not to emphasize women's issues, for any hint that their governments had not fulfilled their promise to emancipate women would have meant the end of their political careers and the accompanying privileges.

In some ways, the status of Eastern women was similar to that of their counterparts in the West, who also exercised very little direct political power and, when they held political office, were relegated to subordinate and stereotypically female functions. Nonetheless, there was a substantial difference in attitudes toward women in politics. In the Western democracies, many women regarded political activity positively, as a means to empower individuals and groups, and therefore worked to increase women's political involvement. Women who lived under communism took a much more negative view of political success, which they attributed less to individual merit than to conformity to the Party's ever-changing doctrines and associated more with corruption than with public spirit. Eastern European women (insofar as their attitudes can be reconstructed) tended to regard politics as a dirty and dangerous game that they were content to leave to men. In all the communist parties, women were a minority. For example, in the Soviet Union, where the Party made an effort to recruit them, their share of the membership rose from 18 percent in the 1950s to 29 percent by 1989.

Though some individual women became prominent politicians, few equated these women's success with the advancement of women as a group. For, with the few exceptions mentioned above, such women usually derived their power from their relationships to important men. For example, when the Romanian dictator Nicolae Ceauşescu took power in 1965, his wife Elena—a mother of three children who had also earned a doctorate—played only the usual role of political consort. However, in the 1970s she acquired a higher profile when she became the President of the National Council on Science and Technology and a leading member of the influential Council of Ministers. At the same time, a cult of personality exalted her as "the first woman of the country" who stood "as star stands beside star, beside the Great Man" and watched over "Romania's path to glory."[11] Naturally enough, the Romanian people resented her undeserved prominence, and blamed her for governmental policies that they disliked.

The satellite regimes of Eastern Europe owed their existence purely to the coercive control of a foreign power, the Soviet Union, and never gained the support of the majority of their people. Popular dissatisfaction, which usually boiled beneath a deceptively tranquil surface, sometimes erupted into open rebellions which the satellite governments themselves were unable to suppress. The fact that they were often compelled to call on the Soviet Union to put down these revolts only confirmed these governments' weakness and unpopularity. The dissident groups who led these rebellions and publicized their people's grievances to the outside world were male dominated, and admitted few women to leadership positions. Nonetheless, in these as in many political movements, a substantial and largely unrecognized portion of the actual work of mobilizing public opinion and providing essential support services was done by women.

In 1977, a group of Czech intellectuals protested against their government's suppression of individuals' freedom of expression and other violations of human rights in a document that they called Charter 77. Though most conspicuously led by men such as the playwright Václav Havel, this movement included a substantial minority of women. Women were 23 percent of those who signed the original document, and statements issued by the group were usually signed by three members, at least one of whom was a woman.

Who were the women who supported Charter 77? Some of them were the wives of prominent dissidents. Josefa Slánská was the widow of Rudolf Slánský, a prominent Communist who had been expelled from the party and then executed in the 1950s. Olga Havlová was married to the author and activist Václav Havel. Others were well-known authors, intellectuals, and artists. Eva Kantůrková studied philosophy and history at the Charles University in Prague and then worked as an editor and author. A prominent spokesperson for the Charter 77 group, she compiled a book of interviews with the movement's leaders. Though censors prevented the publication of this book within Czechoslovakia, it was published abroad and presented a very negative picture of the Czech government. Kantůrková was arrested in 1981 and charged with conspiring to smuggle illegal literature into the country. Although she was eventually released without a trial, the investigation continued until the fall of the communist regime in 1989.[12]

Jiřina Šiklová was a professor of sociology at the Charles University until she published articles that expressed support for the peaceful uprising known as the "Prague Spring" in 1968. Expelled both from her teaching position and from the Communist Party in 1969, she wrote several books on the problems of the elderly and on the position of women while working at a series of menial jobs. In 1977, she used her position as a well-known author and scholar to help other dissidents. She, too, was arrested and charged with "subversion" in 1981, served a jail sentence, and remained under investigation until 1989.[13]

As these prominent women were the first to admit, the democratic opposition depended for its survival on the quiet courage of many thousands of lesser-known people, women as well as men. From the beginning, the leaders of the Charter 77 movement discouraged open defiance of laws or violent uprisings against the government. The history of anti-communist revolts had shown that such actions often produced only suffering and death, not only for individuals but for their families: "even some of the protagonists" of the Charter 77 movement, wrote Šiklová, "feared that they might be needlessly jeopardizing their loved ones or other likeminded people and asked themselves 'Is it worth it?'" She added that the movement's purpose was "to save the nation rather than to sacrifice it."[14] Moreover, heroic actions of which only a few were capable could not form the basis of a mass movement.

In an essay entitled "The Power of the Powerless," which was secretly circulated as an unpublished typescript (or s*amizdat*), Havel proposed a strategy that was less flamboyant but more likely to produce long-term change.

He urged his fellow citizens to create a "parallel society" in which they quietly lived and acted according to their personal convictions rather than the dictates of the official ideology—a way of life which he called "living in the truth."[15] As this counterculture was centered chiefly in the home and the private sphere—which provided at least a partial retreat from the public world of politics—women were among its chief supporters. Whether by copying and circulating typescripts of forbidden literature, providing for families whose male breadwinners had lost their jobs for their political beliefs, encouraging their children to be skeptical of the official truths that they were taught in school, maintaining friendships with people who were under political suspicion, patronizing underground cultural events, and resisting pressure toward political conformity, women supported this quiet revolution. In the 1970s, dissenters were no longer punished, as they had been in the Stalin era, by execution or deportation to labor camps. But many lost their jobs, went to jail, and were denied professional and educational opportunities. Children and relatives of political dissenters also suffered these penalties. Teachers who supported Charter 77 protested courageously against official policies that discriminated against students for their own or their families' political activities.

The dissident group that played the most important role in the downfall of communism throughout Eastern Europe was the Polish labor organization known as "Solidarity." The organization was founded in 1981, as a response to the dismissal of a worker named Anna Walentynowicz from her job in the Lenin Shipyard in the Polish city of Gdansk. Walentynowicz, who was born in 1929, lost her entire family during the Second World War. She escaped from an abusive adoptive family and supported herself and her son by working as a crane operator in the shipyard, where she was honored by the government as a Hero of Socialist Labor. When she was fired for protesting against corruption and unfairness in her workplace, her fellow workers initiated a strike, which quickly developed into a campaign—joined by a wide segment of the population including unionized workers, students, intellectuals, professionals, and Church leaders—for democratization and economic reform. Women took the lead in formulating Solidarity's positions on issues of particular concern to them, such as shortages of food and housing and inadequate social services. Although women made up about 50 percent of Solidarity's membership, only one was elected to the body's National Executive Council in 1981. In that year a Polish general, Wojchiech Jaruzelski, declared martial law in Poland and prohibited Solidarity—an action to which he was instigated by the leaders of the Soviet Union.

Of the thousands of Solidarity activists who were arrested, only 10 percent were women, and thus more women than men remained to keep the movement alive. In the period between 1981 and the legalization of Solidarity in 1989, women played a vital though largely underground and anonymous role. In order to stay in touch with the membership, a group of women led by Helena Lucywo, the editor of a newspaper that had been shut down after the declaration of martial law, published an underground newsletter entitled *The Masow Weekly* (*Tygodnik Masowse*; Masow is a region in the Warsaw area). They set up their editorial offices and printing presses in the attics and cellars of private homes and moved every few weeks to avoid arrest. Women hid Solidarity leaders from the police, carried their messages, and helped them to move around without being detected. For these actions, many paid a heavy price. Lucywo, for instance, sent her daughter to live with grandparents and separated from her husband in order to protect him from being arrested for her activities.[16]

Communist states' official support of women's emancipation was intended to make women into loyal citizens, but it had the opposite effect of calling attention to the wide gap between propaganda and reality. A clash between the rising expectations of a post-war generation and a rigid and conservative political order set off a process of social and political change that eventually contributed to the downfall of the communist systems. But unlike many of their Western contemporaries, most Eastern European women did not channel their political energies into feminism, but joined their men in calling for the basic human rights and freedom of which both men and women had been deprived.

Equal partners? Marriage and the family

A central aspect of the communist agenda was the reform of marital and family relationships. As in the area of politics, the extent of this change differed in individual countries. In Poland, Czechoslovakia, Hungary, East Germany, and parts of Yugoslavia, married women had already gained some rights over their own property and employment decisions. But in Albania and in and parts of Bulgaria, Romania, and Yugoslavia, marriage laws and customs had hardly changed since these areas were part of the Ottoman Empire. Both Muslim and Christian households were organized as extended families in which the male head exercised the power of life and death over his dependents. Marriage transferred women from their fathers to their husbands—a transaction that was sometimes symbolized by the father's ceremonial presentation of a whip and a bullet to his new son-in-law. Alone in a household of strangers, the wife was powerless, and her position was little better than that of a slave.

Since the nineteenth century, a large body of socialist literature had denounced patriarchal marriage as the evil product of capitalism and promised a socialist utopia of true love and gender equality. When they took power, communist governments struck down all laws that subordinated wives to husbands. They proclaimed that men and women were now partners who shared equally in the joys and responsibilities of family life. In the satellite states, most laws were changed to imitate those of the Soviet Union, which since its beginnings in the 1920s had mandated marital equality. Communist governments also undermined age-old religious traditions by making marriage a civil ceremony.

Combined with the restructuring of labor markets and educational institutions, the results of these reforms were striking. As women's rates of literacy and overall educational qualifications rose and they entered the workforce in increasing numbers, some enjoyed a measure of financial independence and personal autonomy of which their mothers could hardly have dreamed. In each country, a female professional elite led independent and privileged lives in and outside of marriage and the family.

But for the majority of women, the promise of gender equality in marriage and the family raised expectations that were never fulfilled. For legal reform and inspirational propaganda alone could not do much to change hallowed customs and well-established ways of life. The most insightful socialist theorists of the past had realized that true gender equality required the restructuring of the household, domestic work, and child-rearing. Many had insisted that the socialist state must transfer the responsibility for services such as cooking, laundry, child-rearing, and household maintenance from the home to public agencies. But apart from child-care that enabled women to work outside the home, communist governments provided few such services. Any truly effective attack on male supremacy in the family would have violated an implicit bargain between the regimes and their male citizens, who in return for obedience to the government continued to enjoy their traditional privileges at home. The foundation of the communist as of the capitalist economies continued to be the unpaid household and reproductive labor of women, enforced by durable and largely unquestioned traditions of male supremacy.

Under these circumstances, what was advertised as "emancipation"—that is, the massive entry of married women into the labor force (a development that will be discussed in the following section)—was more often a crushing burden than an advantage. Except for the wealthy and privileged elite of the communist parties, the occupational category of "housewife" disappeared, and women combined paid labor and household responsibilities for most of their lives. But there was no parallel change in the work and familial roles of men. In fact, economic hardships and shortages reinforced some traditional notions of male and female work. Because most families had little access to the services of builders, plumbers, carpenters, or other tradesmen, men acquired a wide range of do-it-yourself skills, which they used both to remodel their own homes and to earn money in the underground economy. By contrast, housework, cooking, shopping and child-care were defined as female skills, "naturally" suited to women but demeaning to men.

In some ways, the conditions of the communist world resembled those of the Western democracies, where women also entered the paid labor market while continuing their responsibility for the household. But in Western economies that were oriented toward the consumer, household appliances, convenience foods, and many other products made housework easier and less time-consuming. No such luxuries were available to the women of Eastern Europe. Many Eastern European nations had always been poorer than those of the West. Moreover, the central planning agencies that ran the communist economies placed a low priority on supplying goods to the consumer market. Therefore, though standards of living improved, they were low compared to those in the West. In 1956, two-thirds of urban families in the Soviet Union lacked indoor plumbing and had to haul water from an outside tap, and as there were only about 300,000 washing machines in the entire country, almost all women heated water on a wood stove and washed clothes by hand. In rural areas, household technology was almost non-existent. Moreover, food was in such short supply that women spent at least an hour a day shopping, and often had to travel long distances to acquire necessary goods.

By the 1970s, the supply of consumer goods had improved, but refrigerators were found in only one half, and washing machines in two-thirds of Soviet households.[17] Living standards were somewhat higher in other communist countries, but washing machines, refrigerators, freezers, and vacuum cleaners were luxuries that at first were available only to the privileged few, and only gradually became available to the masses. As the Yugoslav journalist Slavenka Drakulić remembered, even those who had a washing machine had to keep their washtubs handy because they could not depend on a reliable supply of detergent. Unpredictable shortages made shopping a daily burden—often, after hours spent waiting in line, women would find that the store had run out of merchandise, and come home empty-handed. And some items were simply not available. Drakulić described how, when returning from the trips to Western Europe in the 1980s, she always filled her suitcase with packages of tampons and sanitary napkins to give to her friends. "After all these years, communism has not been able to produce a single sanitary napkin, a bare necessity for women," she complained. "So much for its...so-called emancipation."[18]

The Eastern European governments all insisted that the family was the foundation of the socialist state. In most communist countries, almost everyone married, usually at a young age. An exception to this pattern was East Germany, where a growing percentage of children were born to unmarried mothers—a trend that was due to policies that enabled women to combine motherhood with study and work and by the culture's tolerance of extramarital sexual relationships.[19] Though families with children received priority in the distribution of housing, they often waited for many years to move into their own apartments. In the Soviet Union in the 1950s, many families' private living space was confined to a single room in a communal apartment. In the 1960s and 1970s, governments devoted considerable resources to building new housing. But even in relatively prosperous countries such as Yugoslavia, families spent years sharing cramped living quarters with parents and in-laws. "The lack of apartments is such a common problem that after a while one simply doesn't notice it," wrote Drakulić. "In fact I have trouble recalling younger people or people of my generation who don't live like that, with their parents, even if they are past forty."[20] Rates of marital breakdown were high—a trend that was partly due to high rates of domestic abuse and male alcoholism as well as to inadequate housing. The number of divorces steadily rose. In the Soviet Union divorce rates doubled between 1963 and 1974, and most of these actions were initiated by women. In Moscow and Leningrad, as in many other urban areas, half of all marriages ended in divorce.[21]

Not surprisingly, women and couples responded to these stressful living conditions by limiting the number of their children. Because contraceptives were always in short supply, the most common method of limiting births was abortion. In the Soviet Union abortion, which had been legalized in 1920 but re-criminalized in the 1930s, was once again legalized in 1955. All of the Soviet satellites except Albania and East Germany followed the Soviet example by permitting terminations when performed during the first three months of pregnancy by a physician in a hospital or clinic. Though all the laws made abortion contingent on indications—such as danger to the mother's life or health or a difficult social situation—in fact these were loosely enforced, and the number of legal abortions climbed rapidly: in Hungary from 8.3 abortions per thousand people in 1956 to 16.3 in 1962; in Bulgaria from 4.9 to 8.7 during the same period.

After the high rates produced by the post-war baby boom, birthrates declined steeply during the years from 1950 until 1962: in Poland from about 30 per thousand population to 19.6; in Czechoslovakia from 22 to 15; in Yugoslavia from 28 to 22; in Hungary from 21 to 12.[22] The decline set in earlier in Eastern than in Western Europe or North America—where birthrates continued high until the mid-1960s—and it raised the prospect of a shortage of adult laborers. As the communist governments mistrusted outsiders, they could not follow the example of the Western European nations, which admitted many immigrant "guest workers" during the 1950s and 1960s. Declining rates of population growth thus constituted a very direct threat to the survival of the nations of the Eastern Bloc.

Governments responded by rewarding child-bearing with cash subsidies and other benefits that were designed to make mothers' lives easier. As a part of their socialized health-care programs, all Eastern European governments provided a wide range of medical services to pregnant women, mothers, and children. In Hungary, mothers-to-be who saw a physician three times before delivery received coupons for low-cost milk and free baby clothes and other supplies. Though these services were unevenly provided, and more available in urban than in rural areas, they reduced rates of maternal mortality and extended female life expectancy, which increased relative to that of men. The average life expectancy of Hungarian women rose from about 64 years in 1950 to about 77 years in 1990, while that of their male fellow citizens rose from 60 to 67 years in the same period, and other Eastern Bloc countries showed similar statistics.[23] Maternity leaves with pay were extended. For example, in the 1980s, Polish mothers received 16 weeks for the first and 18 for subsequent births. Governments also paid cash subsidies to parents, often graduated according to the number of children, and provided special assistance to unmarried and single mothers.

All communist governments subsidized child-care, though the number of children enrolled varied widely. In East Germany in the 1980s, about 63 percent of children aged five months to three years were in nurseries, and about 91 percent of three- to six-year-olds were in all-day kindergartens.[24] In other countries, attendance was lower: in Czechoslovakia only about 22 percent of children under three were in day-care.[25] The Soviet Union provided care for only about 13 percent of children in the 1950s, and for about 22 percent in 1965, when about half of all urban children but only about 12 percent of those in rural areas were enrolled.[26]

Though these services were certainly beneficial, they could not solve the problems of women who had to combine a full-time work schedule with housekeeping and child-care in a situation where all necessary resources— housing, consumer goods, and services—continued to be in short supply. Therefore, in most countries birthrates continued to drop. Communist leaders considered more coercive responses to the birthrate crisis. Most concluded that the re-criminalization of abortion would merely alienate public opinion without doing much to encourage child-bearing. But, as the examples of the East German state, known as the German Democratic Republic (GDR), and Romania show, reproductive policies varied widely.

The GDR was one of only two satellite states (the other was Albania) that had not followed the lead of the Soviet Union in legalizing abortion in the 1950s. The government of the GDR justified this decision by pointing both to devastating wartime losses and to the continued drain on its population caused by the flight of qualified young people to West Germany, which offered them citizenship and employment opportunities. The "Law for the Protection of Mother and Child and the Rights of Women," passed in 1950, allowed the termination only of pregnancies that threatened the life and health of the mother or were likely to produce a handicapped or damaged child. The law required women who wished to terminate pregnancies to submit petitions to a state-appointed committee. In the 1950s, most of these petitions cited economic hardships or medical problems.

But, as the historian Donna Harsch has discovered, the 1960s brought social and cultural changes that were in many ways similar to those that occurred in the West. Petitions from women now complained of the consequences of unplanned pregnancies for their educational and career prospects. A new generation of physicians, many of them women who experienced these problems in their own lives, argued for the liberalization of the abortion law. Meanwhile the Berlin Wall, which was built in 1961, had blocked the flow of refugees from East to West Germany and somewhat calmed official fears of population loss. In 1972, the GDR legalized abortion on demand in the first trimester of pregnancy. This legal reform was one sign that the government was increasingly responsive to the concerns of the population, of which women now constituted an important and influential segment.[27]

The government of Romania took a completely opposite approach, based on the megalomania of its dictator, Nicolae Ceaușescu, and his disregard for the welfare of women, children, and the country as a whole. Though it dropped during the 1960s, Romania's birthrate was still higher than that of some other Eastern European countries, such as East Germany or Hungary. As elsewhere, rates of abortion were high—in 1966, there were about four terminations for every live birth. In that year, Ceaușescu decided that the population of Romania must increase from 19 to 25 million. A new law permitted only those abortions that were necessary to save the life of the mother, to prevent the birth of a handicapped child, to remove the results of rape or incest, or in other rare cases. It criminalized all other abortions, and was enforced by special police units stationed in hospitals. In 1967, the birthrate increased by 92.8 percent, but this effect was brief, and soon birthrates dropped once again. In the 1970s, the government again tried to encourage child-bearing by increasing benefits to pregnant women, but without achieving the desired result. By the 1980s, abortions (now chiefly illegal) once again outnumbered births. In 1984, the government lowered the legal marriage age for girls to 15 and appointed "demographic command units" to examine all women of child-bearing age for evidence of pregnancy, contraceptive use or abortion, to monitor all pregnancies to see that they were carried to term, and to investigate childless women and couples.

In spite of these tyrannical policies, the birthrate of Romania in the 1980s was lower than in the 1960s and only slightly higher than that of neighboring countries. And the consequences were catastrophic: overcrowded orphanages, high rates of maternal and infant mortality, and a generation of children who grew up with inadequate care and education.[28]

Though these reproductive policies theoretically applied to all women, their application often varied according to racial and ethnic criteria. Throughout Eastern Europe, the Roma (commonly known as Gypsies) were a minority who differed in their appearance, language, culture, and way of life from majority populations. Because of their dark coloring and refusal to assimilate, the Roma were often the targets of racial and ethnic prejudice. And there was another difference—unlike the majority populations among which they lived, the Gypsies placed a high value on child-bearing and typically had large families. The suspicion that these detested outsiders received a large share of government subsidies for large families caused widespread resentment. While governments did everything possible to encourage and even sometimes to coerce child-bearing among their majority populations, they took the opposite approach to unpopular minorities. In many countries, laws that permitted voluntary or compulsory sterilization were enforced disproportionately against Roma women. In 1971, the Czech Ministry of Health, Labor, and Social Affairs charged that Gypsy families were producing a large number of retarded children and adopted policies that made abortion easy for Gypsy women and provided financial benefits to those who agreed to sterilization. Social workers threatened women who did not consent with penalties such as the removal of their children to orphanages. Similar policies were in effect in other countries; the number of their victims is unknown.[29]

Despite the communist governments' official support of women's emancipation, both family and state remained patriarchal. Though often discontent with their subordinate status, however, most Eastern European women did not agree with Western feminists that the marriage and family were inherently sexist and oppressive institutions. In a police state where social interactions with strangers had to be guarded and cautious, the home often provided an oasis of intimacy, trust, and spontaneity. A view of the family as an institution ordained by nature or by God often justified resistance to state intrusion and totalitarian control. Eastern European women did not rebel against the family—on the contrary, many wished only to be able to enjoy it.

The double day: mothers and workers

Communist ideology and practice demanded productive labor of both men and women. In theory, the socialist state required all citizens to work according to their abilities and compensated them according to their needs. As a practical matter, the labor of all adults was essential to the state's survival. In the years after the war, a shortage of male labor required the full participation of women in the immense task of post-war reconstruction. By the 1970s, it was clear that the communist nations had fallen behind the West in technology, and a relatively inefficient and unproductive economy required large numbers of workers. Universal employment also served political ends, for the workplace could be more easily supervised than the home.

On Soviet propaganda posters, a robust and smiling female tractor-driver often embodied the emancipated socialist woman. But a decade after the war's end, under 1 percent of Soviet tractor-drivers were women, and this one statistic exemplified a more widespread trend.[30] Why did the massive entry of women into the labor force not promote gender equality? The explanation must lie in two areas: the persistence of notions about "natural" character and abilities and the state's determination to harness both the productive and the reproductive labor of women.

In nations where women workers had traditionally suffered from many forms of discrimination, communism first seemed to promise a new and brighter future. New laws guaranteed women's rights to employment; economic policies enabled them to obtain and keep full-time jobs; and the expansion of education encouraged them to upgrade their qualifications and to gain advancement. Everywhere, women's rates of literacy increased, and an increasing number attended secondary school and university. The most rapid change occurred in Albania, a country where education for women had been almost non-existent, but where in the 1970s women made up about 40 percent of the school population at all levels.[31] In Czechoslovakia, women had comprised only about 20 percent of all university students in 1950 but by 1989 their share of student bodies had increased to about 44 percent of all students, and the average time spent in school by men and women was approximately equal.[32] In 1980, Hungarian girls finished primary school at the same rate as men, and were just as likely to enter a university, although men's rates of graduation were higher.[33] Women's rate of participation in the paid, full-time labor force approached that of men. Among Hungarians between 15 and 45 years of age in 1980, about 83 percent of all women, and 90 percent of all men were full-time workers. In Poland in the 1970s women were about 43 percent of the full-time workforce.[34]

Many governments initiated affirmative-action programs designed to improve women's qualifications and to place them in non-traditional forms of employment. But despite these efforts, women's occupational patterns remained much the same as they had been during the inter-war era. In many fields, male and female spheres were defined by technology. The higher its level of technological sophistication, the more likely a job was to be labeled male. On collective farms women constituted about two-thirds of all workers but they seldom operated machinery. Female industrial workers continued to be concentrated in textile or garment factories, where the work was classified as "light" but actually involved long shifts and stressful conditions. By paying these women low wages, the government subsidized new technology in industries that employed chiefly male workers. Although all but a few vocational training programs were open to both genders, in practice women were admitted only to those that prepared them for conventionally female work. In East Germany in the 1980s, more than 60 percent of all female apprentices went into just 16 of a total of 289 skilled trades.[35]

White-collar women clustered—as they had since the nineteenth century— in jobs that involved education, service, or clerical work. Women constituted 77 percent of all East German workers in education and 86 percent of those in health and social services. In other Eastern European countries, too, almost all nurses, secretaries, and pre-school teachers were women. And in universities, women students were segregated by their choice of major fields. In departments of humanities, education, and medicine (considered a female field) women were the majority of students, while men predominated in specialties such as engineering, mathematics, law, and technical sciences. Though many were highly educated, female professionals such as nurses, medical assistants, kindergarten teachers, and social workers earned very low salaries. Even in these female-stereotyped fields, women were seldom promoted to leadership positions. Surveys of public opinion showed that women as well as men preferred male bosses and believed women to be deficient in leadership ability.

Thus, despite their governments' claim to have raised the status of working women, women in communist economies were as disadvantaged relative to men as those who lived under capitalism. In all sectors, women's average earnings were about two-thirds those of men. Despite state subsidies and benefits for families, those headed by a woman tended to be the poorest.

Labor-market policies reinforced gender disparities in status and income. In the immediate post-war years, a shortage of men created a demand for qualified women in many fields. But in the 1960s and 1970s, declining birth rates created another and equally important priority. Socialist economic policies took into account only productive, or waged labor, and assumed that all workers could devote themselves fully to their jobs without any other obligations—a model that assumed that the worker was a male. These policies took no account of reproductive labor, the production and maintenance of people. And clearly, the very survival of the state depended on a steady supply of new people—a supply that could only be produced by the reproductive labor that biology and custom assigned to women.

The states attempted to raise birthrates by enacting measures designed to induce women to bear children. But unlike Western European nations where labor-market policies encouraged mothers to quit or to cut back to part-time hours, communist states could not do without women's productive labor. Therefore, their policies were designed to enable women to combine full-time paid work and motherhood. The most comprehensive of these legislative programs was enacted in the GDR, which had become well known in both East and West for the high priority it placed on women and their needs. In the 1970s, the workweek of women who had two or more children was reduced from 43.5 to 40 hours, with the explicit purpose of providing time for housework. Mothers were given leaves of 18 weeks or more for the birth of each child, and of four to six weeks to care for sick children. Moreover, mothers—married or single—received preference in obtaining housing, including space in university dormitories, and factories were required to provide day-care on the premises. These measures defined reproductive labor as an entirely female obligation. Fathers, by contrast, were assumed to bear no parental responsibilities, and could claim these benefits only if the mother was absent or incapable of carrying out the duties that were defined as exclusively hers.

The main effect of these policies was to intensify already existing patterns of segregation and discrimination. The woman worker, whom propaganda had once portrayed as a cheerful and capable comrade, now appeared as a burdened and exhausted working mother. Discrimination against all women had a ready-made justification: women spent less time at work, were more likely to be absent, and were generally less reliable. Men used women's entitlements to extra time off and other perks as an excuse to keep them in low-level positions—clearly, they were not their families' primary breadwinners, and their main interests lay outside the workplace. Many policies that were intended to help mothers applied to all female workers, even those without children, and were hardest on the able and ambitious women who, even by hard work and competence, could not overcome the prevailing stereotype. As the sociologist Myra Marx Ferree concludes, the state's need for women's reproductive labor overrode its professed commitment to gender equality.[36] Of course, policies designed to protect mothers also stood in the way of advancement for many women in the capitalist West as well as in the communist East.

The communist nations boasted of having emancipated women through work. But many women took a dim view of this so-called emancipation, which they associated more with coercion than with independence, and more with hardship than success. "Czechoslovakia has a very high level of female employment, in fact one of the highest in the world," stated a position paper of the Charter 77 movement, "but we are all aware that this fact makes a virtue of necessity. Most women do not take jobs because they wish for a fuller life of independence, but rather under economic pressure and out of bare necessity, because their husbands' pay would not ensure a decent life for their families. Consequently, the almost universal employment of women is not a sign of their increased equality, but rather of a higher degree of their dependence."[37] Although surveys of public opinion showed that most women valued their jobs and wished to continue working, many also envied the Western housewife. By their efforts to abolish the housewife role, the communist regimes actually raised its prestige.

Living in the truth: women as producers of culture

Communist governments tightly censored all forms of cultural production. Artists, authors, journalists, and performers who adopted the official line were rewarded, but those who challenged it were subject to supervision and often to harsh penalties, which included deprivation of educational or professional opportunities (often extended to the family members of suspects), loss of employment, and sometimes jail sentences or exile. Among the prohibited themes was feminism, which official policy declared to be irrelevant—after all, socialism had solved the "woman question"—and a sign of decadent and subversive Western influence. Nonetheless, creative people found ways of getting around these constraints by examining gender relations in stories of private and personal life, with political dimensions that were implied rather than directly stated.

The country that produced the largest body of female-authored literature was the GDR, where the government permitted much more open discussion of gender issues than those of the other communist states. As the literary scholar Patricia Herminghouse points out, East German authors of the 1950s depicted women who bucked the opposition of their husbands and co-workers to realize their educational and professional ambitions. Though often openly critical of gender inequality, these stories always featured exemplary heroines who wished only to build socialism, and ended happily when a wise Party official intervened to solve all problems.[38]

However, by the 1960s a new kind of narrative emerged, in which the conflict between the heroine's aspirations and the expectations of husbands or bosses had no simple and politically correct solution. Very often, these stories focused on the "double day" and the consequences of overwork for the working woman herself and for her family.[39] Most authors presented this problem as insoluble, even by magic or supernatural intervention. A story entitled "I Quit" by the author and actress Charlotte Worgitzky introduces us to a woman who manages to combine a fulfilling marriage and a brilliant career only by asking her guardian angel to enable her to do without sleep. But when her husband—presumably turned off by her success—takes up with another woman, she asks the angel to break the spell and cuts back her schedule. As a result, she ends up as a psychiatric patient—a sinister fate in the communist world, where commitment to a mental hospital was one way of dealing with non-conformists.[40]

A chapter from Irmtraud Morgner's novel *The Life and Adventures of the Troubadour Beatriz according to the Testimony of her Minstrel Laura* features a brilliant physicist who can cope with her demanding career and the obligations of single motherhood only by walking a tightrope from her home to her workplace (thus saving the time required for commuting). Eventually she falls to her death.[41] On the surface, these stories were not about politics, but about private life, and women's difficulties in reconciling familial obligations and individual ambition could be seen as a natural consequence of their biology and psychology. Nonetheless, for those disposed to receive it, there was a political message as well: that the GDR's claim to have "emancipated" women was simply a lie—and a lie that often had tragic consequences.

The best-known author who emerged from the GDR was Christa Wolf, who was born in 1929 in a German town that became Polish after the border was changed in 1945. Wolf's family fled westward to Mecklenburg, which became a northern province of the GDR. Having studied German language and literature at the University of Jena, Wolf became an editor and author whose works became known in both East and West Germany and were translated into many languages. In her novel *Thinking about Christa T.*, published in 1968, Wolf broke with literary convention by presenting a woman who was not a hard-working socialist heroine. Instead, this semi-autobiographical figure was like many characters in Western fiction—a troubled individual whose search for happiness put her at odds with social conventions and political constraints. Unable to find a satisfactory way of living, Christa died young, a victim of cancer but also of depression and alienation.[42] Wolf often dealt with the intersection of the personal and the political. In another story, a woman student's love affair with a married professor had a tragic outcome, and not just because the characters themselves made bad choices but also because the university authorities—who like all public officials were agents of the state—unfairly penalized the student and left the professor to pursue his successful academic career.[43]

Defending herself against criticism, Wolf claimed that she supported socialist ideals and wished only to see her society live up to them. But her works also raised the highly subversive themes of individualism, self-determination, and non-conformity. Like other Eastern European authors, Wolf believed that the state's version of "emancipation" was not motivated by real concern for women, but rather by a ruthless intolerance of all human diversity. She called on women to resist cultural pressures to imitate men and to develop their own, distinctively feminine ways of living and thinking. "For there are many indications ... of dissatisfaction among the women of our country," she remarked in 1978.

> Their first concern is no long what they have, but who they are.... Their lust for life is great, their hunger for reality insatiable.... Our society made it possible for women to do what men do; to this, they have predictably raised the question: what *do* men do? And is that really what I want?[44]

Though she did not call herself a feminist, Wolf often resorted to traditional feminist arguments that women's traditions of compassion and non-violence could save men from themselves. "Conditions in our country have enabled women to develop a self-awareness which does not simultaneously imply the will to control, to dominate, or to subjugate, but rather the ability to cooperate. For the first time in their history they are defining their differentness—an immense step forward."[45]

Authors and artists who dealt critically with gender relations were often silenced by censorship, political pressure, and intimidation. The film director Vera Chitilová was a leading figure in the Czech "New Wave" of the 1960s—a group that produced movies that won international acclaim. Innovative in both form and content, her films often dealt with explicitly feminist themes and were much in demand at women's film festivals around the world. After suppressing the uprising that was known as the "Prague Spring" in 1968, the new government tightened censorship and prevented Chitilová from making films and from traveling abroad to show her work and to receive the many prizes that international juries awarded her. In a letter to the President of Czechoslovakia dated October 8, 1975, Chitilová courageously protested against the destruction of her career. She declared that her most recent film had no subversive intent, but dealt only with "the relationship of a man and a woman, the problem of discovering the truth behind this relationship, and the courage to live with this truth." Among the charges that she denied were "that my films were experimental by nature, uncommitted and pessimistic ... that my international prizes came chiefly from western festivals ... that my films had been overvalued by the critics, and that it 'did not appear' that I had 'understood the contemporary cultural policy of the Communist Party of Czechoslovakia.'" Her letter concluded with a promise to "continue to fight for the ideals of a socialist society."[46]

Slavenka Drakulić, a Yugoslav journalist who often traveled abroad and was known as a feminist was "invited" to have coffee with a government censor, who made no open threat but informed her that she was under suspicion. She reflected that the most debilitating effect of official surveillance was on her integrity as a journalist who would censor herself to avoid any further problems.[47] An example of self-censorship was Christa Wolf's story, "What Remains"—an obviously autobiographical account of the surveillance and intimidation to which she was subjected by the East German police. Wolf wrote this story in the 1970s, but did not publish it until 1990, after the fall of communism in East Germany.[48]

Though they often dealt with gender issues, these authors and artists could not explore them with the freedom that was permitted to their Western counterparts. Forbidden to criticize any governmental policy, they could say little about birth control, abortion, wage inequality, and discrimination in schools and workplaces. Also prohibited was the open discussion of homosexuality and of Western feminist movements. Partly because of these limitations, the works of Eastern European women placed less emphasis on gender antagonism than on the concerns that women shared with men. As Slavenka Drakulić commented, "It's hard to see them as an opposite force, men as a gender, it's hard to confront them as enemies. Perhaps because everyone's identity is denied, we want to see them as persons, not as a group or a category or a mass."[49] Like contemporary political dissidents, these authors emphasized the right of all persons (in the words of Havel) to "live in the truth." And, as Christa Wolf pointed out, this was a universally human aspiration. "How can we women be liberated as long as all people are not?"[50]

The failure of emancipation

The post-war communist states contributed to the trend toward gender integration that marks the history of the twentieth century. Their governments deliberately dismantled the barrier between public and private spheres and persuaded or compelled the majority of women to forsake the domestic role and to join men in educational institutions, in the workplace, in politics, and in social and recreational pursuits. Official propaganda equated integration with "emancipation," and indeed many women benefited from the new opportunities that the communist states offered. But others suffered from policies that purported to advance women's well-being but in reality justified exploitation and oppression. Women in the communist world shared some of the problems that beset their counterparts in capitalist Western Europe, where a similar process of gender integration went under the name of "emancipation." In neither communist nor capitalist systems was the transformation of women's familial and work roles accompanied by corresponding changes in male behavior and life patterns. In the absence of any serious attack on male supremacy, the integration of women into the world of men had very mixed consequences, which along with new opportunities also included new forms of disadvantage, discrimination, and exploitation. This was one problem that a new feminist movement would address in the 1970s.

7

The Personal and the Political: Women's Liberation in Western Europe, 1968–1990

In 1968, a woman delegate to the annual meeting of the Students for a Democratic Society in Frankfurt, Germany, rose to speak and criticized her male colleagues' reactionary attitudes toward gender relations. She then pelted the speakers on the stage with tomatoes. In 1970, a group of young women crashed a gynecologists' conference in the Netherlands and lifted their shirts to show the slogan "Boss of my own belly" (*Baas im eigen buik*) written on their bodies. In Paris in 1970, women invaded their country's most revered secular shrine, the tomb of the Unknown Soldier, to consecrate a memorial wreath to that less honored victim, the soldier's wife. And in 1971, three women named Maria published a book that defied the censorship laws of Portugal's police state by detailing in vivid and sexually explicit language the grievances of their country's women. Truly the women of post-war Western Europe, hitherto such hard-working and well-mannered citizens, were behaving in new and disturbing ways. As the Italian feminists exulted, "Watch out, the witches are back!" (*Tremate, tremate, le strege son tornate*).

The feminist movement that began around 1968, reached its peak between 1970 and 1978, and has continued in various forms ever since, is often called the "second wave"—a term that places it in relation to the "first wave" of the nineteenth and early twentieth centuries. The historian Karen Offen rejects this metaphor, which implies that the history of feminism consisted of brief waves of activity surrounded by long troughs of quiescence. Instead, she imagines a volcano, in which feminism is a magma that constantly boils below the surface and erupts through any available fissure.[1] Such a fissure opened in the 1960s, a time of social upheaval when a youthful elite that had reached adulthood after the Second World War aggressively challenged many established structures—governments, churches, universities, economic systems—and called on them to change in accordance with the needs and aspirations of the younger generation.

Among these young activists were many women, who broke with the past history of feminism by giving their movement a new name, "women's liberation." They believed that the struggle for gender equality must begin again, with new ideas and new strategies. Earlier generations of feminists had aimed chiefly to dismantle the legal and political structures that upheld male supremacy. In many countries, they had succeeded to such an extent that feminism was widely assumed to have achieved its goals and outlived its usefulness. And the winning of suffrage and other rights had certainly improved the lives of women in many areas. But these achievements—impressive as they were—had done little to change the structure of male–female relations, which was still firmly based on male supremacy and female subordination. Although women voted, few had gained high positions in government; although women had equal legal rights in the family, most still did the unpaid labor of child-rearing and house-work; although women's job opportunities had expanded, they still clustered in low-paying and female-stereotyped occupations. The woman who did not conform to dominant models of femininity was often regarded as abnormal, even emotionally disturbed. And culture, including movies, television, print media, and advertising, still justified gender inequality through countless images of strong, aggressive men and beautiful, feminine, nurturing women.

Why had male supremacy proved so durable, and how could it finally be overthrown? The new feminists engaged many public issues, and called for legal reforms in the areas of job discrimination, reproductive rights, the family, and many other areas. At the same time, they insisted that these external changes alone could not liberate women. Ultimately, the source of women's oppression was in their own minds, which culture had conditioned to accept its prescribed models of femininity. Liberation, then, must begin with each individual woman, who must be empowered to throw off this crippling psychological burden, to develop a new sense of herself and her possibilities, and to join other women who shared the same vision to create a world where men and women were equal.

The new feminism flourished chiefly in the Western European democracies, but also arose in the Southern European countries—Portugal, Greece, Spain—when they made the transition from dictatorship to democracy during the 1970s. Communist regimes prohibited this and all other dissenting movements, so feminism did not emerge overtly in Eastern Europe until the fall of communism after 1990 (to be discussed in the next chapter). We will look at the origins of the new feminist movements, its organizing strategies, the issues that it addressed, its leading personalities, its theoretical foundations, and its results.

Sisterhood is powerful: organizing for liberation

The Women's Liberation movements that began in 1968 were created by a new generation of activists, many of whom were university students or recent graduates. Most of these activists had been born between 1935 and 1950 and had grown to adulthood in the peaceful, stable, and prosperous post-war era. The youth culture of the 1960s emphasized self-expression, enjoyment, and spontaneity. As they reached adulthood, young people dreamed of transforming society in accordance with these values, and many began their political careers in the established left-wing parties, both communist and socialist. They were quickly disillusioned by these parties' authoritarian leadership style, rigid ideologies, and intolerance of dissent. In the years between 1968 and 1980, several groups—including radical students, environmentalists, and gay-rights activists—broke away from left-wing parties to establish their own organizations. Initially, the women members of these groups worked with their male comrades. But soon, some complained that even these progressive men excluded them from leadership and treated them with condescension, even contempt. Starting in 1968, these young women split off from male-dominated parties or movements to found autonomous all-female groups, which they dedicated to liberating women from male oppression in all areas of life and politics.

The "Women's Liberation" movement proclaimed that sisterhood was powerful and that women were strong together. But organizing women was more difficult that these slogans suggested. From the 1890s until 1968, women's movements had usually been structured by large national "umbrella" organizations in which only a small elite of leaders made policies, which were ratified by a majority vote of the members. Though effective in mobilizing mass support for issues such as suffrage, these organizations also suppressed dissent and often ignored minority groups. In the period 1968–1980, national organizations continued to play an important role in some countries.

But the period's distinctive form of organization was the small group that rejected centralized control and followed diverse agendas that were set by a consensus of its members. The organizational culture of Women's Liberation arose from its central principles. Women must stop looking to men to liberate them and organize around their own oppression. And this process began with each woman, who must recognize and deal with her own situation before taking action on behalf of others. Many meetings focused on a process called "consciousness-raising," in which each woman took turns recounting various aspects of her own experience, especially in intimate areas such as sexuality, family life, and parent–child relationships. The purpose was to gain what the Italians called *autoscienza*—the knowledge of oneself—and also group solidarity based on shared insights.

The young women rejected hierarchical structures and proclaimed that all groups were free to develop their own agendas. If the result was a proliferation of groups, so much the better, for every woman must find her own road to liberation. "In principle, we would not set up a fixed collective political line," wrote the editors of a French periodical, *Histoires d'Elles,* "it is precisely diversity and contradiction that seem to be elements of richness, of life, of openness." [2]

The role of group members was not—as in conventional political parties—limited to electing representatives to act for them in the distant halls of parliament. Rather, the group planned political actions together and held them in public spaces where all those present could observe or participate as they wished. Groups dramatized their demands imaginatively by holding marches and demonstrations, protesting oppressive models of femininity by picketing beauty contests and fashion shows, staging sit-ins and takeovers of women's magazines, and coordinating other forms of protest. For example, one day a group of Danish feminists protested the fact that women's wages were on average only about 80 percent of men's by paying only 80 percent of their streetcar fares, and when penalized paying only 80 percent of the fine.[3]

These strategies were well suited to the conditions of post-war democracies, where mass media were free to cover spectacular or sensational events. Women used the media effectively to publicize their cause. In 1971, the Irish lawyer Mary Robinson and two of her colleagues appeared on a popular television program, the *Late, Late Show*, outlined the many legal disadvantages that Irish women still suffered, and called on their government to pass new laws that mandated equal protection. A Member of Parliament, Garret Fitzgerald, burst into the studio to dispute these shocking allegations, claiming that Irish women had few legal rights because they did not need them. A meeting called by Robinson and her group shortly after the show drew a large number of women.[4]

The relationships of feminist groups to established political parties differed in each country. In Britain, France, West Germany, and Holland, autonomous groups (those with no party affiliation) with names such as Redstockings, Revolutionary Femininists, or Crazy Minas (*Dolle Mina*, the name of a Dutch group that named itself for a famous feminist of the early twentieth century, Wilhelmine Drucker) carried out the most conspicuous actions. These groups soon split to reflect political divisions and other kinds of diversity among their members. Among French groups formed during the period 1970–1975 were *Choisir* (Choice), which focused on abortion rights; *Spirale*, which supported women's creative activity; the *Cercle Dimitriev*, which combined socialist and feminist agendas; and *Psych et Po*, which studied the relationship of feminism to psychoanalysis.

In all countries, left-wing women struggled to reconcile the theories of Marx with those of women's liberation. Some gave up this attempt and committed themselves to a radical feminism that emphasized gender over class oppression, while others tried to advocate both the rights of women and those of the working class—a strategy that they called "double militancy." British women attempted such a strategy in 1969, when feminists and women labor-union activists cooperated in National Joint Action Campaign for Equal Rights. But this movement, too, soon dissolved into a large assortment of autonomous groups.

While some groups seceded from political parties others maintained their connection to these parties. In Italy, dissenters within the communist women's organization, the Union of Italian Women (*Unione donne italiane*, or Udi) rebelled against the party's male leadership. Some left the party to form the Movement for the Liberation of Women (*Movimento di liberazione della donna*, founded in Rome in 1970), and many other autonomous groups—a secession that left-wing men protested with verbal abuse, harassment, and sometimes with violence. Other women, however, stayed in the Udi and eventually gained control of the organization, which in 1981 declared itself an autonomous entity that was open to cooperation with women of all political persuasion. But the Udi still maintained its connection to the Communist Party, which having broken its ties to Moscow in the 1970s became more receptive to women's participation and concerns.[5]

The socialist parties that had governed the Scandinavian countries since the 1930s differed from those of other countries by their openness to feminism and to women, who had held leadership positions since the 1930s. When autonomous women's movements emerged, they had only a brief period of activity, for many of their demands were immediately absorbed into socialist party programs and enacted into law. The close relationship of feminists to the state had both advantages and disadvantages: it made some reforms much easier, but it also cut off the development of a strong, independent feminism in Scandinavia.

Unlike other Western European countries where democracy was well established, Spain, Portugal, and Greece took their first steps toward democracy in the 1970s. Under dictatorial rule, some feminists had worked underground. With the overthrow of dictatorships in Portugal in 1974 and in Spain and Greece in 1975, a multitude of new women's groups emerged and flourished. Some of these were connected to political parties and some were autonomous. In Portugal, the Women's Democratic Movement (*Movimento Democrático das Mulheres*), an organization linked to the Communist Party, published a journal entitled *Mulheres* (Women). A small, autonomous Women's Liberation Movement (*Movimento de Libertação das Mulheres*) campaigned to insert clauses on women's rights into the country's new constitution. In Spain, communist women founded the Organization of Women (*Union Popular de Mujeres*). Anarchists revived a group that had been active in the 1930s, called the Free Women (*Mujeres Libres*). In addition, there was a host of other groups with names such as The Witches (*Las Brujas*) and The Sorcerers (*Las Majas*). Among Greek organizations were the communist Federation of Greek Women, the socialist Union of Greek Women, and some small autonomous groups.

Feminists were divided not only by their political views, but also by other aspects of identity. In consciousness-raising groups that centered on problems such as heterosexual relationships, marriage, reproduction, and motherhood, lesbians felt like outsiders. They separated themselves from heterosexual women and developed their own, distinctive programs and goals. "We must all learn to develop our theoretical understanding of women's oppression from the standpoint provided by our own life situation," wrote a German lesbian in 1975. "We will be able to work with other women when we are also able to deal with our own problems openly and clearly."[6] Lesbians founded their own groups, where they could be themselves, form bonds of community, and develop their own form of feminism in both its personal and political dimensions. Because inequality was built into male–female relationships, some lesbians contended that by living outside these relationships they were able to oppose male dominance more radically than those within them. A manifesto of the French Lesbian Front defined lesbianism as a political struggle by women who refused to "carve out spaces … in a hetero-patriarchal society which objectivizes, oppresses, and kills women," but were instead resolved to "fight the mechanisms of its power."[7] Straight feminists, while explicitly affirming their opposition to all forms of discrimination on account of gender or of sexual orientation, often rejected the claim that lesbian identity, in itself, was a basis for deeper consciousness or more radical activism.

Women of minority racial and ethnic groups also split from white, native-born majorities to formulate their own agendas. The only country in which these women organized conspicuously in the 1970s was Britain, at this time the European country with the largest black and South Asian populations. For women of minority groups, gender and racial or ethnic identities were intertwined. It did not make much sense, wrote the authors of a book on black women in Britain, to talk about "changing life styles and attitudes, when we were dealing with issues of survival, like housing, education, and police brutality." [8] The Organization of Women of Asian and African Descent (OWAAD) was founded in 1978 and held its first conference in 1979. These women's ideology and rhetorical strategies differed from those of their white colleagues. Whereas white feminists often denounced the family as a hotbed of gender oppression, minority women saw it as a source of strength and support. And they were reluctant to denounce their men, to whom they felt strong ties of solidarity. These feminists aimed to raise the status of all members of their communities, not just of the women within them.

The feminist movement attracted a large and talented group of women. A few examples, randomly chosen, illustrate the diversity of their interests and backgrounds. Sheila Rowbotham, born in 1943 in Leeds, England, studied history at Oxford University and taught in adult-education institutions while participating in the Campaign for Nuclear Disarmament, the Labour Party's youth wing, and a variety of radical political groups. In 1969, Rowbotham and other women historians asked a left-wing historians' organization, the History Workshop, to support their research into the history of women. When male colleagues ridiculed this proposal, the women convened a conference at Ruskin College in 1970, which proved to be about more than just history—it established Women's Liberation as a national movement. Always an opponent of separatism, Rowbotham worked to forge liaisons between feminism and other radical movements.[9] She went on to become a professor of history and sociology and to write some of the first books on the history of British women.

Monique Wittig, born in 1935, was a novelist who helped to found one of the first French liberation groups, the Revolutionary Feminists, and collaborated with Simone de Beauvoir and the socialist economist Christine Delphy in producing the journal *Questions féministes* (Feminist Issues). In one of the best known of the era's feminist novels, entitled *The Woman Warriors* (*Les Guérillères*, published in 1969), Wittig used imagery taken from the world's mythologies to depict a war of women against men.[10] Wittig, who became a pioneering theorist of lesbian feminism, moved to the United States in the 1970s, where she held a number of academic positions.

The German journalist and activist Alice Schwarzer, born in Wuppertal in 1942, came of a less privileged background than many feminists. She was the daughter of a single mother from the lower middle class, and worked as a secretary before she became a journalist. In 1970, having moved to Paris, she joined the French Women's Liberation Movement, and in 1972 interviewed Simone de Beauvoir. When she returned to Germany, she helped to organize a similar movement there, and in 1975 published *The Little Difference and its Huge Consequences* (*Der kleine Unterschied und seine grossen Folgen*), a frank exposé of the unhappiness and abuse that many women suffered in their intimate relationships with men.[11] The book, which contained interviews with 17 women, set off a storm of outrage, and its author was pilloried as a man-hating pervert. In 1977, Schwarzer founded a highly successful magazine, *Emma*, which carried the dedication "from women, for women" and dealt with a wide range of feminist issues.

Simona Mafai, an Italian born in 1928 who in her youth worked in the anti-Fascist resistance movement, was a parliamentary delegate of the Italian communist party and edited a journal called *Women and Politics* (*Donne e politica*) that interpreted feminism to communist women. Though she supported the transformation of the Union of Italian Women from a communist to an autonomous feminist organization, Mafai opposed gender segregation and urged women to work alongside men toward the many goals on which they agreed. In 1979, she led a procession of Sicilian women to the civic center of Palermo to protest the crimes of the Mafia, which she denounced for its violence against women as well as other forms of criminality.[12]

In 1971, three Portuguese women, all in their thirties and all named Maria, met twice a week for several months to collaborate on a book that they called *New Portuguese Letters* (*Novas Cartas Portuguesas*). Maria Isabel Barreno and Maria Fátima Velho da Costa both worked as researchers in their country's Ministry of Economics; Maria Teresa Horta worked as a journalist for a Lisbon paper and had also published a volume of poetry. The inspiration for the book was a French novel of the seventeenth century that contained letters supposedly written by a seventeenth-century Portuguese nun (also named Maria) to her French lover, who had abandoned her after a passionate affair. For the three Portuguese women, the trapped and grieving nun was a symbol not only of the oppressed Portuguese woman but also of Portugal itself, still ruled by a fascist police state and isolated from Europe and the Western world. The book, entitled *New Portuguese Letters* (*Novas Cartas Portuguesas*), contained poems, essays, and short stories on themes that included "passion; feminine seclusion and sisterhood; the act of writing; man and woman as strangers to each other; the couple; a national and personal sense of isolation and abandonment."[13] When the book appeared in 1973, the police immediately banned it and arrested the authors for "abuse of the freedom of the press" and "outrage to public decency." The case became an international *cause célèbre* as women's rights advocates in many countries and international writers' organizations such as PEN came to the defense of the "Three Marias," as they came to be known. In 1974, all charges against the authors were dropped—a victory both for women and for freedom of expression that anticipated the fall of the dictatorship in that same year.[14]

Its individualist and anti-hierarchical spirit was the wellspring of the feminist movement's creativity. But it was also the movement's greatest weakness. In the absence of leadership, groups often dissolved amid chaos and recrimination. A British activist, Judith Barrington, described a typical meeting in London. "The room smelled of sweat and was thick with cigarette smoke. Someone raised the question of office hours and someone else wanted to discuss ordering books to sell. Within minutes, women were interrupting each other and shouting in frustration, some even getting up to leave when they failed to be heard."[15] The fragmentation of the movement into a diverse array of "feminisms"—socialist, radical, lesbian, to name just a few—raised obstacles to working together. In the consciousness-raising groups, veteran members complained that the constant need to initiate newcomers distracted them from their own quest for personal growth and feminist consciousness.

Inevitably, some women placed feminism in the service of personal ambition. Antoinette Fouque, a Parisian psychoanalyst, was a prominent member of a group called *Psych et Po*, which founded a publishing company and several bookshops. By 1979, Fouque had registered the name "Women's Liberation Movement" (*Mouvement de Libération des Femmes*, or MLF) as a commercial trademark, forbidding any other group to use it. Other French activists denounced Fouque for attempting to transform the diverse and vibrant women's movement into a quasi-religious cult centered on a charismatic leader.[16]

Partly because of these factional divisions, Women's Liberation maintained its identity as a united movement for only a short period, from about 1970 until 1978. During this era, it engaged a very large number of women. The historian Gisela Kaplan estimates that (out of a total population of about 100 million adult women in Western Europe) about 1 million were movement activists, and an additional 12 million could be mobilized to express their support for demonstrations and other militant actions.[17] Certainly, the composition of this group differed from that of the population as a whole—many were middle-class, educated, and economically secure enough to be able to devote time to unpaid political work. But by contrast to their American counterparts, European feminists often maintained links to left-wing parties, labor movements, and other groups with blue-collar constituencies. Through these connections, a substantial number of less affluent and educated women were drawn into feminist groups and activities.

"The fight of all of us?" Emancipation and autonomy

"You are not a feminist if you only work for the improvement of your own position," stated an editorial in the Dutch journal *De Bonte Was* (*Colored Laundry*). "The oppression of your sister is your own oppression. The only fight is the fight of all of us."[18] But, given women's diversity, who would lead "the fight of all of us?" Feminists defined their goal—gender equality—in different and sometimes contradictory ways. One dimension of equality was emancipation: equal access to all the rights, privileges, and opportunities that men enjoyed. Another dimension was autonomy, the control over specifically female functions such as pregnancy, sexuality, and motherhood. In these areas, liberation was not defined as formal equality with men, but rather as the freedom of women to live as they chose, free of male domination. Feminist groups argued both about the relative importance of these goals, and about the best ways of working toward them.

In some countries, women continued the struggle that their great-grandmothers had launched in the nineteenth century. In Switzerland, where women could still not vote, long-established national organizations and newly founded radical groups worked together, though not without friction, to complete the work of the suffrage movement. In 1968, the Zurich Woman Suffrage Association celebrated the 75th year of its founding. Its members, many of whom had grown old in the struggle, were offended when a young woman seized the microphone and complained that as long as Swiss women did not have the right to vote, there was nothing to celebrate. A new group called the Swiss Women's Liberation Association, which was founded in 1968 and consisted chiefly of university students, downplayed the importance of suffrage and pushed a much more radical agenda that included abortion rights. Nonetheless, the younger feminists joined their elders in a march on the country's capital city, Bern, in which many thousands of women demonstrated for suffrage. This demonstration probably influenced Swiss lawmakers' decision to grant women the vote in 1971.[19]

In many other countries, too, women of diverse social backgrounds and political allegiances worked together to complete long-standing feminist campaigns that had been interrupted by war and dictatorial rule. In 1976, a new Portuguese constitution gave women the right to vote and equal rights in marriage, the family, and the workplace. Other laws protected women against employment discrimination and instituted civil divorce. Maria de Lurdes Pintasilgo founded a governmental commission charged with the enforcement of these rights that in 1978 became the Commission for Women's Condition (*Comisão da Condição Feminina*).[20] In Spain, too, a new constitution and new legislation gave women equal rights in many areas, and a governmental commission staffed by women (*Subdirección General de la Mujer*, or Women's Subdivision of the Ministry of Labor) oversaw the implementation of these provisions.

In the 1970s, Italian feminists campaigned successfully for changes in their country's legal system. Laws that defined adultery as an offense for wives but not for husbands were repealed, and women gained rights to legal equality in family relationships and to civil divorce.[21] In France and Germany, too, women won an equal legal status in marriage and parenthood in the 1970s. Irish feminists spearheaded successful campaigns to overturn "marriage bars" which barred married women from many civil service jobs and to pass laws that mandated equal pay and employment opportunities. They failed to secure the right to civil divorce and equality for women in the marriage relationship.

Other feminists asserted that women's liberation required more than formal and legal equality with men. For them, liberation meant autonomy, or freedom from male control. They agreed with Simone de Beauvoir and others that the root of women's subordination lay in their specifically female sexual and reproductive functions. The most important objective, many agreed, was to wrest the control of these functions from man-made laws and institutions and restore it to women themselves.

The issue around which feminists of this era most successfully coalesced was the legalization of abortion. In 1970, abortion was legal only in the Scandinavian nations, Britain, and the Netherlands, and even there under restrictive circumstances that put physicians rather than women in charge of the decision. Abortion was a problem with which everyone was acquainted, for in a period when contraception was unavailable or unreliable most women had aborted illegally or knew someone who had. But it was a taboo topic that all but a very few feared to mention. The first step toward liberation was to break this guilty silence. In the Netherlands, where some abortions were already legal, the group calling itself *Dolle Mina* championed the liberalization of the law with slogans such as "Boss of my own belly," and "Stay away from my body!" In 1971, 343 French women including Simone de Beauvoir published a sensational statement in the French newspaper *Le Nouvel Observateur*. "About a million women abort every year in France," stated the French women. "No one ever mentions these millions of women. I declare that I am one of them. I declare that I have had an abortion." [22] Later in that same year, a similar announcement appeared in the popular West German magazine, *Stern*.

On abortion as on other issues, feminists disagreed, and those who were practicing Catholics often upheld prohibitions against it. Still, even in some predominantly Catholic countries such as France and Italy, support for abortion rights was strong. Women throughout Western Europe joined in massive demonstrations, and found many other ways to publicize their cause. In 1972, a French group that called itself Choice (*Choisir*) defended four women who were arrested for assisting a girl to obtain an abortion after she had been raped by a schoolmate. Gisèle Halimi, the lawyer for the defense, used the trial as a platform to challenge the 1920 law against abortion—a law that she claimed fell more heavily on the poor than on the rich, who could afford to obtain abortions discreetly. [23] The women were found guilty, but let off with a small fine. In 1974, when the police tried to close an abortion clinic in Holland, a group drawn chiefly from the *Dolle Mina* group held them off for two weeks and prevented the closure. [24] In Italy, communist women openly defied their party's male leadership to work for legal abortion and other reproductive rights.

Reproductive freedom was one of a very few causes around which feminists united across lines of class, politics, and nationality, and their success indicated that sisterhood could indeed be powerful. During the years from 1970 until 1980, pressure from women's organizations resulted in the legalization of abortion during the early months of pregnancy in many countries: in France in 1975, in Denmark in 1973, in Italy in 1978, in Norway in 1979. In Sweden, Great Britain, and the Netherlands, where some abortions were already legal, laws were liberalized to broaden access. But abortion-rights campaigns did not succeed everywhere. A draft law that would have legalized abortion on demand in the first trimester was ruled unconstitutional by West Germany's Supreme Court in 1976, and the law that was finally passed allowed abortion only according to certain indications. Abortions that did not meet these requirements remained illegal, though they were not punished if the woman showed proof that she had consulted a counsellor. In Spain, Portugal, and Greece, abortion was not legalized until the 1980s, and then under very restrictive conditions; in Belgium, not until the 1990s. And in Ireland, opponents of abortion passed a constitutional amendment in 1983 that protected life from the moment of conception.

The demand for reproductive self-determination was part of a broader claim to autonomy. Feminists stressed women's right to live as they chose—with men or apart from them, in or outside families, with or without children. Through the ages, men had often controlled female members of their households by physical force. Starting in the mid-1970s, women's groups set up the first shelters for victims of domestic violence—a project that they supported at first with private funds and volunteer labor. At the same time, they broke the silence on this taboo topic by showing how widespread the abuse of women and children was. Feminists castigated police forces and courts for their loose and negligent prosecution of the crime of rape, which was often blamed more on the victim than the perpetrator. In 1984, Italian women joined together to protest a new law that stiffened penalties for rape, but exempted husbands from prosecution![25] Rape crisis centers offered counseling and other services to victims of sexual assault.

Male harassment of women on the street was a major threat to women's autonomy everywhere, but particularly in southern Europe where in some places women hardly dared to appear in public without a male escort. In 1976, Italian women declared their resolve to "take back the night." In several cities, thousands of women turned out and marched arm in arm, proclaiming "We enjoy the evening, and we want to go out in peace!" [26] At the same time, they encouraged women to learn techniques of self-defense in order to resist violence and harassment.

But when the "take back the night" movement spread to other countries, it sparked a controversy that split the feminist movement. The marches often targeted commercial venues that sold pornography, which feminists charged was an incitement to sexual violence against women. Some feminists urged local governments to forbid or limit the sale of pornography; others opposed censoring any publication, however offensive. At a national conference in 1978, British activists argued so bitterly about these questions that no further such meetings were convened, and feminism continued only on a local basis.

Another divisive issue concerned women's "traditional" work as mothers and homemakers. Despite the advances made by women, the greatest injustice of all—the expectation that they would spend their lives doing unpaid and often compulsory labor—still persisted. But how should this labor be reorganized? Many feminists advocated the socialization of child-rearing and housework. In Germany, parents cooperated in running nurseries, called Kid Shops (*Kinderläden*) because they were often located in empty storefronts, where men and women worked together to provide child-care. And everywhere, the commune—a household composed of adults and children who shared household chores—became a popular way of life among young radicals. But other women objected to this critique of the family, which they cherished as a realm of intimacy and caring. Women needed public facilities, wrote the Italian Mariarosa Dalla Costa, but also wanted to "have time to stay with children and with older people, and with the sick when we want, and to have the means to work less." [27] Should housework be abolished and replaced by public services, or should it be dignified by some form of payment and recognition by the state? Like other debates, this one reached no definite conclusion.

Speaking for herself: feminist theory

The organizing strategies and political agendas of Women's Liberation Movement started out from the basic assumption that there was a group called "women." But no sooner had this identity been asserted than it began to fracture as individuals and groups proposed widely varying notions of what it was to be a woman and what women needed, wanted, or demanded. Was it possible even to speak of a group called "women"? If so, how could this group be defined? A new intellectual enterprise, which in English is called "Women's Studies," arose to answer these and other questions.

The new scholarship flourished in new institutional settings. Throughout history, women had studied and learned outside of academic institutions, most of which admitted only men. And when women entered universities, they found that curricula seldom included the female half of the human race. Protesting against women's invisibility in existing academic disciplines, feminist intellectuals investigated all aspects of women's situation in past, present, and future. They pursued this new inquiry outside universities in all-women settings such as community centers, libraries, and bookstores. Among the most famous of these venues were the Women's Research and Information Center (*Frauenforschungs- und Informatizionszentrum*, or FFBIZ), founded in Berlin in 1980 and the Woman's Bookstore (*Libreria della Donna*) of Milan, founded in 1982. The first university courses in Women's Studies were summer schools and other events outside the regular curriculum. The field of Women's Studies was extraordinarily broad and used the methods and insights of a wide variety of academic disciplines to explore the status, living conditions, and thoughts of women in past and present.

For many generations, philosophers and others had asked what defined a woman, and had answered the question in two basic ways—by referring to what women had in common with men, and to what made them different. In both of these arguments, maleness had been assumed to be the norm, and femaleness the exception. The influential theorist Simone de Beauvoir had depicted female biology as a prison from which women longed to escape into what she imagined as the male realm of freedom and self-determination. Though some theorists of the new feminism agreed with de Beauvoir, others objected that to encourage women to imitate men merely reinforced male-supremacist norms. "Women must not be defined relative to man," stated the Italian group Women's Revolt (*Rivolta Femminile*). "Liberation for women does not mean leading the life man leads... on the contrary, it means expressing her own sense of existence." [28]

Women who had always been the object of male theorizing now emerged as subjects who demanded the right to define themselves. This required a break with the communist or socialist Left, to which most European feminist theorists initially belonged. Left-wing parties often asserted that gender inequality was not a problem in itself, but was merely an evil consequence of capitalism that would disappear with the establishment of the socialist state. Rightly perceiving socialists' dismissal of feminism as a way of keeping women party members subservient to their male leaders, feminists struggled to find an alternative way of looking at gender relations.

The rebellious women confronted their socialist comrades in debates that often took on a bitter and strident tone. Against the socialist theory that class was the fundamental contradiction, and gender merely its by-product, feminists argued that patriarchy (a system of male supremacy in family and state) was the primary form of human inequality, and women always the oppressed class. "There are many forms of patriarchy," reflected the central figure of a widely read German novel, Verena Stephan's *Shedding* (*Häutungen*, published in 1973) "but all of them are directed against women and children who want to live, not just to survive."[29] Some resurrected ancient myths of glorious prehistoric matriarchies and their defeat by the forces of patriarchy to explain the origins of the male–female divide. Socialist feminists objected that this exclusive emphasis on gender difference trivialized class conflict and other forms of inequality and injustice. Some engaged in "double militancy," combining socialism and feminism. But unable to make themselves heard within the male-dominated ranks of the Left, such women often shifted their main allegiance to feminism.

But what exactly was this primordial difference from which all other forms of inequality had arisen? In some languages, the use of the term "gender" rather than "sex" implied that male–female differences were due more to culture than to biology. Some feminist theorists insisted that gender had no basis in reality, but was a purely constructed category. Among these was Germaine Greer, the Australian author of a feminist classic entitled *The Female Eunuch*, which appeared in 1970. Greer dismissed all theories about gender difference as mere myths designed to trap women in subordination and servitude. She urged women to throw over these crippling conventions and refuse to be co-opted into marriage, motherhood, and other female roles. But what women should aspire to, apart from rebellion, Greer could not say. Certainly, she did not counsel women to imitate men, for men too had been deformed by artificial stereotypes. But she admitted that the very notion of a woman free of male domination was so remote as to be unimaginable.[30]

Other theorists, though like Greer rejecting conventional stereotypes, denied that gender difference was imaginary. Indeed, they claimed that women's biological functions differentiated them from men in a positive way. Though they purported to be original, some of these arguments in fact reverted to an older tradition that glorified women's motherly vocation as a source of distinctively female values such as compassion and non-violence. Whereas many feminists denounced motherhood as a trap that was best avoided, others reclaimed it as woman's defining experience: "The transmission of life, respect for life, awareness of life are intense experiences for women and values that she claims as her own," stated the manifesto of an Italian group, Women's Revolt (*Rivolta Femminile*) in 1970.[31]

In order to experience motherhood or any other distinctively female function in freedom, these theorists insisted that women must penetrate through the ideology imposed on them by millennia of patriarchy and discover their own, authentic feelings. "But what a mother is, only a mother can say."[32] How could women find the words through which to discover their feelings and express them? Since prehistoric times, both language and discourse had been molded by male-dominated cultures that had systematically devalued women and silenced their voices. Monique Wittig's fictional women warriors began their struggle by refusing to speak this male language. "The women say, I refuse henceforward to speak this language, I refuse to mumble after them the words lack of penis lack of money lack of insignia lack of name. I refuse to pronounce the names of possession and non-possession." [33]

The relationship of women to male-dominated language and culture was explored in theoretical debates too complex to be adequately summarized here. Feminist scholars in France and Italy framed their theories in the context of a broader philosophical inquiry known as post-modernism, which challenged modern ways of thinking and their basis in rationality and objectivity. Jacques Derrida, a French philosopher, denied that anyone (man or woman) can know reality directly. Rather, he claimed, knowledge of the world is mediated by language and therefore by culture. The French psychoanalyst Jacques Lacan pointed out that human individuals understand themselves and the world in the context of a "symbolic order" created by language. And as language and its symbolic order are the products of a male-dominated culture that since its inception has excluded and silenced women, women literally have no words in which to develop or express an authentically female subjectivity. Lacan went so far as to say that such a female subjectivity could not exist within male language and culture. [34]

However, feminist philosophers such as the French Julia Kristeva, Luce Irigaray, and Helene Cixous contended that women could, in fact, create a female language and symbolic order (to which they referred as "the feminine" or "the feminine Imaginary"). But first it was necessary to subvert the entire structure of Western philosophy, which was based on the world of rational thought and academic knowledge from which male culture had always excluded women. By contrast to the logical structure that she identified as male, Irigaray presented an alternative model of female writing: playful, evocative, emotional, enigmatic, and open-ended. And she insisted that a female symbolic order must be based on the female body and its functions, and particularly on women's ways of enjoying sexuality—an enjoyment of which they had been deprived by male exploitation of the female body for reproductive ends. [35] The French philosophers often used mythological figures, such as the snake-haired Medusa who turned any man who looked at her to stone, to represent the power of the unchained "feminine Imaginary" to shake the foundations of patriarchy. [36]

Influenced by Irigaray, Italian philosophers took their search for the "feminine" into the realm of personal relationships. Charging that male-dominated culture had sundered women's ties of solidarity and love, some Italian philosophers charted a route to authenticity through the rediscovery and revaluation of all forms of female intimacy. The Italians criticized the egalitarian ideology of "sisterhood is powerful," which had rejected all forms of hierarchy as un-feminist. Women's groups who followed this principle and rejected all forms of leadership were often too disorganized to achieve much. According to the philosopher Luisa Muraro, the mother–daughter relationship could provide a model for a new style of leadership known as "entrustment" (*affidamento*), in which women voluntarily entrusted themselves to others who were qualified through expertise or experience. Under such wise leadership, women could find solidarity, strength, and unity.[37]

But many other French and Italian feminists indignantly rejected arguments that pictured "men" and "women" as separate groups whose identity was defined by their anatomy and biological functions. Did such concepts not recall the very gender stereotypes that feminists were trying to overcome? Monique Wittig, who defined herself as a lesbian feminist materialist, asserted that male and female were artificial categories created by what she called the "straight mind," which had produced "the difference between the sexes as a philosophical and political dogma." She refused to define lesbians as women. "It would be incorrect to say that lesbians associate, make love, live with women, for "woman" has meaning only in heterosexual systems of thought and heterosexual economic systems. Lesbians are not women." [38]

Though critical of male intellectuals and their obscure and pedantic debates, feminist thinkers too became entangled in esoteric discourses. In fact the feminist movement produced an intellectual elite that was often as narrow, factional, and contentious as any male academic clique. Nonetheless, some of the philosophers' questions were important. What, after all, was the female "consciousness" upon which the movement's agenda was initially based? And what would be the end result of women's rebellion against patriarchal culture? To share with men some "human" identity beyond gender? Or to be a fully authentic and self-realizing woman? The fact that neither of these outcomes could be visualized showed how strong the grip of patriarchy on the imagination still was.

The 1980s: progress or stagnation?

As the decade of the 1970s came to an end, commentators in the media often dismissed the Women's Liberation Movement as a thing of the past. Indeed, in most countries feminism lost its public image as a mass movement, and dissolved into diverse groups pursuing separate agendas. But though in less conspicuous ways, these groups consolidated and extended the achievements of the 1970s.

Along with this process of consolidation went a shift in ideological orientation. In the heyday of Women's Liberation, the most vocal women were those who broke with established political parties and founded autonomous, all-female groups. But, less conspicuously, others worked to increase women's representation and power within political parties and the governments that they headed. As a result of their efforts, some governments created ministries (central government departments) devoted to women and their concerns. The Dutch government established an official Committee on the Status of Women in 1974. In the same year, the well-known French journalist Françoise Giroud was appointed as France's Secretary of State for the Condition of Women, and in 1981 this office was expanded to create a Ministry of Women's Rights, headed by the socialist and activist Yvette Roudy. Germany's ministry of Health, Family, and Youth added "Women" to its official title in 1986. In Sweden, where women's rights had been a government concern for many years, Anna Gradin, the Minister of Equal Opportunity, brought men into the picture by setting up a committee on the role of the male in 1983.

Women in governmental positions placed many projects initiated by autonomous women's groups on a secure footing by providing public funding. Local and municipal governments integrated shelters for abused spouses and rape crisis centers into public social service programs. Many countries passed or strengthened laws mandating equal employment opportunities and equal pay for women. The Netherlands also became a pioneer when in 1982 it passed a law that prohibited discrimination on the basis not only of sex but of marital status and sexual orientation. In some countries—Germany, Britain, France, and the Netherlands—the first Women's Studies programs and centers were incorporated into state-supported universities. Though governmental sponsorship certainly assisted these feminist institutions—many of which could not have survived without it—it also changed them. In the 1970s, their founders had mistrusted the state as an instrument of patriarchy and male domination, and had aspired to create an autonomous women's community. Now, most feminist activists conceded that the state might be an ally rather than an enemy. As the critics of government became its employees, the original dream of a separate, autonomous women's community faded, and feminism was increasingly integrated into the political mainstream. Some feminists welcomed this trend, while others resisted what they saw as an attempt to make their movement respectable and dull its radical edge.

Under the influence of feminist educators and politicians, school curricula adopted sex education courses and contraception, financed by national health insurance, became widely available. Abortion—once such a radical demand—was provided by some national health systems. The Scandinavian countries, France, the Netherlands, and Great Britain legalized the procedure during a specified period in early pregnancy, though sometimes with a counseling requirement. And unlike the United States, where the *Roe* v. *Wade* decision prevented governments from interfering with some abortions but imposed no obligation to provide them, some European governments assumed the more positive responsibility of assuring access to the procedure for women who needed it. For example, in France publicly supported hospitals are required either to offer abortion services themselves or to refer patients to another facility. However, as we have seen, abortion did not become widely accessible in all European countries.

Along with these legal and social reforms went a change in consciousness that was not limited to self-identified feminists, but shared by an increasing segment of the public. Abortion, rape, and domestic violence—once taboo topics—now emerged into the light of public discussion. Political parties realized that women were citizens whose votes could not be taken for granted, and incorporated gender issues into their programs. News media, popular entertainment, and a flood of books and articles kept gender issues in the public eye.

Nonetheless, there was still a wide gap between the appearance of advancement and the reality of continued disadvantage. Despite equal-pay legislation, women's income was still substantially less than that of men; despite laws against employment discrimination, labor markets were still segregated by gender; and despite the introduction of a few women's studies programs, the number of women on university faculties remained small. Moreover, a movement that had claimed to speak for all women had left many untouched. Among these were most of the immigrants who by the 1980s constituted a large minority group in many European countries. Unlike their American counterparts, who at the urging of black and Hispanic women had recognized that their movement must take account of racial and other differences among women, white feminists in most European countries (except Britain) made few attempts to communicate with foreign-born women or those belonging to minority groups.

Finally, there were the women who were simply not convinced. In a letter to a feminist publication, a Berlin woman, who was married and the mother of two, responded skeptically to what she understood as the feminist message: that women could do everything that men could do and could live without men. "Well," she concluded, "I don't want to live without men, and I don't want to imitate them, either." [39] For this woman as for many others, the journey toward autonomy was too individual and personal to be guided by ideology.

8

Democracy without Women: The Post-Communist Transition, 1989–Present

"Bliss was it in that dawn to be alive." [1] The response of the British poet William Wordsworth to the first phase of the French Revolution captures the euphoric mood that swept Eastern and Central Europe when the communist governments of the Soviet Union and its satellites collapsed during the years 1989–1991. But exhilaration soon gave way to anxiety and a sense of disorientation. "We are experiencing cultural shock," wrote the Czech sociologist Jiřina Šiklová. "The shock originates in the fact that one has been uprooted and is suddenly living in a totally new environment in which he must quickly adapt." [2] Many women soon realized that although communism was dead, patriarchy was still alive and well. "We women should not wait; we must act," wrote the Russian feminist Anastasia Posadskaya in 1993, "We cannot depend on someone else to better our situation on our behalf. We ourselves have to think about what changes we want and work for them ourselves. Democracy without women is not real democracy." [3]

Partly because they are so recent, the events surrounding the fall of communism and the transition to capitalism and democracy are open to a variety of interpretations. Though some historians claim that this transition liberated women as well as men, others argue that women actually lost many of the advantages that they had enjoyed under communism. Both of these arguments are one-sided. Communist governments claimed to have emancipated women by forcing them into the workplace and providing social benefits and services that helped them to combine work and family life. The policy-makers of the regimes that succeeded communism likewise claimed to have emancipated women by leaving them free to make their own choice of home or workplace. In fact, gender inequality was built into both of these systems. In this chapter, we will look at the effects of the post-communist transition in the areas of politics, employment, and the family.

"Emancipation is to blame for everything": women and politics

Looking back on the events of 1989, an East German feminist remarked to the American sociologist Myra Marx Ferree that "the time of chaos was the best."[4] In the late 1980s, Soviet Premier Mikhail Gorbachev relaxed his government's formerly strict control of political speech and organization. His policies of *perestroika* and *glasnost* (restructuring and openness) encouraged citizens to assemble, to speak publicly, and even to criticize their government. In every nation of the communist bloc, women greeted this new era by forming groups, reading formerly forbidden Western feminist literature, and formulating political programs. In the Soviet Union, a multitude of new groups joined the communist women's organization to form the Free Association of Feminist Organizations. When the fall of the Berlin Wall in November of 1989 signaled the collapse of the communist dictatorship in the German Democratic Republic, East German feminist groups joined together in the Independent Women's Movement (*Unabhängiger Frauenverband*, or UFV). The UFV began immediately to make its presence felt by founding shelters and women's centers, initiating consciousness-raising groups, and issuing newspapers and periodicals.

In this early phase of the transition, the governments that assumed power after the fall of the communist regimes encouraged women's aspirations by sponsoring many new institutions, some associated with universities and some independent. Even before the fall of the Berlin Wall in 1989, the Center for Interdisciplinary Research on Women had opened at East Germany's most prominent university, the Humboldt University in Berlin. Similar centers opened in other formerly communist countries in 1990: the Minsk Center for Gender Studies in the new nation of Belarus; the Women's Studies Center in Budapest; the Women's Studies Center in Vilnius, Lithuania; and the Women's Studies Center at the University of Lodz, Poland (to mention only a few). Many of their founders had pursued an interest in gender issues even in the hostile communist environment. Anastasia Posadskaya, the founder of the Moscow Center, was born in 1958 to unmarried parents and as a child shared one room in a communal apartment with her mother and grandparents. As a student at Moscow University, she was at first forbidden to write a thesis on the problems of Soviet women—problems that the Soviet Union had supposedly solved!—but finally found a professor who would supervise her. In the more liberal atmosphere of the Gorbachev era, she obtained a position at the Institute of Socioeconomic Studies of Population, where she was first exposed to feminist literature from the West. Benefiting from the political influence wielded by the head of this Institute, who had been a classmate of Gorbachev, she was able to found the Moscow Center for Gender Studies in 1989. As the Russian language lacked a word for "gender," Posadskaya invented one.[5]

In other countries, however, feminist groups received little support from their own governments, and were financed chiefly from abroad. In Prague, Czechoslovakia, four new women's organizations founded the Gender Studies Center in the apartment of Jiřina Šiklová, a sociologist who had recently regained the academic position that she had lost because of her opposition to the communist government. Though at first unfamiliar with feminism, Šiklová became a convert after the fall of the communist government, when the lifting of press censorship allowed Western feminist literature to be imported and sold.[6] Funding for the Center, of which Šiklová was the first director, came from American feminist groups and from the *Frauen-Anstiftung*, the women's organization of the German Green Party.

Exhilarated by the rapid pace of political change and with high hopes for the future, women's groups demanded an active role in the creation of the newly independent states. In 1989, huge street demonstrations in all the major East German cities called for the resignation of the communist government. Demonstrators carried a sign that proclaimed, "Our country needs new men." The UFV responded indignantly that "You can't create a state without women." [7] Representatives of the UFV joined the New Forum (*Neues Forum*), a group of prominent civic leaders that met to set policy for what they hoped would be a reformed East German socialist state. Among the founders of this group was Bärbel Bohley, a painter and peace activist who in communist times had served several prison terms for advocating freedom of discussion and contacts with Western organizations. Hans Modrow, the head of a short-lived provisional government of the GDR, appointed prominent women to his cabinet. The UFV also drafted a Charter of Social Rights—a document that called on the state to guarantee both individual liberty and social security—that was later adopted by the provisional government, which also appointed an Equal Opportunity Commission.

In 1991, as the Soviet Union disintegrated and Russia emerged as a national state under the presidency of Boris Yeltsin, the Russian Free Association of Feminist Organizations held its first Women's Forum in Dubna. "Our main concern was to show that a women's independent voice did exist in the country, that women were setting up their own new organizations and initiatives. ... The Forum's final document ... spoke of the many forms of discrimination against women, both during the period of state socialism and during the perestroika years," recollected Posadskaya.[8] Later in the same year, a second forum entitled "From Problems to Strategies" focused on practical steps to protect the rights and advance the interests of women at the state, regional, and municipal levels and in all branches of the economy. By this time, the Russian women's movement had grown so rapidly that the program had to be extended in order to enable representatives of all the groups in attendance to speak.

Václav Havel, the new President of Czechoslovakia, paid tribute to the courage and political wisdom of his country's women by appointing several to high office. Eda Kriseová, an author and journalist whose works had been prohibited due to her support of dissident groups, became an advisor to the President. Another new Presidential advisor was Věra Cáslavská, a champion gymnast who had won seven Olympic gold medals in the 1960s but had then been forbidden to compete abroad because of her open opposition to the Soviet Union's invasion of her country in 1968. Rita Klimová, an economist whom the communist government had also silenced for her political opinions, became ambassador to the United States. In other transitional states, too, women briefly held influential positions in government, the economy, and cultural life.

But the next step toward democratic state-formation—the election of new representative bodies at the national and local levels—disappointed female politicians' hopes. Most communist governments had apportioned seats to women according to a quota (usually 30 percent) and thus women had played a visible parliamentary role. Of course, with the fall of communism these quotas were abolished and representatives were chosen through elections in which multiple parties competed. In 1990–1991, many women ran for parliamentary seats, some as representatives of political parties and others as independents. Despite the high visibility of women's organizations and issues, however, women candidates who were unschooled in campaign strategy and lacking in funds were unable to mobilize voters. The election results showed a dramatic decrease in the number of women delegates to national legislative bodies. In Czechoslovakia, women gained only 19 percent of parliamentary seats; in Poland 13 percent; in Yugoslavia about 4 percent; in Hungary about 7 percent; in Albania 3.5 percent. There was no substantial increase in these numbers in subsequent elections.

In an election held in the German Democratic Republic (or GDR, as the East German state was called) in March of 1990, the UFV allied itself with the East German Green Party, which focused on environmental issues. This coalition opposed immediate unification with West Germany and advocated a separate East German state. But in this election, parties that were funded from West Germany and held out the bright promise of freedom, prosperity, and unification won a large majority of votes. The UFV and Greens won only 2 percent of the vote and eight seats, none of which were occupied by feminists. These results discredited feminism by revealing the narrowness of its base of support; most women, like most men, voted for the Christian Democratic Union (CDU), West Germany's governing party. East and West Germany were united in October of 1990. The East German feminist movement soon fragmented, though its members continued to be active in many projects, including political lobbying groups, non-governmental organizations, and community centers and organizations.

Some commentators refer to these electoral disappointments as the exclusion of women from politics, implying that they had once been included.[9] But considering that under the communist regimes parliamentary delegates (male or female) had exercised very little power, it would be more accurate to say that the powerlessness of women, once veiled by their token presence in legislative bodies, was now starkly revealed by their absence.

The few women who were elected to national parliaments were often so disappointed by their reception that they wondered whether politics was worth the immense time and effort that it required. In Romania, the percentage of women in the lower house, or Chamber of Deputies, ranged from about 3 percent in 1990 to about 5.5 percent in 1995 (during that period, only two women served in the upper house, or Senate). In 1992, the political scientist Mary Ellen Fischer interviewed five of these deputies, who represented a range of political parties. All of them complained that their male colleagues did not take them seriously, that their own party leaders refused to choose them for important committees, that there was little attention to women's issues—even the Commission for Labor, Health, Social Protection, and the Status of Women was headed by a man—and that the hectic schedule of a politician was hard to combine with the responsibilities of a wife and mother. In an interview conducted five years later, Fischer found that these politicians had matured. They took a more realistic view of parliamentary politics, and focused less on their disadvantages and more on developing strategies to reach their goals. But these strategies often required deference to their male colleagues.[10]

A major obstacle to women's success in politics was a widespread assumption, shared by politicians across the party spectrum, that politics was a male job for which women were not well suited. "None of the new political parties has a plan to involve women in political life, and not one of them yet plans to adhere to the principle that women should be represented alongside men in decision-making levels. Our democrats are quite happy to use women in the old conservative way—to carry out the work," complained the Russian Olga Voronina in 1994.[11] And many researchers found that women themselves agreed, declaring that they themselves would never wish to be involved in a game so sordid and treacherous as politics. Of course, this situation is not unique to the post-communist world. In many well-established democracies, including those of the United States and Britain, women candidates for elective office face similar obstacles.

However, Eastern European attitudes toward women in politics were also shaped by their experience under communism. Communist regimes encouraged most of their citizens, men as well as women, to be politically passive. Individual self-assertion in any form was risky, for it could easily be taken for dissidence or subversion. Women received "emancipation" as a gift from above, to be gratefully accepted rather than actively sought. And the very word turned out to be a piece of Orwellian double-speak, for in fact most women experienced the communist version of "emancipation" as coercion and oppression rather than as freedom (see Chapter 6). After communist governments fell, feminist leaders urged women to participate in politics in the name of a new ideal of "emancipation." But women who had always associated "emancipation" with the deprived and laborious lives that they had led under communism were unable and unwilling to grasp any other definition of this word. "Having been convinced all their lives that their exploitation is 'emancipation,'" remarked Kira Reoutt, a Russian-American feminist, of the Russian women she knew, "they are unable to understand what true emancipation is, and it's rare that they will listen to you when you try to explain otherwise." [12]

Women who had deeply resented the communist women's organizations mistrusted those who tried to enlist them under the new banner of feminism, which many feared would prove to be a merely a new party line. The option of leaving organizations and retreating to private life was very attractive to people who had been denied privacy for so long. The constant police surveillance exercised by communist governments had raised the prestige of the family, which for many had become a locus of privacy and personal freedom. Women who had been active opponents of communism sometimes rejected feminism because they prided themselves on working with men. "I don't like those women who are fighting for independence," wrote the Czech political activist Eva Kucerová, "they should be fighting for improvements in the economy, better services, since women would then be automatically better off." [13]

Eastern European women's attitudes toward feminism also arose from the very new circumstances in which these women encountered their Western counterparts and traveled to Western countries. Living behind the Iron Curtain, prevented from traveling to the West, and deprived of free access to news media,

Eastern European women had developed an idealized view of the West—a view that was based largely on their reading of the glamorous women's magazines that, although officially forbidden, were nonetheless widely available. With the lifting of these restrictions, these women were soon disillusioned. The Western society that they had imagined as a utopia of universal prosperity proved in fact to be pervaded by inequality, poverty, alienation, and violence. Moreover, the combination of democratic rights of free speech with capitalist greed could produce some very unpleasant effects—pornography, prostitution, and the sex industry flourished everywhere. If after two centuries of struggle Western feminists had not been able to free the women of their own countries from violence and misogyny, then how effective were the ideologies and political strategies that they now urged upon Eastern European women.

Encounters between Eastern and Western women, first greeted with enthusiasm, soon became fraught with conflict and misunderstanding. Western feminist organizations played an important role as the sponsors and mentors of the many fledgling institutions, such as gender studies centers, shelters for battered women, and community services, that could not have survived without their contributions. But the very wealth and generosity of these Western women gave them and their ideas a dominant position that their beneficiaries often resented. In addition, some Eastern European women were very dubious about the model of emancipation that many Western feminists embodied. The stereotypical image of the Western feminist as the single, childless professional was deeply unappealing to many women who prized the familial relationships that their overburdened lives had left them little time to cultivate. Western feminists' view of the family as the primary locus of women's subordination hardly fit the experience of women for whom the home had been the only retreat from the coercive pressures of a totalitarian society. A rational discussion of these issues might have resulted, if not in perfect harmony, then at least in mutual respect and tolerance.

But in the polarized political atmosphere of the transitional period, little rational discussion was possible. In all the post-communist countries, a wide variety of political speakers held up the Western feminist as a symbol of every danger that threatened the new nations. A religious revival gave the leaders of both the Roman Catholic and the Orthodox churches enormous influence in politics. Most of these leaders used their newfound freedom of speech to denounce feminism as the evil offspring of communist atheism and Western secularism and to urge a return to a religious version of traditional family values. Nationalist leaders likewise warned against feminism as a pernicious foreign import that threatened newly reconstructed national cultures. And women themselves felt the pull of religion and nationalism. Many new women's organizations emphasized domesticity, family, and motherhood.

Therefore, hostility to feminism—whether identified with communism or with capitalism—soon pervaded both political discourse and popular culture. In an article entitled "Why Western Feminism Isn't Working in the Czech Republic," Jiřina Šiklová recalls that her grandson once asked her "Granny, are you a feminist?" "And what do you think that is? How do feminists behave?" she inquired. "Feminists think that they are better than men," the boy responded confidently. "And they want to kick us out and live on their own."[14] This hostile stereotype was often openly or implicitly homophobic. According to the Budapest sociologist Maria Adamik, most Hungarians defined feminists as "women who hate men and children, are sexually voracious, don't wear bras, and above all are very unhappy and lesbians."[15] The Russian activist Valentina Konstantinova wrote in 1993 that her country's media made feminism an object of paranoia, claiming that "emancipation is to blame for everything."[16] And the use of "feminism" as an epithet to discredit any individual or group that organized women for political action or placed gender issues on its agenda silenced women and excluded them from the political arena.

The events of the 1990s thus justified Konstantinova's fear that the new democracies of the transitional period were "taking shape without the parti- cipation of women."[17] However, some feminists and political activists hope that this pattern will change. They point out that it would have been unreal- istic to expect totally inexperienced women to adapt immediately to the highly competitive political culture of the new democracies. Moreover, it is clearly impossible to organize a group that is divided by religion, nationality, class, and many other aspects of identity around any single definition of feminism or unified political agenda—a fact that is as obvious in the "mature" Western democracies as in those of Eastern Europe. Though most Hungarian women rejected feminism, observed Marie Adamik, they were nonetheless aware that the new political order had brought some new disadvantages, both in the home and in the workplace.[18]

"Pretty girl under 25": work and employment

Among the most dramatic consequences of the transition was the change in employment patterns, particularly those of women. In large measure, this was a result of the change from communist central planning to the capitalist free market. Communist full employment policies had been dictated both by the economic and the political needs of the totalitarian state. By comparison with the capitalist West, technology was not up to date and manufacturing processes inefficient and labor intensive. By providing jobs for everyone, requiring almost all adults to work, and making pay and advancement contingent on political loyalty the state had controlled its population. After the fall of communism (though at rates that varied widely from country to country) this command economy was dismantled, state-controlled enterprises were transferred to private ownership, and trade barriers that had isolated industries from global markets and competitive pressures fell.

In many cases, this process affected women more than men. Unemployment, unknown in the days of communism, now rose rapidly as state-owned enterprises were closed down or reorganized under private management, which usually upgraded technology and fired workers who were no longer needed. Women, who had constituted about one half of the labor force, were well over half of the unemployed: according to official statistics, in 1991 about 62 percent in Bulgaria and about 70 percent in Russia; in 1994, about 60 percent in Lithuania, and in 1995, about 63 percent in East Germany.[19] Of course, these figures included only those who were still looking for work or eligible for unemployment benefits—the total number was probably much higher. Women's participation in the labor force diminished. In the former GDR, the number of working women decreased from about 4.5 million in 1989 to around 2.8 million in 1995.[20] In newly independent Latvia, the percentage of young women from 20 to 24 years of age who were working dropped from 80.6 percent in 1989 to 46.1 percent by the end of 1996.[21]

What accounted for this rise in female unemployment? Women were vulnerable chiefly because their position in communist labor markets had already been disadvantaged. Industries that employed large numbers of women, particularly the textile industry, had been among the least efficient and technologically advanced. When the trade barriers that had protected communist state-owned enterprises from competition fell, these inefficient plants were the first to be closed, and their unskilled female workers found few other employment possibilities. Another large group of women had worked in social services, particularly in the health and educational sectors. When these sectors were reorganized, many services were privatized, cut back, or eliminated. These measures affected women severely, as they were chiefly in lower-level positions without the qualifications that would have helped them to find similar positions in the new governmental bureaucracies. Women, too, were the majority of workers in agriculture, and when collective farms were transferred to private ownership, most lacked the resources to buy land and set up as independent farmers. Besides, few wished to continue to live in rural areas where poverty, male alcoholism, domestic violence, and marital breakdown were common.

Governmental policies increased the impact of these structural changes. The new policy-makers shared the perception that was already prevalent in the communist era that the level of female employment under communism had been too high, that women had often been forced or pressured to work outside the home, and that if given the choice many women would prefer the life of full-time housewives. A prominent proponent of this view had been Mikhail Gorbachev himself, who as the Soviet head of state was the first to loosen governmental control of the economy and to encourage private enterprise. After paying tribute to the hard-working women of the Soviet Union, Gorbachev regretted that they no longer had "enough time to perform their everyday duties at home—housework, raising children, and the creation of a good family atmosphere" and hoped to "make it possible for women to return to their purely womanly mission."[22] Policy-makers who shared these views did not regard unemployment among women as a problem, but rather as the return of a natural and beneficial order.

Because few women legislators, cabinet ministers, or organized groups spoke for women, no effective measures were taken to combat employment discrimination or to provide new opportunities. To be sure, laws still guaranteed "equal opportunity," but their only specific provisions required protection for pregnant women and shorter workdays for mothers—measures that forced women workers to give priority to domestic over occupational roles. In all this legislation, there was "not a word about measures to help promote women to decision-making levels, or about shielding women from the unemployment that has now become a reality for them," objected the Russian Olga Voronina in 1993.[23]

Therefore, job discrimination was rampant, and justified by every timeworn gender stereotype. Job advertisements usually specified the sex of the employee, and most employers preferred men. In Poland in 1991, for example, job openings existed for one in every 17 employed men, but for only one in 59 unemployed women. In the Slovak Republic (one of the two states into which the former Czechoslovakia split in 1991), only 29 percent of the vacancies listed by governmental employment agencies in 1991 were for women.[24]

Prospects were particularly poor for women over 40, many of whom were highly qualified professionals who had worked in governmental agencies that were dismantled after communism fell. In industry, women in management positions generally lost them, for private employers associated business success with stereotypically male qualities such as aggression, initiative, and competitiveness. "Requirements: young, dynamic, handsome male able to work with people," stated an advertisement for a sales representative in a Lithuanian newspaper in 1994.[25] Older women found that selling their qualifications and experience on this new labor market was a well-nigh impossible task. Government-sponsored retraining programs favored younger people. Most of the retraining opportunities open to older women were provided by private women's organizations which—adapting their expectations to the harsh economic environment—emphasized lower-level skills such as sewing, hairdressing, and domestic work. As women usually retired earlier than men and lived longer, more depended on government-supplied pensions, the value of which had been seriously eroded by inflation. When the former GDR was absorbed into Germany, the government offered unemployed East German women over the age of 55 early retirement if they promised to withdraw permanently from the workforce. About half accepted this offer, even though their meager pensions put most below the poverty line.[26]

Younger women found more job opportunities, but faced discrimination in even more disheartening forms. Most white-collar opportunities for women were in clerical or office work, and the qualifications were not all job-related. Typical advertisements in a Russian newspaper in 1994 called for "attractive girls with office experience, aged 18–22, at least 168 cm tall," and "secretary/personal assistant... with knowledge of English: pretty girl under 25."[27] Openly or covertly, job interviews tested out the applicant's willingness to provide sexual services. And although of course there was no statistical evidence on sexual harassment, women testified that it was widespread. In Russia, it was aggressive enough to be called "sexual terror." "This particularly affects women who are the sole breadwinners for their family," remarked an anonymous woman in a Russian newspaper interview. "It is these women who are transformed into office prostitutes. Those who refuse any proposition are simply chucked out."[28]

The new capitalist economies gave free rein to the commercialization of sex and women's bodies. In the days of communism, Eastern European women had enviously admired the glamorous models featured in Western fashion magazines. Now the fashion industry offered prestigious job opportunities. To beautiful girls, the agencies held out the most coveted reward of all—a modeling job in Western Europe, with high pay, luxurious working conditions, and star status. Girls, particularly those from the poorest areas of Eastern Europe and the former Soviet Union, fell easily for these treacherous promises. Some alleged employment agencies were actually prostitution rings, and others recruited for the pornography industry.

Prostitution and pornography, though of course they had existed under communism, had been officially forbidden and hidden from public view. But in free-market economies, the sex business was free to expand. In Riga, the capital of Latvia, a survey taken in 1997 indicated that about 5 percent of all women between 14 and 59 years of age worked in the sex trade.[29] When asked why they chose this kind of work, most women spoke of economic hardships, including unemployment and inflation. Indeed, prostitution became a source of supplementary earnings for women in many occupations—including teaching, office work, and nursing—that did not pay enough for them to live on. Much of the lucrative trade in female bodies was controlled by the organized criminal gangs that flourished in the chaotic atmosphere of the collapsing communist police states. These gangs supplied the huge flesh markets of Western Europe. Girls who were lured by the promise of legitimate jobs and a better life in the West often found themselves in involuntary confinement and forced into prostitution, unable to complain to the police for fear of being identified as illegal immigrants and sent home. The fact that those who were sent home often wished to return, even under the same conditions, suggests just how hopeless their situation seemed.

But despite the darkness of this picture, it would be misleading to portray the women of the post-communist states chiefly as victims. For the collapse of planned economies opened new vistas to those who were energetic, enterprising, and able to create their own opportunities. In some countries, such as Slovenia and Hungary, the privatization of the economy was far advanced by the mid-1990s, and unemployment was low for both sexes. Privatization offered many new opportunities to women with entrepreneurial skills. Some founded their own businesses—in Slovenia, for example, about 30 percent of new businesses are owned by women—that include travel agencies, data management firms, beauty shops, and a variety of retail enterprises.[30] "I began to work on realizing my dream of opening up my own sauna with a fitness center and solarium," said an East German woman, Petra P., to the American researcher Dinah Dodds in 1991. "The only thing I'm waiting for now is a place where I can build."[31]

During communist times, many Hungarian women had supplemented their family incomes by working in the "underground economy," and the skills that they acquired in fields such as catering, hairdressing, and dressmaking served them well. Foreign companies that launched joint ventures with Eastern European firms often considered women ideal employees, for they tended to be more reliable, flexible, and receptive to the new workplace culture than men. Professionals, too, could sometimes make a new start. Haiderun Lindner, an East German physician and therapist, opened a private practice. "I've become a businesswoman," she told Dodds. "I work twelve to fourteen hours a day and attend seminars on weekends." The interviewer added that

Lindner "was clearly pleased with the way things were going for her profession-ally." [32]

In the transitional period, many predicted that women who felt overworked and exploited under communism would welcome the opportunity to return to full-time domesticity. For example, the Czech author and activist Eva Kantůrková was certain that "feminism has been eradicated in our society by having been brutally transformed into a new form of women's slavery: oblig-atory work. Thus, if there is one thing that a woman wishes to obtain for herself, it is to recover her undistorted feminine essence." [33] However, Eastern European women have not rushed to give up their jobs and put on their aprons. To be sure, many responded to public-opinion surveys that they did not wish to imitate the employment patterns of men, particularly in the pressured and insecure environment of the new capitalist economies. But, by large majorities, they valued their jobs and their identities as workers and had no desire to leave the workforce permanently. In 1991 a Czech researcher, Hana Navarová, concluded that "women obtain status, experience, skills in their jobs, they find financial independence, many of them fulfill themselves in and identify with their work." [34] Elżbieta Oleksy, a Polish professor and activist, observed that many women who had initially been willing to quit work if their husbands could support their families placed more value on their jobs when unemployment among women increased. Young women, she added, were less eager than their mothers to marry and raise a family. [35] Even more than in the past, women faced the problem of combining work and familial obligations.

Mothers of the nation: family, sexuality, and reproduction

In 2000, a 35-year-old Polish woman who was severely near-sighted sought an abortion after three ophthalmologists had agreed that the continuation of her pregnancy could cause the further deterioration of her vision. But these physicians refused to grant her a certificate for a therapeutic abortion, although her serious health condition clearly qualified her for one. Having suffered a retinal hemorrhage, the single mother became permanently disabled, and was forced to support her family on the tiny disability compensation of 140 Euros a month. Nonetheless a Polish court refused to hear her criminal complaint against the physicians, claiming that the charge was unfounded. In addition, she faced harassment by anti-abortion groups. This woman, whose case is now before the European Court of Human Rights, is one of many victims of a massive turn to conservative and religious values in some post-communist countries—a trend that, although it affects many aspects of life, focuses particularly on gender and family issues.

The strength and effectiveness of this religious revival varied widely among post-communist nations. In some countries, such as predominantly Protestant East Germany and Catholic Czechoslovakia and Slovenia, a strong trend toward secularization had begun in communist times and continued under the new democracies. But in Catholic Poland and Croatia and Orthodox Romania and Bulgaria, churches had gained prestige as centers of resistance to widely resented communist governments. When communist regimes collapsed, religious leaders in these countries immediately used their considerable financial resources in the political arena, sponsoring candidates, exerting pressure on legislators, and saturating the media with propaganda that associated national strength with religious faith. To name only one example, the Romanian patriarch Teoctist declared in 2000 that the Romanian Orthodox Church was "the unified moral conscience of the Romanian People."[36] Though led by men, the religious revival was supported by the many women who had found in their churches a partial refuge from the pressures of the totalitarian state. In the 1990s, church attendance declined in Western Europe but increased in Eastern Europe by about 10 percent, and in some countries by more than 20 percent.[37]

The churches found many allies among secular leaders and political parties. Many religious leaders threw their authority behind a return to the "traditional" family—a unit that was, once again, based on the division of labor between male breadwinner and female housewife and mother. As we have seen, secular policy-makers found this view of the family very convenient because it justified the removal of women from the labor market and their replacement by men, who were now encouraged to take their rightful place as household heads. Both religious and secular media exalted "traditional" gender roles. In Russia, new manuals on child-rearing urged parents to model correct male and female behavior. Fathers, they insisted, must be strong and mothers submissive and feminine.[38] The high incidence of domestic violence in these patriarchal homes did not receive much attention from the media or from legislators.

Nationalism was another agenda that gained both religious and secular support. Starting in the communist era, governments had had responded to declining birth rates by putting pressure on women to bear children. This pressure increased when the ethnic tensions that had boiled below the surface of communist states emerged to tear apart many of the newly independent nations. As the nation of Yugoslavia dissolved into warring ethnic states, nationalist demagogues warned that women's only acceptable political stance was as "heroic mothers, who devoted the lives of their sons for [sic] the great historic goal of their nation...celebrated as shining examples of national pride."[39] In newly independent Latvia, leaders exhorted Latvian women to produce enough children to ensure their own group's dominance of an area which, in Soviet times, had gained a large Russian population.[40]

Christian leaders, both Catholic and Orthodox, joined secular nationalists in denouncing communist policies that they alleged had encouraged low birth rates by alienating women from their motherly role. And Western-style feminists, who in Hungary were often referred to as the "murderers of mothers," were also numbered among the demons to be driven from the body of the nation.

The revival of traditional "family values" had consequences for women in many areas of life. Combining paid work and motherhood, normal in communist times, became increasingly difficult. In part, this problem was due to economic factors: the paid maternity leaves that were affordable in communist economies marked by full employment and low wage levels became more expensive in the competitive capitalist environment. But the total absence of effective measures against gender discrimination added to the economic vulnerability of pregnant women and mothers. Young women who had children or seemed likely to become mothers were usually not hired. Though laws that mandated paid maternity leaves remained on the books, they were not enforced, and employees who took time off for pregnancy or motherhood were often fired or found that their jobs were eliminated the day after they returned to work. Likewise, local and municipal governments, which lost much of the funding that they had received under the old system, were no longer in a position to support public child-care centers. For example, between 1990 and 1993, almost half of all child-care centers in Lithuania closed.[41] Those that remained open charged fees that most working mothers could not afford.

The newly empowered religious right demanded a return to what it nostalgically portrayed as traditional standards of sexual morality. Overlooking the fact that Soviet-bloc regimes had assigned a very low priority to contraception and sex education, religious leaders attributed both to godless communism as well as to feminism and other dangerous Western influences. In many post-communist states, birth-control providers faced a barrage of hostile propaganda. In Russia, a revived Communist Party joined forces with religious and nationalist groups to denounce International Planned Parenthood and similar organizations as a "Jewish-Masonic" conspiracy that aimed to destroy the nation by corrupting its morals and reducing its population. The result was that access to contraceptive advice and technology was limited: in 1999, 41 percent of married women in post-communist countries did not use contraception (compared to 23 percent in Western Europe).[42] Extremists also warned that sex education in schools would destroy the Russian family by teaching children to spurn Christian morality and to adopt alien values. In the face of a frightening growth in AIDS infections, nationalist and religious leaders and even some physicians denounced sex education as a still more deadly plague.[43] As a result, in 1998 there were few school-based sex education programs in Eastern Europe.

In Roman Catholic countries, abortion was the issue that most clearly pitted the forces of religious conservatism against those of secularism. In Poland, the Catholic Church had actively opposed legalized abortion since the 1950s. In the 1980s Solidarity, Eastern Europe's most powerful and popular anti-communist resistance movement, had rallied behind the Polish Pope John Paul II, who on his visit to Poland in 1991 equated abortion and the Holocaust, calling Europe a "vast graveyard of unborn children."[44] Conservative political groups backed by the Church introduced legislative proposals that would have banned all abortions and condemned physicians who performed the procedure to the loss of their licenses and a two-year prison sentence.

But such legislation was not popular among the general public. Even in pious Poland, the majority was opposed to banning the only widely available method of family limitation. According to polls taken in 1991, only about 20 percent of the population favored a total ban on abortion, and a majority of 70 percent believed that the Church had no right to write religious values into secular legal codes. A feminist group, the Polish Women's League, asked how all the unwanted children who would be born could be provided for amid the economic crisis facing the country, and warned that women would be endangered by illegal abortions. A Parliament dominated by religious parties and powerful individuals, such as the charismatic leader of Solidarity, Lech Wałesa, refused to allow the issue to be decided by popular referendum. But by 1993, Catholic leaders were alarmed by a decline in church attendance. They accepted what they called a "compromise" measure, which allowed the termination of pregnancies that were caused by rape or incest, that endangered the mother's life or health, or that were likely to produce defective offspring. But physicians who were personally opposed to abortion or afraid of being exposed to public disgrace and condemnation often refused to perform abortions even for the few women who "qualified" under this law. And the results were predictable: an increase in illegal abortions, "abortion tourism" by women who could afford to travel to other countries; and a rising incidence of child abuse and abandonment.[45]

In other countries, however, religious conservatism did not prevail. Organizations such as International Planned Parenthood gained a footing in some countries, such as Czechoslovakia and East Germany. Despite widespread rhetoric that lamented falling birthrates and the imminent death of their nations, Czech and Hungarian women preserved their right to choose abortion, although with the privatization of medical services the procedure became much more expensive than in communist times. In Romania, the severe anti-abortion law which was the centerpiece of the dictator Nicolae Ceaușescu's campaign to raise birth rates had been so unpopular that the new regime legalized abortion on December 26, 1989—the day after the hated tyrant's execution. In Slovenia, despite its Catholic tradition, large majorities of both women and men opposed the criminalization of abortion, and a new constitution written in 1990 guaranteed the right of women to make decisions about child-bearing. However, conservative religious groups and politicians continued their effort to ban abortion. First-trimester terminations remained legal and free of charge in Russia, although gaining access to publicly funded abortions was so time-consuming and humiliating that most women preferred to pay for an abortion in the private, largely illegal market.[46]

In the newly unified Germany, the usual confrontation of the religious East with the permissive West was reversed, for the East stood for reproductive choice and the West for restriction. The two states that came together to form the Federal Republic of Germany in 1990 had very different abortion laws. In the GDR, abortion in the first trimester had been widely available on demand, but West German laws allowed it only according to indications that were certified by a physician. East German women's groups, joined by some of their Western colleagues, pushed for extending the permissive East German law to the entire country. But the conservative Christian Democratic majority in the West German parliament (or *Bundestag*) upheld the West German law, and some deputies moved to make it even more restrictive. Fearing that this controversy might derail the entire unification process, Chancellor Helmut Kohl decreed that each area should retain its own laws until the first all-German *Bundestag* decided on a single law for all of Germany.

The parliamentary elections of 1990 brought a large group of women delegates—20.5 percent of all deputies—to the *Bundestag*. However, these women were too bitterly divided by political, religious, and local loyalties to form a united front on abortion or any other issue. Male politicians, the majority of whom belonged to the conservative party (the CDU) dominated the *Bundestag's* Special Committee for the Protection of Unborn Life, which considered proposals for a new national abortion policy. As the committee's very name suggested, its deliberations gave less attention to the rights and needs of women than to the legal status of fetuses, the definition of life, and the technicalities of criminal law. The committee produced what it called a compromise proposal, which actually resembled the Western rather than the Eastern law. Under this proposal, abortion would remain illegal in principle, but could be performed by a physician in the first trimester of pregnancy if the woman had spoken with a counselor.

Immediately after the *Bundestag* voted this bill into law, a large group of parliamentary deputies appealed it in Germany's Constitutional Court. Referring to a clause in the German Basic Law that places all human life under the protection of the state, the Court made the law still more restrictive. Henceforth, the Court decreed, abortion would be illegal except in cases of medical problems, fetal deformity, or rape. Abortions performed in the first 12 weeks would nonetheless remain exempt from punishment if the woman received counseling that the Court ruled must be directed toward preventing the abortion and preserving the life of the fetus. As an illegal act, abortion could not be covered by health insurance except in cases of financial need, when it could be funded by social welfare payments. This confusing law now applied to the entire united German state, depriving Eastern women of some reproductive options to which they had become accustomed.[47]

In all post-communist countries, restrictions on reproductive choice fell most heavily on the poorest and most vulnerable women. Even where abortion was legal, rising prices due to the privatization of medical services drove many poor women to dangerous, illegal practitioners. Many still suffered involuntary pregnancy and all its consequences. Among these was a new traffic in human beings: the sale of babies. In communist Romania, children who were abandoned to orphanages were often sold to foreign adoptive parents—a trade that, because it brought in valuable Western money, was authorized by the government. After the fall of communism, foreign adoptions continued, now often sponsored by Western humanitarian organizations that were justifiably appalled by the situation of these children. Because governmental regulatory agencies were corrupt and inefficient, a flourishing market in "private" adoptions emerged, in which individual buyers often purchased children directly from their parents. Especially for Gypsy families—the poorest segment of the population—the sale of children became a source of ready cash, and women were often put under pressure by their husbands to "produce" children for foreign purchasers.[48]

Racial and ethnic prejudice, which the lifting of totalitarian restrictions on speech and political activity brought into the open, also limited some women's reproductive choices. Gypsy women in the Czech Republic complained in the 1990s that compulsory sterilization, though now prohibited by law, still continued in practice, usually immediately after a hospital delivery. Sometimes physicians deliberately deceived women by assuring them that the sterilization procedure could be reversed later.[49]

Attitudes toward another kind of sexual self-determination—a preference for same-sex relationships—varied greatly among the former countries of the Soviet bloc. East Germany, where laws that penalized (male) homosexual behavior were abolished in 1967, had been the most tolerant of the communist countries. Before the fall of communism, lesbian groups began to meet under the protection of some Protestant churches, and in 1990 30 gay organizations formed an umbrella group, the Gay Association of the GDR (*Schwulenverband der DDR*). In Czechoslovakia and Hungary, laws against homosexuality were also repealed in the 1960s. After the fall of communism, gay communities flourished in the large cities of all these countries.

But many post-communist societies were much less tolerant. Though Russian legal prohibitions on homosexual conduct were abolished in 1993, public opinion remained strongly homophobic, and media demonized lesbians as women who lived outside patriarchal control and rejected motherhood. A small but determined lesbian movement in Moscow and St. Petersburg promoted its members' artistic and literary works and advocated tolerance and rights for gay people, but had little funding or visibility outside these large cities. Likewise in Slovenia, homophobic prejudice that was encouraged by the revival of Catholic religious practice prevented many lesbians from "coming out" and justifies laws forbidding gay couples, male or female, to adopt children.

Romanian politicians and church leaders stubbornly defended their right to criminalize homosexuality. After the fall of the Ceauşescu government, a law that had prohibited most kinds of homosexual conduct was modified in 1996 to apply only to behavior that was publicly offensive. Though an improvement over the old legislation, the new law still permitted police harassment of gay individuals and meeting places.[50] In 1998, three years after Romania had applied for membership in the European Union, the European Parliament passed a resolution that denied membership to any country that discriminated on the basis of sexual orientation. In response, representatives of all Romania's Christian churches petitioned the EU to recognize their country's laws against homosexuality as part of its "traditional Christian identity."[51] But when the petition failed, the Romanian government eliminated the law in 2002.

Laws and policies intended to fortify the family, increase birthrates, and uphold religious morality actually undermined these goals. As of 2000, marriage rates were lower and divorce rates higher in Eastern than in Western Europe. In the period 1990–2004, birthrates per thousand population dropped steadily: in the Czech Republic from 13.4 to 9.0; in Poland from 14.3 to 9.9; in Romania from 13.6 to 10.7.[52] These figures, among the lowest in the world, suggest that abortion rates have risen, although few reliable statistics exist. As feminists and others have pointed out since the early twentieth century, restrictions on women's labor-market opportunities often discourage motherhood by depriving women of the financial means to raise a family. In 1992, an investigation of an enormous increase in sterilizations at a clinic in Magdeburg (in the former GDR) revealed that many young, childless women were requesting the procedure because employers would not hire them without proof that they would never become mothers.[53] And propaganda that demonized homosexuality did not seem to have converted the younger generation to conservative "family values." As the Russian physician and well-known sex reformer Igor Kon remarked, "any attempt by the state, church, or local community to forcibly restrict young people's sexual freedom is doomed to failure. The militant position of the Orthodox clergy may even have a boomerang effect." [54]

The exploitation of the female body in the service of nationalism reached a horrifying climax in the wars that split Yugoslavia into five republics during the years 1991–1995. The republics of Croatia and of Bosnia-Herzegovina included some areas inhabited primarily by people of Serb ethnicity. When Yugoslavia disintegrated and these republics declared independence, Serb nationalist militias fought fiercely to annex areas inhabited by Serbs to their own nation, which they called "greater Serbia." In areas of mixed population, these militias launched brutal campaigns of "ethnic cleansing," designed to drive out members of other groups and create all-Serb enclaves. Though the main responsibility for the violence rests with the Serbs, Croatian and Muslim fighters also committed atrocities in Bosnia-Herzegovina.

Along with massacre and the destruction of entire villages, rape was among the tactics that these soldiers used to terrify civilians and to impel them to leave their homes and to flee.[55] In many towns, women were separated from men—many of whom were massacred by firing squads or held in concentration camps—and confined in "rape camps," where they were assaulted repeatedly by gangs of soldiers. The International Red Cross produced a list of 42 such camps, and reliable estimates place the number of rapes in both Croatia and Bosnia at 20,000. Some estimates are higher.[56]

In these as in other wars, rape dramatized the subjection and domination of enemy territory. By forcing the victims to bear their own, ethnically Serb children, the rapists aimed not only to defeat the conquered people, but also to destroy their ethnic identity. Women who became pregnant from rape were often well fed and forbidden to leave the camps until it was too late to abort the pregnancy.[57] Therefore, some observers claimed that rape was an instrument not only of conquest, but of genocide.[58] Although the Bosnian Serb leadership and the Yugoslav head of state Slobodan Milošević, denied that they had authorized these crimes, they clearly bore much of the responsibility for financing and arming the militias who fought to create "greater Serbia." The Dayton Peace Accords of 1995, which concluded the war in Bosnia, left Bosnian Serbs in control of about 49 percent of Bosnian territory. Most of the people displaced by ethnic cleansing have not returned to their homes.

Among the few Serbs who protested against nationalist violence was a group calling itself the "Women in Black." In the streets and squares of Belgrade and of many other cities in Serbia and its allied state of Montenegro, women wearing black as a sign of mourning stood in silent protest. Their motto was and still is "not in our name." Serb mothers also banded together to demand an end to the military recruitment of their sons. As the news of rape and other sexual violence came in, the protesters shifted their focus to the female victims of the war. But, vilified by their own government as traitors and subversives and deprived of international support by the media boycott of Yugoslavia, these courageous women could have no effect on their country's ethnic or military policies.[59]

Conclusion: women and a new social contract

Although the transition from communist totalitarianism to capitalist democracy is usually portrayed as a process of rapid and radical change, for women it had many elements of continuity. As under communism, women remained second-class citizens. Their troubles were increased by the return of some elements of the pre-communist past: nationalism, conservative religion, and unregulated "gangster" capitalism. Nonetheless, many Eastern European women resented being stereotyped as victims or losers and stressed the positive effect of the recent changes. "We are happy that we have bid farewell to Communism," wrote the Russian feminist Valentina Konstantinova in 1993, "but...is it not time that we launched an attack on patriarchalism?" [60]

In some ways, the 1990s in Eastern Europe resembled an earlier decade, the 1920s. In 1920 as in 1989, most women in Western Europe were full of optimism about democracy, which they idealistically believed was a system that would empower individuals regardless of class, gender, or social status. In the 1920s as in the 1990s, these hopes were disappointed: natalist pressures, discriminatory employment policies, and a culture that glorified misogyny restricted women's personal liberties and economic opportunities, and feminism declined amid a revival of domesticity and religious conservatism. But the backlash of the 1920s could not permanently turn back the clock, and women continued the struggle to improve their status, advance their interests, and improve their lives and those of their children.

We can thus expect that Eastern European women will find ways to place gender issues on the political agenda and to work toward equality and justice. The European Union, which many post-communist countries eagerly aspired to enter, requires its member nations to guarantee the rights of women and minority groups. Through a global communications network, moreover, women can now find alternatives to conservative national and religious traditions. In this international context, what might a new feminism look like? Most Eastern European feminists reject certain Western feminist ideologies, which in their opinion place too much emphasis on gender antagonism, separatism, and the imitation of men. Many define feminism in the context of a new kind of citizenship—one that rejects the narrow national, ethnic, and religious identities that have had such destructive consequences and views gender difference as one form of diversity among many. "If we strive to uphold the principles of the social contracts that come with citizenship as a concept that both the majority and the minority can adhere to, feminists included," wrote Jiřina Šiklová in 1999, "we will give women of various races, nationalities, and social groups an opportunity to find themselves and maintain their own identities and thereby ensure the maintenance of a pluralistic society." [61]

9

From Equal Rights to Gender Mainstreaming: Women in the European Union, 1980–Present

Many women experienced the twentieth century, despite all its horrors, as a hopeful period. Successive generations struggled to raise women's status and improve their lives. By the end of the century, they had gained results that their nineteenth-century foremothers could hardly have imagined: the abolition of legal patriarchy in marriage, control over reproduction, and vast improvements in educational level and occupational qualifications. But gender equality was still a dream deferred. In 2003, Anna Diamantopolou, the European Union's Commissioner for Employment and Social Affairs, declared that although the laws of the EU nations guaranteed women equal rights, "in practice we are far away from claiming to have reached parity in numbers and influence. There are simply not enough women in high political decision-making posts to ensure that women's perspectives are adequately represented in all areas of life." [1]

Diamantopolou and many other prominent speakers challenged the women of the twenty-first century to develop new goals and aspirations. As the earlier chapters have shown, the twentieth century had developed its own gender order to replace the nineteenth-century regime of legal inequality and separate spheres. The twentieth-century paradigm involved legal equality plus integration in many areas—the workplace, educational institutions, social and cultural life. But in addition to change, the century saw much continuity. Though the status of women changed, that of men remained substantially the same. The entrance of women into the male sphere was not paralleled by a symmetrical movement of men into the female world of home, family, and child-care. In fact, many twentieth-century states reinforced the female identification of these tasks by making motherhood a public function with distinctive privileges, constraints, and obligations. Women who carried family responsibilities might join men in work, education, labor or politics, but were seldom able to compete with them for power or leadership. Many women aspired to "emancipation" from the condition of femininity; few men assumed that masculinity was a condition from which anyone needed to be emancipated.

Though they might complain of the dangers of too much emancipation, male elites of the twentieth century often accepted this gender regime, and many actually affirmed it. For it made women available to the state—not only as homemakers and mothers, but also as trained and educated workers, voters, and military personnel—without any threat that they would actually gain political and economic power. At the close of the century, however, many policy-makers recognized that this regime no longer served the interests of states or societies. Indeed, leaders of the European Union and of its member states now identify gender inequality as a major obstacle to their societies' growth and prosperity, even to their survival. At the turn of the century, they formulated a new objective: "gender mainstreaming" or "parity," defined as the equal participation of both genders in all aspects and at all levels of political and economic life, and especially in decision-making positions. There is a growing consensus that both male and female behavior must change.

This chapter will look at the reasons for this policy change and at the prospects for its success in the countries that belong to the European Union. The EU, founded in 1957, at first committed only six countries—France, Germany, Belgium, Luxemburg, the Netherlands, and Italy—to move toward free trade and economic cooperation. Since then, its membership has expanded. In 1980, the EU took in nine and in 1995 six more member nations in Western and Southern Europe and in Scandinavia. In 2006 it accepted twelve further members, including ten nations of the former Eastern Bloc; and in 2007 two more post-communist nations.[2] Several other post-communist countries have applied for EU membership. The organization, which is administered from its headquarters in Brussels, Belgium, is governed by the European Commission, its executive body, the Council of Europe, composed of officials of the member governments, and a European Parliament that is elected every five years by all citizens of the member states. Over the years, the EU has broadened its mandate, and now makes policy in many areas: the environment, labor, immigration policy, and human rights. The jurisdiction of the EU extends chiefly to issues that overlap national boundaries and its actual authority in any member country is limited. But in a Europe that functions more and more as a unit, the EU exercises considerable influence on its member states' internal policies.

Work/life balance

The old model of "emancipation" has become obsolete chiefly because of the immense change in the life course of women in rich Western countries over the course of the twentieth century. Starting with the biological parameters: in 1900, the average life expectancies of women in Europe ranged from about 35 years in Portugal to about 55 years in Sweden; by 1990, the Portuguese figure had approximately doubled to reach 78 years and the Swedish figure had increased by more than 50 percent to 80 years. Women's life expectancies increasingly outstripped those of men: Portuguese women lived on average two years longer than men in 1900 but eight years longer in 1990, and in Sweden the difference grew from three to six years in the same period.[3] Meanwhile, the number of children produced by each woman declined. In 1900, total fertility rates (the number of children per woman) were 2.8 in France, 4.8 in Germany, 4.9 in Spain, and 7.1 in Russia. By 2000 these rates had dropped sharply, to 1.89 in France, 1.36 in Germany, 1.24 in Spain, and 1.21 in Russia.[4] These figures signaled two novel historical trends: the first was the association of falling birthrates with rising prosperity and high expectations rather than with catastrophes such as war or famine; and the second was the transformation of child-bearing from the inevitable destiny of the majority of women to a choice to be accepted or avoided.

The combination of lengthened life expectancies and falling birthrates have created new opportunities and new problems for women themselves and for the societies that depend for their continuance on women's productive and reproductive work. One consequence was already apparent by the 1950s, when the Swedish social reformer Alva Myrdal remarked that women devoted only about a third of their lives bearing and rearing children, and would have to develop another focus for their post-parental years. By 1979, the French sociologist Évelyne Sullerot estimated that women devoted on average only one seventh of their lives to full-time motherhood.[5] As the notion that women's chief or only occupations were those of wife and mother gradually fell into obsolescence, women's lives changed dramatically.

The change did not consist merely of rising rates of employment—for at the beginning of the twentieth century many women already worked for pay—but rather in the relation of paid work to women's identity, aspirations, and life course. Around 1900, the typical worker was a young, unmarried woman, who usually gave up her job when she married and had children, and (though she often did some kind of paid work) did not return to full-time employment. Married women and mothers who continued to be employed were likely to be poor, uneducated, and working under the control of their husbands in family businesses or on family farms. But by 2000, women were more than half of all students in the tertiary education sector of most European countries, and their educational levels equaled or surpassed those of men. Educated women were now more likely than those with less education to be employed, and women's patterns increasingly resembled those of men—they, too, tended to spend the greater part of their adult lives in the labor market.

But though women's opportunities had improved, striking inequalities remained. Partly due to their rising educational levels and their lifetime laborforce participation, the wage levels of women rose and the gender gap in pay narrowed, especially in Western Europe and Scandinavia. But women still earned less than men. By 2004, the average woman in the EU (which now included eight formerly communist countries) earned about 15 percent less than the average man, and the gap ranged from about 6 percentage points in Belgium to about 25 in Latvia.[6] Moreover, average wage levels do not tell the whole story, for they do not account for the clustering of women in low-paying jobs. Around 2000, women and children still made up the majority of poor people.[7] In many Western European countries, women were significantly more likely than men to work part-time; in the EU countries in 2002, 41 percent of employed women, but only 10 percent of employed men, were part-time workers.[8] Because of women's rising educational qualifications, their representation in professional and managerial positions increased, but they were still much less likely than men to rise to senior or leadership positions.

In addition to wage inequality the European labor market was and still is characterized by strong job segregation, which increased with the expansion of the welfare state. Women are much more likely than men to hold government or civil service jobs; in fact 31 percent of full-time women and 19 percent of all full-time men in the EU countries were employed in the public sector in 2002. Most female public employees are still in traditionally female occupations—teaching, child-care, medical and social services—that offer secure employment in return for relatively low wages. By contrast, men have moved into private-sector jobs that require technological expertise, personal initiative, and competitiveness, and offer good prospects for pay and advancement.

What explains the persistence in 2000 of some of the same gender stereotypes that were current in 1900? Although female gender roles had changed greatly over the past century, the corresponding male roles remained much as they were in 1900. Men saw themselves primarily as breadwinners, and gave priority to paid work over familial obligations. This mentality persisted despite the reality that families now depend on the earnings of both partners. Women were expected to care for home and children, even though most were also breadwinners. Although marriage and parenthood now no longer kept women out of the labor market, they still had the effect of limiting their earning power and possibilities of advancement. Female employment patterns, including long career breaks, part-time hours, and failure to progress to higher levels, were largely due to the pressure to combine labor market and familial responsibilities. These, to be sure, were personal choices, but they were heavily influenced by the cultures of both family and workplace.

The "family-friendly" policies of European welfare states reinforced some kinds of gender inequality. Natalist concerns that arose during the first years of the twentieth century decreased somewhat during the prolific years of the post-war baby boom, but returned as birthrates began to drop again in the 1970s and 1980s. In these decades, welfare states in the communist east as well as the democratic west further expanded the services and protections that they allotted to employed mothers. These programs rested on varying social and political principles. Scandinavian states used highly progressive taxation and generous benefits to redistribute wealth and level class differences. Germany and France provided many universal entitlements, but in forms—such as pension benefits and unemployment insurance based on a percentage of the worker's salary—that preserved class differences. After the reforms of the 1980s Britain, like the United States, provided fewer universal entitlements and more means-tested benefits designed only for the poor.[9]

But despite these philosophical differences, all of these policies rested on the basic assumption that mothers—but not fathers—were responsible for children and required help in combining child-rearing and paid work. Prospective mothers received paid maternity leaves; mothers were given paid and unpaid time off for child-rearing (sometimes with the promise that they could have their jobs back when they returned); and family allowances enabled some families temporarily to do without mothers' incomes. Some countries (such as Germany), operating on the assumption that most families were headed by male breadwinners, offered tax breaks to households where only one parent worked. Others, chiefly in Scandinavia, aimed to enable women with children to live independently of men by supplementing mothers' incomes. For single mothers, welfare policies emphasized familial over work responsibilities: in Germany, for example, single mothers who received social assistance were not required to work for pay until their children were 12, in the UK not until their children were 16.[10] These measures sometimes served another purpose—to reduce the unemployment that plagued most countries after 1970 by encouraging women to withdraw from the labor force.

Certainly, these forms of assistance did a great deal to reduce poverty, to improve the living conditions of mothers, children, and families, and to enable women to combine careers with family life. But they did not solve the problem of gender inequality in the workplace. Women who took long career breaks often could not make up for the lost time, and fell permanently behind their male colleagues. Those who worked part-time sacrificed the possibility of moving ahead. Employers often assumed that young women (regardless of marital or parental status) would require time off and other concessions and were reluctant to hire and promote them to responsible positions. Gender segregation, too, increased as women were drawn to the public sector where—because of tighter state regulation—a "family-friendly" environment was guaranteed. Simply making benefits gender neutral did little to change these patterns. In the 1990s, Scandinavian countries made parental leave available to fathers as well as to mothers. Very few fathers took advantage of this "benefit," for fear of being regarded as slackers, placing their prospects for promotion and advancement in jeopardy, or losing out to their competitors. Women who adopt a "male" work ethic and rise to leadership positions are much more likely to be unmarried, divorced, or childless than other working women or than their equally successful male colleagues. Women still occupy a minority of all senior and managerial positions: in France 30 percent, in Germany 25 percent, in Sweden 32 percent.[11]

At the century's end, European labor market policies rested on an assumption—that mothers, unlike fathers, were willing to set back their careers and earning potential in order to care for children—that was increasingly out of step with changing patterns of reproduction and household formation. Most young women still wished to become mothers: for example, a survey taken in the 1990s in several Western European countries showed that the average young woman born between 1965 and 1975 planned to have two or more children.[12] However, fewer women than ever before were able or willing to rely on a male breadwinner. After a peak in the 1960s, rates of marriage declined steadily, and people got married at ever later ages—in 1998, the average age of women who married for the first time in the EU was 27.[13] An increasing number of children were born outside marriage, although this pattern varies enormously: in the 1990s, 58 percent of all Swedish, but only 4 percent of all Italian and Hungarian children were born to unmarried parents.[14] Whether married or unmarried, by

2000 many women regarded themselves as primary breadwinners, and—like men—sought career stability and financial independence before having children.

In earlier decades, policy-makers feared that women who had good employment opportunities would be less willing than others to have children. But at the century's end, the correlation between women's career success and their fertility was strongly positive. In countries where working-age women's labor force participation was high relative to that of men (71 percent of women and 88 percent of men in Norway, 53 percent of women and 68 percent of men in France in 2000) and income disparities were narrow, completed fertility rates (the average number of children per woman) were also relatively high: 1.89 children per woman in France and 1.72 in Scandinavia in 2000. In countries such as Italy and Spain, where relatively few women were employed (39 percent of women and 68 percent of men in Italy, 40 percent of women and 70 percent of men in Spain) and income disparities were wide, birthrates dropped further and faster. In Italy in 2000 the completed fertility rate was 1.21, and in Spain 1.24.[15] But nowhere in Europe does average family size reach the level that most young women say they desire—two or more children. Among the complex causes of this trend is certainly the fact that motherhood still entails career setbacks and financial insecurity—disadvantages that an increasing number of young women are no longer willing to accept.

Dwindling birthrates contribute to another social problem—the rising ratio of non-working to working people. Since the beginning of the twentieth century, both average life spans and expenditure on retirement pensions have increased rapidly, and these two trends are now on a collision course. Aggravating the problem is an ever more widespread expectation of early retirement, which depletes the labor force and enlarges the number of pensioners. Governments now face an unwelcome choice between increasing the already high taxes on working people to support the aged, or reneging on commitments to retirees. By far the most desirable solution to this dilemma is to increase the ratio of workers to retirees by raising retirement ages, increasing birthrates, and employing working-age adults who are unemployed or working part-time. Two of these three measures depend on women, who are both the producers of children and the largest group of unemployed or underutilized workers.

In addition, due to inequities in pay and employment opportunities, women—and especially single mothers—make up a large percentage of poor and marginal members of society. The best means of reducing poverty and social exclusion is to integrate these women into decently paying and stable employment. And the state's heavy investment in educating women—who now outnumber men in higher education—is wasted if they are prevented from using their training and potential to the fullest possible extent.

In the 1990s, EU governments and policy-makers adopted the policy of "gender mainstreaming," which aimed "to make equal opportunities for women and men an integral part of all areas of policy." [16] "Employment growth in the EU, the key to our future prosperity, has become hugely dependent on the increased participation of women in the labor market," declared Padraig Flynn, a member of the European Commission (the EU's executive body) in 1999.

"Member States must create the conditions that will enable the European economy and the European workplace to benefit fully from the creativity, talents and skills of women and to enable men and women to have greater balance in their working and family lives." [17]

The EU's employment strategy aims not only to bring women into the labor market—the Lisbon summit of 2000 envisaged a 60 percent female employment rate throughout the EU area by 2010—but also to enable them to rise to leadership positions in business, industry, and government agencies. EU leaders urged member nations to initiate affirmative-action programs, aggressively enforce laws against gender discrimination, recruit women into traditionally male occupations, and increase the availability of child-care services. However, the EU operates according to the principle of subsidiarity: its jurisdiction ends where those of its member governments begin. Except in areas related to intergovernmental relations, the organization has little power—though substantial influence—over its member states' domestic policies.

Most member states—even those that until recently rejected public child-care as an assault on "family values"—have now committed themselves to increasing their expenditure on these services. But the extent to which they are actually available varies widely. In 2000, 48 percent of all Danish, but only 5 percent of all Italian children under three were enrolled in public day-care centers. [18] In Spain and France, pre-school education for children from three to six years of age is well established and popular, but nurseries for younger children are less available. [19] The conservative government of the British Prime Minister Margaret Thatcher (1979–1990) cut back funding for social services, and only after the victory of the Labour Party in 1996 did the government, alarmed by the threat of a "demographic time bomb," increase public support for child-care. German governments since 1995 have committed themselves to creating a kindergarten place for every child, but this promise is still a long way from fulfillment. In Poland and other post-communist nations, of course, the transfer of previously public day-care centers to private ownership has raised their cost, made them unaffordable for most families, and led to many closures. [20]

However necessary and desirable, services such as child-care that are designed chiefly to help working mothers will not suffice to achieve gender mainstreaming in the workplace. Scandinavia, where public child-care is widely available, still has a highly segregated labor market and a substantial pay differential, especially in the private sector.

Rather, the goal must be to move away from the traditional notion of "emancipation"—the assimilation of women to male life patterns—and toward a new concept of gender equality that also encourages men to take on traditionally female roles. Only if both sexes share work both outside and within the home on an equal basis will the artificial distinction between male "breadwinners" and female caregivers become truly obsolete, leaving men and women equally free to engage in both work and family life. "We must conclude," writes the influential Swedish sociologist Gøsta Esping-Andersen, "that true gender equality will not come about unless, somehow, men can be made to embrace a more feminine life-course. Whether or not such a scenario would truly conform to the prevailing choice set of today's men and women is pretty unclear." [21]

But as the political scientist Nancy Fraser points out, this would amount to a total "deconstruction of gender"—an objective that goes far beyond the mandate of the EU or of its member states.[22] The ability of any government to regulate personal choices is, and should be, limited. With the memory of totalitarianism still fresh, public opinion will not tolerate a return to the coercive policies of the past. Apart from educational campaigns, the only way that governments can encourage men to share child-care is by manipulating parental leave policies, which in some countries grant a government-subsidized paid leave of a year or more to new parents. Scandinavian governments now grant the full period of parental leave only if a portion of it is taken by the father. Though fathers pushing baby carriages have become a more common sight on city streets, the effects of this measure have been limited—in Denmark in 2004, fathers took an average 3.6 weeks, and mothers 42.3 weeks, of leave.[23]

Some social reformers oppose these policies, claiming that what Europe needs is not more meddling by the "nanny state," but rather cuts in government spending and deregulation of the labor market—measures that they hope will enhance the economic success of both women and men. But even some conservatives who are normally sympathetic to these arguments make an exception for parental leave policy. Ursula von der Leyen, a member of the conservative Christian Democratic Party (CDU), is the Minister for Family, Senior Citizens, Women and Youth Germany. She herself is the mother of seven children. When asked to justify a new policy requiring fathers to take at least 2 months of a 12-month paid parental leave, she admitted that it was not the business of the state to tell families how to raise their children. However, she added, most women were employed when they had their first children, and wanted to continue with their careers. Young fathers were willing to take an active role in raising their children. A state that did not help young couples to fulfill these wishes faced "the risk that no one will want to have children any more."[24]

"Liberty, equality, parity"

During the first decades of the twentieth century, suffrage movements in almost every European country struggled to secure for women the rights to vote, to run for office, and to hold parliamentary and governmental positions. Suffragists were confident that the achievement of these rights would bring steady progress toward the integration of women in politics and all areas of public life. But they were disappointed, for women gained only a token presence in most parliaments. In 1989, women held about 30 percent of parliamentary seats in Denmark and Finland, but their share of seats was only 16 percent in the West German *Bundestag*, 5.7 percent in the French National Assembly, and 6.5 percent in the British House of Commons. In the final decades of the twentieth century, the under-representation of women in politics and government appeared in a new light, no longer as a result of "natural" gender differences but as a flaw in the political system that could threaten the survival of democracy itself.

For some feminists, the inclusion of women in mainstream politics was a new and still controversial idea. The women's movements of the 1970s had mistrusted conventional party politics and formed alternative, countercultural political movements. The decline of separatist feminism in the 1980s made way for a more pragmatic attitude toward women's political role. But still, feminists did not support all of the women politicians who succeeded in gaining their parties' nomination and winning elections.

The prime example of the successful woman politician, of course, was the British Margaret Thatcher. First elected to Parliament as a representative of the Conservative Party in the 1950s, Thatcher advanced into the Party's leadership in the 1960s, served as Secretary of State for Education from 1970 to 1974, and held the office of Prime Minister from 1979 to 1990. Thatcher's relationship to both femininity and feminism was complicated. She owed nothing to the women's movement—most of which supported her opposition, the Labour Party—and paid little attention to feminist issues or to advancing the careers of women in government. She got her start in politics by presenting herself as a housewife and mother who was concerned with saving money, preserving the family and the nation, and encouraging hard work and sound moral values. But in fact, Thatcher was far from motherly. As Secretary of State for Education, she made the quintessentially unmaternal decision to abolish free milk for school children, and was reviled as "Maggie Thatcher, milk snatcher." As Prime Minister, she reduced public expenditures and privatized the economy, in the process eliminating or cutting some of the benefits—such as child allowances and medical services—upon which disadvantaged women and children had relied. But the very fact that this talented politician could gain the respect of her male peers did much to broaden women's horizons. And by stimulating the growth of the British economy, Thatcher's government opened career opportunities to capable and ambitious women as well as to men.

Unlike Thatcher, some other women who occupied high offices had a background in the feminist movement and continued their engagement with women's issues. Gro Harlem Brundtland, a socialist physician who had headed Norway's ministries of health and environmental policies, held the position of Prime Minister during the 1980s (1981 and 1986–1989) and from 1990 until 1996. Brundtland, who was an advocate of reproductive rights and other feminist causes, appointed several women to her cabinet and enforced a regulation that required at least 40 percent of the parliamentary candidates on her party's ballot to be female.[25] Mary Robinson, a lawyer who as a feminist leader in the 1970s had supported the legalization of abortion and rights for homosexuals, was elected President of Ireland in 1990 and served until 1997, when she left office to become the United Nations High Commissioner for Human Rights. Despite the high visibility of these exceptional women, politics remained a male sphere.

In the 1990s, the leadership of the European Union resolved to change the conventional image of the politician as a man in a gray suit. Since its founding in 1957, the EU had officially supported equal rights for women in many areas. But its leading elite was almost wholly male—a fact that did not go unnoticed by Europe's feminists. In the 1970s, the Norwegian historian Ida Blom and the other members of her group opposed Norway's joining the EU because of "the fact that it was led by men only!"[26] In 1992, the Maastricht Treaty, which deepened European integration by providing for European as well as national citizenship, a common monetary system, and a common foreign and security policy, was sent to the member countries for ratification. The Treaty proved unexpectedly controversial—Danish voters rejected it (in 1993, they accepted it only with a clause that allowed Denmark to opt out of some provisions) and French voters ratified by a very narrow majority. The wave of "euro-skepticism" expressed the alienation of the many Europeans—including the women who made up a majority of voters—from an organization which they did not believe represented them or their interests. Fearing for the future of European unity, the EU re-evaluated both its image and its policies. The goal of gender mainstreaming, which the EU adopted in the 1990s, required not only "the inclusion of equal opportunities for men and women in all aspects of policy," but also "positive activities (the specific promotion of women) until equality has actually been achieved." [27]

Many national governments and political parties also committed themselves to gender mainstreaming. Like the EU leadership, national governments were concerned about voters' alienation, as reflected in declining participation in elections and increasingly negative views of politics and politicians. In France, feminist politicians took advantage of this sour public mood to point out that women had good reason to mistrust a national parliament in which women held less than one in every ten seats. In 1996, a group of French feminists issued a manifesto demanding a constitutional amendment that affirmed the principle of "parity"—that is, the equal representation of women and men in governmental and legislative bodies. Adopting the motto "liberty, equality, parity," they based their arguments both on gender equality and on gender difference—women were entitled to participate in all decisions both because they were men's equals and because they brought distinctively feminine concerns into the political arena.

In France as in some other European countries, many legislative elections are conducted by proportional representation—a system in which each political party submits to the voters a list of candidates, and the number who are actually seated is determined by that party's percentage of the total vote. The proposed law required each party to place an equal number of male and female candidates on each list, in alternating positions. This proposal was controversial, and many feminists rejected it, arguing that it insulted women by implying that they could not succeed on their own. But it gained broad support among French political leaders and voters. In 1998, an amendment to the French constitution required "equal access by both men and women to elective office and positions," and a law of 2000 imposed the quota system on all political parties. Penalties for non-compliance might include de-certification of a list or cuts in the campaign funding that the government provides to each political party. The results to date have been uneven, and women have made greater gains at the local and municipal than at the national level.[28] In Belgium, too, a quota regulation requires all political parties to allot at least one-third of their list positions to women. Some other governments provide financial and other incentives to parties that develop strategies to promote women. Although the number of female officeholders has risen substantially, only in Scandinavia does their representation in parliaments and governments approach 50 percent.[29]

Feminism in many EU countries moved from the counterculture to the mainstream. In the 1980s, new national ministries were set up to promote the rights and interests of women, and sometimes also of children and families. These ministries, which are typically headed by women, have provided employment to a new political class of feminist civil servants and officials, or "femocrats." Under pressure to reduce taxes, cut budgets, and downsize public sectors, governments have transferred many responsibilities from public agencies to private organizations. Among these are feminist groups, which often receive full or partial state subsidies to perform a wide variety of services to women and families—family planning clinics, day-care centers, shelters for women, community centers, libraries, educational programs, shelters for abused women, rape-crisis centers, and a host of others. Though happy to receive public funding, some feminists are uncomfortable with their movement's new dependency on the state, which creates strong pressures to refrain from radicalism and to subordinate feminist principles to the practical constraints of working within the system. Also, many are aware that privatization, though it may empower some feminists, is often detrimental to the interests of clients, who may face a cutback in the availability or an increase in the cost of the services they need.[30]

To what extent have these new directions in public policy affected the actual lives of women? Women's status still varies widely among EU countries. Though women have increased their visibility in the political life of Western European nations, there is no similar development in the post-communist east, even in countries such as Poland which have recently joined the EU.

Moreover, the EU's policies on gender equality still leave many controversial issues to member states. Among these is reproductive choice. Most EU members have now legalized abortion (see Chapter 7), although both the laws and the actual availability of services differ widely across national boundaries. Ireland, however, prohibited all abortions except those that are necessary to save the life of the mother in a constitutional amendment passed in 1983. Ireland attached a special protocol guaranteeing its right to prohibit abortion to its ratification of the Maastricht Treaty of 1992. In that same year, Ireland defended its national sovereignty in a case that became an international *cause célèbre*. The Attorney General of Ireland issued a court order to prevent a 14-year-old rape victim and her parents from leaving the country to obtain an abortion in England. As feminists pointed out, this action violated the right guaranteed by the EU to freedom of movement among member nations. The nation's Supreme Court struck down this ruling because the pregnancy endangered the life of the girl, who had threatened suicide, but did not alter the law. A national referendum of 1992 guaranteed the right of Irish citizens to travel but upheld the constitutional amendment. Organizations that provide information on abortion providers in Britain still face harassment by the police and anti-abortion groups.[31]

Diversity of opinion among and within member nations complicates EU deliberations on some other gender issues. Although in 1991 the EU issued a policy statement that identified sexual harassment as a form of gender discrimination, national policy-makers have often been reluctant to pass and enforce laws against this offence.[32] Freedom of movement among some EU countries works to the advantage of many women but exposes others to exploitation and violence. A booming traffic in women supplies the prostitution and pornography industries. Since the fall of communism and the Iron Curtain, traffickers recruit most of their victims from Russia and Eastern Europe, and take advantage of open borders and lax enforcement of immigration laws to move them into and around Western Europe. EU authorities and national governments recognize the evil but disagree on the appropriate remedy. Feminists and advocacy groups urge member governments to crack down on the sex trade, which they consider a major offence against human rights, by stiffening penalties for pimping as well as by providing social services and drug-rehabilitation programs to prostitutes and sponsoring sex-education curricula that emphasize non-exploitative sexual relationships. In 1999, the Swedish government affirmed these principles by defining all prostitution as sexual exploitation and making the purchase—though not the sale—of sexual services a criminal offence, to be punished by fine or imprisonment. But a more prevalent current of opinion distinguishes between forced and voluntary prostitution, regards the latter as a legitimate occupation, and while supporting laws against illegal trafficking resists broader limitations on the sex industry.[33]

The ability of the EU and its member governments to realize their new definitions of gender equality is thus limited. Nonetheless, the ever more widespread recognition of gender equality not simply as a desirable but also as an urgent policy goal reflects the new power exercised by women as voters and citizens. A political party, government, or institution that does not include women in its leadership now risks a loss of popularity that may threaten its very existence. A century after the first European women won the right to vote, they may be finally be able to use the ballotbox to exercise a power proportionate to their numbers.

Unity in diversity

Advocates of gender mainstreaming often assume that all that is needed to defend the rights and serve the interests of women is to place women in decision-making positions. But women differ widely in their ideas and interests, and what is good for one woman is often not good for another. In nations where the population is now increasingly divided by religion, race, and nationality, the goal expressed by the EU's new motto, "unity in diversity," has yet to become reality.

In the acceptance of one kind of diversity—difference in sexual orientation and gender identity—some European countries have set an example to the entire world. In the 1970s, homosexual acts between consenting adults were decriminalized in most Western European countries, and in the 1980s Scandinavian nations took the further step of giving legal recognition to same-sex unions. Dutch single-sex couples gained the right to enter "registered partnerships" in 1989, and many other nations followed this example—for example, in 1999 France made a legal "*pacte civil de solidarité*" (civil union) available to both same and opposite-sex couples, and Germany passed a similar law in 2002. In 2001, the Netherlands became the first country to eliminate all legal distinctions between gay and straight couples by striking all references to gender in the laws on marriage. At least in large cities, single-sex couples are increasingly integrated into middle-class society. Anne-Marie Thus, a native of Amsterdam who married her partner, Helene Faasen, in 2001, declared in a newspaper interview that the couple and their children were glad to live in a neighborhood where "people know that they don't have to be afraid of us."[34]

But not all neighborhoods are so tolerant. Though discrimination against gay people continues everywhere, it is most serious in Eastern Europe. Although forced when they applied for EU membership to repeal laws that criminalized homosexual behavior (see Chapter 8), many post-communist governments still do little to protect their gay citizens from intimidation and violence. In 2000, a new European Charter of Fundamental Rights prohibited discrimination on the grounds of sexual orientation or gender identity. An organization known as ILGA-Europe (Equality for Lesbian, Gay, Bisexual, and Transgender people in Europe) receives EU funding for its campaign to dismantle all remaining forms of discrimination. The organization supports the access of gay and transgender people to employment, government benefits, medical services, and rights of political asylum. It champions their right to organize, to assemble, and to express themselves freely. And it claims equal status for same-sex couples in marital and parental relationships.[35] In 2004, the European Parliament called for the recognition of gay unions in all member states, and Spain followed the example of the Netherlands by legalizing gay marriage.[36]

A still more difficult set of issues have been raised by the integration of another substantial minority, that of immigrants and their descendants. In most European countries, citizenship is defined by common ethnicity, language, and cultural heritage—a definition that feminist movements often reinforced by claiming rights for women on the basis of their membership in a national or ethnic community. Current campaigns to provide career opportunities for women and encourage motherhood carry an ethnocentric subtext, for an increase in the number of native workers means less need for immigrants to swell the depleted ranks of the labor force.

Most foreign-born residents or their parents entered Europe under the "guest-worker" programs of the 1950s and 1960s, when booming post-war economies created the need for laborers in many branches of agriculture, manufacture, and construction. Though originally admitted only on a temporary basis, guest workers frequently found ways to stay, although more often as resident aliens than as citizens. Although the "guest-worker" programs ended in the 1970s, many immigrants have now become permanent residents, and have brought family members to live with them. The younger generations of these families have often spent their entire lives in Europe. The immigrant population is diverse, including people of many racial, religious, and national groups. But the group that is now most conspicuous traces its origins to the Muslim countries of North Africa, the Middle East, Turkey, and South Asia. Though they constitute a small minority of the EU's inhabitants, Muslims are concentrated in a few urban areas, where their presence is highly visible, and their birthrate is three times that of non-Muslims. In several European countries, including France, Germany, and the Netherlands, a large portion of the younger generation is Muslim, and by 2030 this group may constitute one-third of these states' populations.

In Muslim as in many immigrant communities, familial tensions pit an older generation that remains attached to its ancestral culture against young people who feel both the pull of tradition and the lure of assimilation. Many of these family conflicts focus on women, upon whom the continuation of the family's biological and cultural heritage depends. Young women who violate their families' norms of dress and decorum, escape from the control of their fathers and brothers, and adopt the alien ways of their host cultures become objects of a resentment which sometimes becomes violent and abusive, even murderous. Hatun Sürücü, the daughter of Turkish Kurds who lived in Berlin, was forced to leave school after eighth grade and marry a man whom her parents chose. Having separated from her husband, Sürücü took refuge in a women's center, entered a vocational training course, and took advantage of her new independence to abandon her Islamic head scarf and wear sexy Western clothes. In 2004, three of her five brothers murdered her only a few days before she could receive her diploma. Seyran Ates, a lawyer of Turkish background who runs a women's center in Berlin, estimates that about half of all daughters of Turkish families in Berlin are forced into marriage. Obviously, this and other practices—such as excluding young women from educational and vocational opportunities and denying them the freedom to live independently of their parents—violate the norms of gender parity to which the EU and its member states are committed.[37] However, governments often hesitate to intervene for fear of being accused of improper meddling in their citizens' private lives or of religious or cultural intolerance.

A role model for Islamic women who aspire to assimilation is the courageous Dutch politician and feminist Ayaan Hirsi Ali. Hirsi Ali, who was born in Somalia and spent much of her youth in Kenya, escaped the marriage that her father had chosen for her and sought asylum in the Netherlands. Having gained Dutch citizenship, she attended university, received a degree in political science, and entered politics and became a Member of Parliament for the Liberal Party. Hirsi Ali makes no secret of her rejection of her religion and native culture, both of which she calls backward and misogynist, and her admiration of Western Europe. Her political positions on such issues as immigration policy and women's rights have alienated her from her own people, including her family. "That is how perverse religion can be," she wrote, "it interferes with intimate relationships and forces parents to choose between their children and their god."[38] Hirsi Ali decries the policies of the Dutch government, which in the name of tolerance and multiculturalism funds Islamic schools and neighborhood centers. She accuses these publicly-supported institutions of reinforcing religious traditions of male supremacy and female subservience, and contributing to "the continuation of a hopeless tyranny over women and children."[39] In 2004, Hirsi Ali partnered with the producer Theo van Gogh to create a film entitled *Submission* that showed Koranic verses inscribed on the recumbent and nude body of a woman. After a Muslim extremist expressed his rage by murdering van Gogh, Hirsi Ali was forced to hide from killers who threatened her life. The

Netherlands, for decades one of Europe's most peaceful, stable, and humane societies, witnessed an outburst of ethnic and religious hatred.

While Islamic women who reject religious tradition are often persecuted by their own families and communities, those who uphold it incur the hostility of their non-Muslim neighbors. In 1989, three high-school students who signaled their religious identity by wearing head scarves were expelled from a school in Creil, a suburb of Paris. The headmaster justified this action by invoking a central principle of the French state—that religious expression had no place in secular public schools. This and similar incidents are part of a global conflict between the secularism of Europe, where the vast majority, though nominal Christians, no longer practice any religion, and the wave of religious fervor in the Islamic world—a cultural clash in which both sides use women as symbols. In a concession that some commentators angrily compared to the appeasement of Nazi Germany, a government decree reinterpreted the French law to apply only to religious proselytizing, not to passive expressions of belief, and allowed the girls to return to their school. Controversies about attire and other expressions of religious belief, always involving girls and women, continue to disrupt schools and other public institutions and attract widespread attention in the media of France and other countries.

The *affaire du foulard* (or head-scarf controversy) also stirred up controversy among feminists. Some upheld the ban on head scarves in the name of both women's rights and religious freedom, asserting that the wearing of religious attire was often not a truly free choice, but rather the visible sign of the subordination of women and girls. By creating a religion-free zone, schools provided their students with the opportunity to throw off the symbols of oppression and to enjoy the liberty, equality, and fraternity that the French republic guarantees to all its citizens. But others pointed out that young people from immigrant backgrounds experienced these ideals more as promise than as reality. In fact, despite their educational achievements, young Muslims face discrimination in the workforce and exclusion from the majority culture. According to the feminist Christine Delphy, girls who were ostracized by their French peer group had little choice but to adopt the alternate identity signaled by the head scarf. The problem could not be remedied simply by prohibitions—more positive measures were needed. France must

> begin to struggle against discrimination, first by realizing that we practice it and that it is evil, and then by taking measures specifically designed to stop discrimination. And if we reintegrate the young people whom we have excluded, and continue to exclude, maybe after some time they will feel included. . . . But we could also react by repression, and continue to create a society based on caste which will be more and more violent as . . . the young women in head scarves of today . . . become the Islamic radicals of tomorrow.[40]

However, some Muslim women see the combination of Muslim and Western identities not chiefly as a negative response to discrimination, but as a positive assertion of both difference and equality. By wearing a head scarf while attending a French school, a young woman invents a hybrid (mixed) identity—that of a French Muslim. Western society holds many attractions for Muslim women, who outstrip their male co-religionists in both educational achievements and career success. Teachers remark that Muslim girls are often the most motivated of all students because they have the most to gain from academic qualifications: escape from the crowded, run-down housing projects where immigrant families are clustered and from control by fathers, brothers, and neighborhood gangs.[41] These young women try to find ways of belonging to both their native and adopted cultures. "While, on the one hand, I want to be loyal and maintain the culture my parents have brought me up in," wrote a Bengali Muslim who lived in Britain, "I also want to embrace the good parts of the one I see around me in Britain. This includes the respect that British culture gives to women, allowing them to be more independent."[42]

A concept of citizenship that is based on assumed rather than on native identity is profoundly threatening to the vocal groups who support extreme right-wing parties in many European countries. In 1984, the National Front (*Front National*, or FN), led by the retired French military officer Jean-Marie Le Pen, burst on the European political scene by capturing a substantial 11 percent of the votes in elections for the European Parliament. Its support in France ranges from ten to twenty percent of the electorate. The FN warns that immigration is a danger to the cultural survival of both France and Europe, and strongly advocates measures such as preventing the admission of members of immigrants' families to France (family reunions), denying social benefits to foreign-born citizens, and deporting all illegal immigrants. Returning to a traditional obsession of the French right, Le Pen also decries falling birthrates, which he attributes to such evil tendencies as feminism and women's employment. The FN therefore advocates banning abortion and increasing subsidies to large families of French ethnicity.[43] Likewise, the far-right Flemish Block (*Vlaams Blok*), which appeals to Flemish (Dutch-speaking) Belgians, combines anti-immigrant with natalist propaganda, campaigning for bans on abortion, the revival of religious values, and financial support for Flemish families.[44]

Though most are led by men, some of these extremist parties feature women in conspicuous leadership roles. The youthful and dynamic Pia Kjaersgaard heads the Danish People's Party (*Dansk Folkeparti*), which since its founding in 1995 has stridently asserted that "Denmark belongs to the Danes." The Party's platform declares that Denmark will never become a multicultural society, and promises to restrict immigration, take Denmark out of the European Union, support traditional Protestant values, and protect native Danish families. Though it gains only about 12 percent of the vote, the People's Party is highly visible, and in 2006 polls identified Kjaersgaard as Denmark's most powerful woman.[45]

The women who support these parties are likely to be poor, uneducated, and without secure employment. Like their male counterparts, women are divided by class, and the most vulnerable look upon immigrants as competitors for jobs and social benefits, and thus as a threat to their well-being. Many are also more attracted by the prospect of financial aid to families than by feminist ideals of gender equality, which appeal more to educated, privileged women than to those without qualifications or career prospects. And such women often blame the European Union for processes of economic rationalization that they believe have destroyed jobs, fractured communities, and raised the cost of living. The long-standing European traditions of xenophobia, racism, and religious hatred are still alive and well and still threaten progress toward European unity, gender equality, and racial and ethnic harmony.

In the present as in the past, feminists aspire to gender equality not only as an end in itself but as a means to the even greater end of creating a just, peaceful, and harmonious society. Of course, there is nothing inevitable about this outcome. In fact, when women gain positions of political leadership, they show a wide variety of behaviors: progressive or conservative, warlike or pacific, compassionate or harsh. Therefore, women who commit themselves to work for equality and justice will be guided not by some innate gift for nurture and non-violence, but rather by lessons learned from their history. For many generations, women have known what it is to be defined by their difference from the male norm, and have experienced that difference sometimes as a stigma and sometimes as a source of positive energies. They have usually understood equality not as uniformity or sameness, but as a set of rights that includes the right to be different. This distinctively female and feminist perspective informs the philosopher Rosi Braidotti's conception of "a new, post-nationalist definition of European identity." Braidotti criticizes not only nationalism but many other aspects of the European cultural heritage, including prejudices that classify non-white and non-European people as different and therefore inferior. A new, flexible definition of citizenship must honor both traditional attachments to home and native soil and the transnational communities and hybrid identities that result from migration and global communication.[46] If this new community has any hope of becoming reality, women, the traditional builders of community, must take the lead in creating it.

Conclusion: Emancipation as Myth and Reality

The twentieth century was indeed the best of times and the worst of times. Women as well as men experienced war and peace, prosperity and poverty, progress and backlash, hope and despair. Obviously, we can gain no balanced or authoritative perspective on events that happened so recently—their interpretation must be left to future generations. Here, we can only revisit some of the issues and questions that our story has raised.

As we consider these questions, we must remember that our knowledge of the history of women in this and any period can only be partial and fragmentary. In 1929, the British novelist Virginia Woolf wrote that her effort to find out about women in the past had ended in total frustration. "One knows nothing detailed, nothing perfectly true and substantial about her. History scarcely mentions her." Woolf called on historians to create a new account of the past, in which women might "figure ... without impropriety," but compared their task to lighting "a torch in that vast chamber where nobody has yet been. It is all half lights and profound shadows like those serpentine caves where one goes with a candle peering up and down, not knowing where one is stepping." [1]

Since Woolf wrote, and especially since the 1970s, when the field of women's and gender history finally became part of college and university curricula, a great deal of excellent research has illuminated this dark chamber. It is this research that provides the basis for this and many other books. Still, we are not now, nor will we probably ever be, in the position to create any authoritative "master narrative" of the history of women (or indeed, of any other history). There is too much that has yet to be discovered, and too much that, having never been recorded, is forever lost. Moreover, history is produced by those who are empowered to write and speak, and up until now only a small group of women have been in a position to interpret the history of the twentieth century. As new groups of speakers come onto the scene, new versions of the past will emerge. Here we can speak only about ourselves and how our understanding of the story this book has told shapes our own attitudes and expectations.

At the beginning of the twenty-first century, one popular view of women in the past century expresses an optimistic faith in inevitable progress—an attitude that was expressed in a cigarette commercial of the 1970s which showed a thin, fashionable woman smoking a cigarette over the caption "You've come a long way, baby." Women in the West—including North America as well as Europe—learn from the media, politicians, and popular histories that the twentieth century was an era of emancipation, in which women emerged from total and abject subjection into freedom and equality. The many people who believe this story often insist that women have already attained all the rights for which past generations worked, and see no more need to continue the struggle or even to be vigilant in preserving the gains already made. The history recounted in this book should encourage us to look critically at emancipation as a goal, and particularly at claims that the twentieth century saw the fulfillment of this goal.

Certainly, twentieth-century women experienced a process of change that was one of the most rapid and thorough in all of history. The forces that shaped the modern world—expanding states, dynamic economies, devastating wars, lengthening life spans, reduced fertility, and ever-changing technology—also transformed the lives of women. Some of these forces undermined traditional ways of life and brought an increasing number of women into occupations and activities once reserved for men. Of course, feminists did not cause this process of modernization, though they sometimes succeeded in influencing it. Nonetheless, both those who applauded and those who opposed these changes in women's status often associated them with the feminist project known as "emancipation"—that is, the freeing of women from the legal, political, economic, and other disadvantages that they had suffered because of their sex. The dominant view of emancipation defined its goal as the admission of women to the rights, privileges, and activities of men. This view was often contested, even by feminists. Indeed, some feminists in both Eastern and Western Europe urged women to pursue their own individual and collective goals rather than to imitate or compete with men. Still, the most common measure of women's progress continued to be their success in entering secondary school or college, the professions, the labor market, the halls of parliament, organized sports, the military, and other areas that had traditionally been identified as male.

According to this definition, the twentieth century was indeed the era of emancipation. We began this book with the First World War, when as a result of the wartime emergency women violated conventional boundaries between the sexes by taking male jobs and by acting as heads of families. In the aftermath of the war, women gained the rights of citizenship in many countries and entered another quintessentially male-defined area—that of politics and the state. The Russian Revolution of 1917 ushered in what its leaders portrayed as a utopia of gender equality, where women had the rights of citizens, marriage was a relationship of equals, and higher education and all forms of labor were open to both sexes. Though its claims to have emancipated women were more propaganda than reality, the Soviet Union did indeed bring women into many formerly male areas of work, politics, and military service. In the Second World War, women's participation not only in labor but also in the armed forces expanded in all countries.

In Western Europe, the post-war era brought new household technologies that enabled women to combine what were called their two roles, in the home and in the workplace. The repeal of laws that had blocked access to contraception allowed the limitation of births and the planning of pregnancies. Legislatures gradually dismantled laws that had made men the heads of their family, giving women an equal legal status in marriage. Starting in the 1970s, a new feminist movement advocated many other rights—to terminate unwanted pregnancies, to be free from employment discrimination, to live openly in same-sex relationships. In the communist world, where no feminist movements were permitted, women nonetheless improved their educational qualifications and status in the workforce. On both sides of the Iron Curtain, states provided benefits that improved women's health and standards of living.

Therefore, we are justified in seeing the history of women in the twentieth century as a story of progress and improvement. Nonetheless, the process of emancipation was flawed and incomplete, for it placed the burden of adjusting to this changing gender order much more on women than on men. Indeed, as we have seen, twentieth-century women changed their lives in many ways—by learning new job skills, improving their educational qualifications, running for political office, leading organizations, and taking on exhausting schedules that combined domesticity and full-time work. But though women were often successful in transforming themselves, they were less successful in changing men or in dismantling male supremacy. Men's behavior and attitudes, particularly in areas involving marriage, the family, and gender relations, changed much less than those of women. Men continued to hold most of the power in politics, religion, the economy, culture, the military, and many other aspects of life. Even in areas in which the law made the sexes equal, custom, tradition, and economic forces still preserved male dominance.

The result was that the "emancipated" woman entered a male-dominated world where, for the most part, she could hold only a subordinate position. In many cases, this new world exposed her to new dangers and new vulnerabilities. As citizens, women endured political repression and persecution; as fighters on the "home front" or the battlefield they suffered violence and death; as workers, they faced job discrimination and sex-stereotyping; in politics, they played a marginal role. What was presented as emancipation often imposed new disadvantages. Though women emerged into many fields that were formerly reserved for men, there was no corresponding movement of men into the female realm of domesticity and child-rearing. To the many women who combined a paid job with marriage and domesticity—a way of life that became increasingly normal in the latter half of the century—their new opportunities brought long workdays and severe emotional conflicts. The fact that so many women bore this "double burden" prevented them from gaining leadership positions in government, business, or the professions.

Their winning of the right to vote, to run for office, and to organize politically did not give women political power proportionate to their numbers. For women were much too divided by ethnicity, religion, class, political convictions, and many other differences to engage in any common struggle. Moreover, the process of emancipation itself sometimes deepened these antagonisms, for it offered opportunities to educated, professionally qualified women while leaving the majority behind.

Therefore, women's gains in the areas of political rights, economic advancement, personal autonomy, or reproductive self-determination were never secure, but always depended on the approval of a power structure that remained largely male dominated. The process of emancipation was often halted or turned back. Sometimes the backlash resulted from an economic crisis, such as the

Great Depression of the 1930s, when angry male workers called for laws that kept women, and especially married women, out of desirable jobs. Totalitarian regimes, such as those of Mussolini, Hitler, and Stalin, abridged many rights that the women of their countries had gained in order to exploit their labor and reproductive capacity. Some democratic governments also encouraged misogynist backlash. The most blatant example is the post-communist transition in Eastern Europe, where the fall of totalitarianism and the advent of democracy has (at least in the short term) undermined the employment and reproductive rights of women, deprived them of essential social services, and exposed many to sexual exploitation and violence. Even in the more prosperous countries of Europe, right-wing parties threaten to cut back the reproductive rights and social benefits for which feminists throughout the twentieth century struggled.

The trajectory of women in the twentieth century did not lead steadily onward and upward to equality, but was often delayed, halted, or reversed. Even now, some European leaders—and not only feminists—note with concern that women have not advanced into decision-making positions in government and industry. Nor, despite educational achievements that by now outstrip those of men, have they overcome disparities in pay and income. And modern developments that make travel and communications easier have made many women even more vulnerable than before to sexual exploitation and violence.

Despite all the progress that they have made, the women of the twentieth century did not advance into a utopia of equality and justice, and the struggle for gender equality must continue. One objective of this struggle must be to reassess the twentieth-century gender order that brought women into the male world of labor and politics while also leaving them in charge of the female world of home and family. As long as women are pulled between two realms and two roles, they can never gain equality with men. But the task of reconstructing the relationship of work-place and family cannot be left to women—it also requires the active cooperation of men. Only the emancipation of men can complete the emancipation of women.

Notes

Introduction: The Best of Times, the Worst of Times

1. Charles Dickens, *A Tale of Two Cities* (Geneva: Edito-Service, 1970), 1.
2. Rachel G. Fuchs and Victoria Thompson, *Women in Nineteenth-Century Europe* (Houndmills and New York, 2005).
3. Kevin J. Kinsella, "Changes in Life Expectancy, 1900–1990," *American Journal of Clinical Nutrition* 55 (1992): 1196–1202.
4. Göran Therborn, *Between Sex and Power: Family in the World, 1900–2000* (London: Routledge, 2004), 230.
5. Karen Offen, *European Feminisms, 1700–1950: A Political History* (Stanford: Stanford U. Press, 2000), 25–26.

1 Women and the First World War, 1914–1918

1. Millicent Garrett Fawcett, "To the Members of the National Union," *The Common Cause*, August 7, 1914, quoted in Susan Groag Bell and Karen M. Offen, eds., *Women, the Family, and Freedom: The Debate in Documents*, 2 vols (Stanford: Stanford U. Press, 1983), vol. 2, 260–261; Helene Lange, "Die grosse Zeit und die Frauen," *Die Frau* 21 (September 1914): 709–714 (quotation 710).
2. Vera Brittain, *Testament of Youth: An Autobiographical Study of the Years 1900–1925* [1933] (New York: Penguin Books, 1994), 7.
3. Hubertine Auclert, "La fonction maternelle rétribuée" [1914] in Hubertine Auclert, *Les Femmes au Gouvernail* (Paris: Marcel Giard, 1923), 307–316 (quotation 309).
4. Brittain, *Testament of Youth*, 213–214.
5. Letter from Katharine Furse to serving VAD nurses, 1914, "Voluntary Aid Detachment," http://www.spartacus.schoolnet.co.uk/FWWnurses.html.
6. Minna Stöckert, quoted by Regine Schulte, "The Sick Warrior's Sister: Nursing during the First World War," trans. Pamela Selwyn, in Lynn Abrams and Elizabeth Harvey, eds., *Gender Relations in German History: Power, Agency and Experience from the Sixteenth to the Twentieth Century* (Durham: Duke U. Press, 1997), 121–141 (quotation 130).
7. Brittain, *Testament of Youth*, 280.
8. Ibid., 166.
9. Aletta Jacobs, *Memories: My Life as an International Leader in Health, Suffrage, and Peace*, ed. by Harriet Feinberg, trans. Annie Wright (New York: Feminist Press, 1996), 82.
10. Helena Swanwick, *Women and War* (London: Union of Democratic Control, 1915), 2.

11. "L'Affaire Hélène Brion au Conseil de Guerre," *Revue des Causes Célèbres*, May 2, 1918, 152–154, excerpted and trans. in Bell and Offen, eds., *Women, the Family, and Freedom*, vol. 2, 273–275 (quotation 274)

12. See Ann Taylor Allen, *Feminism and Motherhood in Western Europe, 1890–1970: The Maternal Dilemma* (New York: Palgrave, 2005), 128–133.

13. For more statistics, see Allen, *Feminism and Motherhood in Western Europe*, 113–114.

14. Jane Misme, "Les hommes ne sont pas raisonnables," *La Française*, December 16, 1916.

15. Peggy Hamilton, *Three Years or the Duration*, quoted in Claire A. Culleton, *Working-Class Culture, Women, and Britain, 1914–1921* (New York: St. Martin's, 1999), 34.

16. Madline Ida Bedford, "Munition Wages," in Catherine Reilly, ed., *Scars upon my Heart: Women's Poetry and Verse of the First World War* (London: Virago Press, 1981), 8.

17. René Viviani, "An Appeal to French Women," quoted in Margaret Darrow, *French Women and the First World War* (Oxford and New York: Berg, 2000), 178.

18. Quoted in Françoise Thébaud, *Les Femmes au Temps de la Guerre de 14.* (Paris: Stock, Laurence Pernoud, 1986), 137.

19. Henriette Herzfelder, "Unsere Berufsfrauen und der Krieg," *Der Bund* (January 1915): 1–8 (quotation 1).

20. Mary Gabrielle Collins, "Women at Munition Making," in Reilly, ed., *Scars upon my Heart*, 24.

21. Hugo Sellheim, *Was tut die Frau fürs Vaterland? Nach Kriegsvorträgen an der Universität Tübingen und im Deutschen Frauenverein vom Roten Kreuz für die Kolonien in Stuttgart* (Stuttgart: Verlag von Ferdinand Enke, 1915), 14.

22. Marie-Monique Huss, "Pronatalism and the Popular Ideology of the Child in Wartime France: The Evidence of the Picture Postcard," in Richard Wall and Jay Winter, eds., *The Upheaval of War: Family, Work and Welfare in Europe, 1914–1918* (Cambridge and New York: Cambridge U. Press, 1988), 329–367, illustrations, 342 and 346.

23. Susan Pedersen, "Gender, Welfare and Citizenship in Britain during the Great War," *American Historical Review* 95 (October 1990): 983–1006.

24. Women's Cooperative Guild, comp. *Maternity: Letters from Working Women* (London: G.Bell and Sons, Ltd., 1915), 53.

25. Ibid., 78.

26. Ibid., 16. See the interpretation of Susan R. Grayzel, *Women's Identities at War: Gender, Motherhood, and Politics in Britain and France during the First World War* (Chapel Hill: U. of North Carolina Press, 1999), 113.

27. WCG, *Maternity*, 15.

28. Marguerite de Witt-Schlumberger, "Le devoir particulier des femmes," *La Française*, May 12, 1916.

29. Alice Salomon, *Charakter ist Schiksal: Lebenserinnerungen* (Weinheim: Beltz Verlag, 1983), 149.

30. See Belinda J. Davis, *Home Fires Burning: Food, Politics, and Everyday Life in World War I Berlin* (Chapel Hill: U. of North Carolina Press, 2000).
31. L.D. Trotsky, *The History of the Russian Revolution*, trans. Max Eastman, 3 vols (Ann Arbor: U. of Michigan Press, 1964), 1, 109, quoted in Richard Stites, *The Women's Liberation Movement in Russia: Feminism, Nihilism, and Bolshevism* (Princeton: Princeton U. Press, 1978), 291.
32. Françoise Thébaud, "The Great War and the Triumph of Sexual Division," in Françoise Thébaud, ed., *A History of Women in the West, Volume V: Toward a Cultural Identity in the Twentieth Century* (Cambridge and London: Belknap Press, 1994), 21–75.

2 Women as Citizens in the Inter-war Democracies

1. Catherine Gasquoine Hartley, *Woman's Wild Oats: Essays on the Re-Fixing of Moral Standards* (New York: Frederick A Stokes, 1920), 12, 17, and 18.
2. Dora Russell, *The Right to be Happy* (New York and London: Harper, 1927), 166, 169.
3. Wilma Meikle, *Towards a Sane Feminism* (New York: Robert M. McBride and Co., 1917), 127.
4. Camilla Jellinek, "Vom Kochtopf und von der geistigen Arbeit," *Neue badische Zeitung*, May 25, 1921.
5. "Die deutsche Reichsverfassung vom 11 August 1919," in Herbert Michaelis and Ernst Schraipler, eds., *Ursachen und Folgen vom deutschen Zusammenbruch, 1918 und 1945, bis zur staatlichen Neuordnung Deutschlands in der Gegenwart: Eine Urkunden- und Dokumentensammlung*, vol. 3, Article 119 (Berlin: Dokumenten-Verlag, 1979), 464–492, #119.
6. Bunreact na hÉireann, # 41(1), quoted in Sharon Lambert, "Irish Women's Emigration to England, 1922–1960: The Lengthening of Family Ties," in Alan Hayes and Diane Urquart, eds., *Irish Women's History* (Dublin: Irish Academic Press, 2004), 152–167 (quotation 153).
7. Russell, *The Right to be Happy*.
8. Wilhelm Stekel, "Frigidity in Mothers," quoted in Sheila Jeffreys, *The Spinster and Her Enemies: Feminism and Sexuality, 1880–1930* (London: Pandora Press, 1985), 170.
9. Angelika Schaser, *Helene Lange und Gertrud Bäumer: Eine politische Lebensgemeinschaft* (Köln: Böhlau Verlag, 2000).
10. Lida Gustava Heymann, with Anita Augspurg, *Erlebtes—Erschautes: Deutsche Frauen kämpfen für Freiheit, Recht und Frieden*, ed., Margrit Twellmann (Frankfurt: Ulrike Helmer Verlag, 1992), 77.
11. Gisela Bock and Pat Thane, eds. *Maternity and Gender Policies: Women and the Rise of European Welfare States, 1880s–1950s* (London and New York: Routledge, 1991), 17.
12. John B. Watson and Rosalie Rayner Watson, *Psychological Care of Infant and Child* (New York: Norton, 1928), 15.
13. Marie Stopes, *Mother, How Was I Born?* (London: Putnam, 1922), 16, 22.
14. Helena Swanwick, *The War in its Effect upon Women* (New York: Garland Publishing, 1971), 8.

15. Renate Bridenthal, "Something Old, Something New: Women Between the Two World Wars," in Renate Bridenthal and Claudia Koonz, eds., *Becoming Visible: Women in European History* (Boston: Houghton Mifflin, 1977), 422–444.

16. Simone de Beauvoir, *Memoirs of a Dutiful Daughter*, trans. James Kirkup (New York: Harper & Row, 1974).

17. Ursual Nienhaus, *Nicht für eine Führungsposition geeignet: Josefine Erkens und did Anfänge weiblicher Polizei in Deutschland, 1923–1933* (Münster: Westfälisches Dampfboot, 1999).

18. The Open Door International for the Economic Emancipation of the Woman Worker, *Manifesto and Charter*, Berlin, June 16, 1929, I.

19. Melissa Feinberg, "Democracy and Its Limits: Gender and Rights in the Czech Lands, 1918–1938," *Nationalities Papers* 30 (December 2002): 553–570.

20. Bund deutscher Frauenvereine, "Frauenarbeit und Wirtschaftskrisis: Erklärung des BDF April 1931" in Landesarchiv Berlin, B-Rep. 235-0, Petionen zu Wirtschaftsfragen, April 1931, Fiche 2848.

21. Bunreact na hÉireann, # 41 (2), quoted in Pauline Conroy Jackson, "Managing the Mothers: The Case of Ireland," in Jane Lewis, ed., *Women and Social Policies in Europe: Work, Family and the State* (Aldershot: Edward Elgar, 1993), 72–91 (quotation 75); see also Yvonne Scannell, "The Constitution and the Role of Women," in Brian Farrell, ed., *De Valera's Constitution and Ours* (Goldenbridge, Dublin: Gillard Macmillan, 1988), 123–136.

22. Doctoresse Houdré Boursin, *Ma doctoresse: Guide practique d'hygiène et de médecine de la femme moderne* (Strasbourg: Éditorial Argentor, 1928), 95.

23. Quoted in Martin Pugh, *Women and the Women's Movement in Britain 1914–1959* (Houndmills: Macmillan, 1992), 173.

24. Quoted in Karen Offen, *European Feminisms 1700–1950: A Political History* (Stanford: Stanford U. Press, 2000), 328.

25. Virginia Woolf, *A Room of One's Own* (San Diego, New York, London: Harcourt Brace Jovanovich, 1929), 26.

26. Christine Bard, *Les filles de Marianne: Histoire des féminismes 1914–1940* (Paris: Fayard, 1995), 186–205; Mary Louise Roberts, *Civilization without Sexes: Reconstructing Gender in Postwar France, 1917–1927* (Chicago: U. of Chicago Press, 1994), 46–52.

27. Victor Margueritte, *The Bachelor Girl*, trans. Hugh Burnaby (New York: Knopf, 1923), 143.

28. Katherine Mansfield, "At the Bay," [1922] in Lorna Sage, ed., *The Garden Party and Other Stories* (New York and London: Penguin Books, 1997), 5–37 (quotation 19).

29. Vera Brittain, *Honourable Estate: A Novel of Transition* (New York: Macmillan, 1936), 516–517.

30. Quoted in Vibeke Rützou Petersen, *Women and Modernity in Weimar Germany: Reality and its Representation in Popular Fiction* (New York and Oxford: Berghahn Books, 2001), 47.

31. Ibid., 30.
32. Virginia Woolf, *Women and Writing* [1931], ed., Michele Barrett (San Diego, New York, London: Harcourt Brace, 1979), 61–62
33. Lesley Hall, *Sex, Gender, and Social Change in Britain since 1880* (New York: St. Martin's Press, 2000), 114.

3 Women in the Authoritarian and Totalitarian States of the Inter-war Years

1. Vladimir Ilyich Lenin, "Speech at the First All-Russian Congress of Women, 9 November, 1918," excerpted in Susan Groag Bell and Karen Offen, eds., *Women, the Family, and Freedom: The Debate in Documents* (Stanford: Stanford U. Press, 1983), vol. 2, 287–289 (quotation 288).
2. Adolf Hitler, "Speech to the *Nationalsozialistische Frauenschaft*, 8 September, 1934," excerpted in Bell and Offen, eds., *Women, the Family, and Freedom*, vol. 2, 373–378.
3. "The Soviet Decree on the Legalization of Abortion, 18 November, 1920," excerpted in Bell and Offen, eds., *Women, the Family, and Freedom*, vol. 2, 302.
4. On Kollontai's life and work, see Barbara Evans Clements, *Bolshevik Feminist: The Life of Alexandra Kollontai* (Bloomington: Indiana U. Press, 1978).
5. Barbara Evans Clements, "The Utopianism of the Zhenotdel," *Slavic Review* 51 (Autumn 1991): 485–496.
6. Richard Stites, "Women and the Revolutionary Process in Russia," in Renate Bridenthal, Claudia Koonz, and Susan Stuard, eds., *Becoming Visible: Women in European History* (Boston: Houghton Mifflin, 1987), 451–471. See also Wendy Z. Goldman, *Women, the State, and Revolution: Soviet Family Policy and Social Life, 1917–1936* (Cambridge and New York: Cambridge U. Press, 1993).
7. Barbara Alpern Engel, *Women in Russia, 1700–2000* (Cambridge: Cambridge U. Press, 2004), 148–165.
8. Wendy Z. Goldman, "Industrial Politics, Peasant Rebellion and the Death of the Proletarian Women's Movement in the USSR," *Slavic Review* 55 (Spring 1996): 46–77.
9. Engel, *Women in Russia*, 173–175.
10. *Pravda*, quoted in Gail Warshofsky Lapidus, *Women in Soviet Society: Equality, Development, and Social Change* (Berkeley: U. of California Press, 1978), 112.
11. Rudolph Schlesinger, comp., *Changing Attitudes in Soviet Russia: The Family* (London: Routledge and Kegan Paul, 1949), 256.
12. Engel, *Women in Russia*, 175–180.
13. J. Arch Getty, Gabor T. Rittersporn, and Viktor N. Zemskov, "Victims of the Soviet Penal System in the Pre-War Years: A First Approach on the Basis of Archival Evidence," *The American Historical Review* 98 (October 1993): 1017–1049.

14. Evgenia Semyonovna Ginzburg, *Journey into the Whirlwind*, trans. Paul Stevenson and Max Hayward (New York: Harcourt, Brace, 1967), 367.

15. Robert W. Thurston, "The Soviet Family during the Great Terror, 1935–1941," *Soviet Studies* 43, 3 (1991): 553–574.

16. Kevin Passmore, "Introduction," in Kevin Passmore, ed., *Women, Gender, and Fascism in Europe, 1919–1945* (New Brunswick, NJ: Rutgers University Press, 2003), 1–10.

17. Anne Cova and Antonio Costa Pinto, "O Salazarisme e as Mulheres: Uma Abordagem Comparativa," *Penelope* 17 (1997): 71–84.

18. Carol S. Lilly, "Serbia," in Passmore, ed., *Women, Gender, and Fascism in Europe*, 95–100.

19. Mara I. Lazda, "Latvia," in Passmore, ed., *Women, Gender, and Fascism in Europe*, 124–147.

20. Maria Bucur, "Romania," in Passmore, ed., *Women, Gender, and Fascism in Europe*, 57–78.

21. Cova and Costa Pinto, "O Salazarisme."

22. Dubrochna Kalwa, "Poland," in Passmore, ed., *Women, Gender, and Fascism in Europe*, 148–167 (quotation 161).

23. Lilly, "Serbia," (quotation 105).

24. Irène Flunser Pimentel, "Une Organisation féminine de l'état nouveau portugais: L'oeuvre des mères pour l'éducation nationale 1936–1974," in Gisela Bock and Anne Cova, eds., *Writing Women's History in Southern Europe, 19th–20th Centuries* (Oeras: Celta Editora, 2003), 161–168.

25. Mária M. Kovacs, "Hungary," in Passmore, ed., *Women, Gender, and Fascism*, 79–90 (quotation 87).

26. Bucur, "Romania."

27. Quoted in Victoria de Grazia, "How Mussolini ruled Italian Women," in Françoise Thébaud, ed., *A History of Women in the West, vol 5: Toward a Cultural Identity in the Twentieth Century* (Harvard: Belknap Press, 1994) 120–148 (quotation 130).

28. Ibid.

29. Ibid.

30. Ibid., 144; Victoria de Grazia, *How Fascism Ruled Women: Italy 1922–1945* (Berkeley: U. of California Press, 1992), 234–271.

31. De Grazia, "How Mussolini ruled Italian Women," 144.

32. Perry Wilson, "Italy," in Passmore, ed., *Women, Gender, and Fascism in Europe*, 11–32.

33. For more on this subject, see J.D. Zimmerman, ed., *Jews in Italy under Fascist and Nazi Rule, 1922–1945* (Cambridge: Cambridge U. Press, 2005).

34. Benito Mussolini, "Speech of the Ascension," May 26, 1927.

35. Lesley Caldwell, "Madri d'Italia: Film and Fascist Concern with Motherhood," in Zygmunt G. Baranske and Shirley W. Vinali, eds., *Women and Italy: Essays on Gender, Culture, and History* (New York: St. Martin's, 1991), 43–63.

36. Adolf Hitler, "Speech to the *Nationalsozialistische Frauenschaft*," November 9, 1934.

37. Cf. Claudia Koonz, *Mothers in the Fatherland: Women, the Family, and Nazi Politics* (New York: St. Martin's, 1987).
38. In this text, I will use the term "German" to refer to people whom the Nazis defined as German—those who did not fall into a persecuted ethnic or religious group. Of course, this was a lie—many members of these groups had been German citizens before the Nazis deprived them of full citizenship.
39. Gertrud Scholtz-Klink, "Speech to the *Nationalsozialistische Frauenschaft*, 10 September, 1935," excerpted in Bell and Offen, eds., *Women, the Family, and Freedom*, vol. 2, 378–381 (quotation 379–380).
40. Jill Stephenson, *Women in Nazi Society* (New York: Barnes and Noble, 1975).
41. Gisela Bock, "Nazi Gender Policies and Women's History," in Thébaud, ed., *A History of Women in the West*, vol. 5, 148–177.
42. Gisela Bock, "Antinatalism, Maternity, and Paternity in National Socialist Racism," in Gisela Bock and Pat Thane, eds., *Maternity and Gender Policies: Women and the Rise of the European Welfare States, 1880s–1950s* (London and New York: Routledge, 1991), 233–255.
43. Gisela Bock, "Racism and Sexism in Nazi Germany: Motherhood, Compulsory Sterilization, and the State," *Signs: Journal of Women in Culture and Society* 8 (1983): 400–421.
44. Marion A. Kaplan, *Between Dignity and Despair: Jewish Life in Nazi Germany* (New York: Oxford, 1998).
45. Guenter Lewy, *The Nazi Persecution of the Gypsies* (Oxford and New York: Oxford U. Press, 2000), 30–35.
46. Documents on Emmy Freundlich are in the Hull University Manuscripts and Archives Database, Records of the Women's Cooperative Guild and Records of the International Women's Cooperative Guild. I thank Amanda Capern for bringing these documents to my attention.

4 Women in the Second World War

1. Penny Summerfield, "Women and War in the Twentieth Century," in June Purvis, ed., *Women's History: Britain, 1850–1945: An Introduction* (London: UCL Press, 1995), 307–332 (quotation 326).
2. Winston Churchill to Secretary of State for War, December 1, 1941, excerpted in Auxiliary Territorial Service, www.spartacus.schoolnet.co.uk.
3. J.W.N., "'Mixed' Batteries," *Journal of the Royal Artillery* 69 (1942): 199–206 (quotation 206), quoted in D'Ann Campbell, "Women in Combat: The World War II Experience in the United States, Great Britain, Germany, and the Soviet Union," *The Journal of Military History* 57 (April 1993): 301–323 (quotation 309).
4. Quoted in Campbell, "Women in Combat," 309–310.
5. Ibid., 309.
6. Dwight D. Eisenhower, *Crusade in Europe*, quoted in "Auxiliary Territorial Service."

7. "The Second World War Memories of Miss G. Morgan," quoted in Campbell, "Women in Combat," 308.
8. Brenda Beeton, interviewed in *Women Who Went to War*, excerpted in "Auxiliary Territorial Service."
9. Nina Masel, April 24, 1941, excerpted in "Auxiliary Territorial Service."
10. Lesley A. Hall, *Sex, Gender, and Social Change in Britain since 1880* (New York: St. Martin's, 2000), 133–149.
11. Campbell, "Women in Combat," 314–318.
12. "The Lotta Svärd Organization in Finland," www.kevos4.com/lotta_svard.html.
13. Campbell, "Women in Combat."
14. Quoted in "Raskova and the Soviet Women Pilots of World War II," www.ctie.monash.edu.au/hargrave/soviet_women_pilots.html. See also Campbell, "Women in Combat," and Barbara Alpern Engel, *Women in Russia, 1700–2000* (Cambridge: Cambridge U. Press, 2004), 209–230.
15. Quoted in "Raskova and the Soviet Women Pilots of World War II," 13.
16. See Engel, *Women in Russia*, 225–230.
17. Roger Chickering and Stig Förster, "World War II and the Theory of Total War," in Roger Chickering and Stig Förster, eds., *A World at Total War: Global Conflict and the Politics of Destruction, 1937–1945* (Cambridge: Cambridge U. Press, 1995), 1–18.
18. Penny Summerfield, *Women Workers in the Second World War: Production and Patriarchy in Conflict* (London and New York: Croom Helm, 1984), 29.
19. Ibid., 196.
20. Summerfield, "Women and War in the Twentieth Century."
21. The best account of German women's work in wartime and related areas of policy is Leila J. Rupp, *Mobilizing Women for War: German and American Propaganda, 1939–1945* (Princeton: Princeton U. Press, 1978). See also Jill Stephenson, "Women's Labor Service in Nazi Germany," *Central European History* 15 (September 1982): 241–265.
22. Felicja Karay, "Women in the Forced Labor Camps," in Dalia Ofer and Lenore J. Weitzman, eds., *Women in the Holocaust* (New Haven: Yale U. Press, 1998), 285–309.
23. Susan K. Foley, *Women in France since 1789: The Meanings of Difference*, (Houndmills and New York: Palgrave Macmillan, 2004), 219; Victoria de Grazia, *How Fascism Ruled Women: Italy, 1922–1945* (Berkeley: U. of California Press, 1992), 282–283.
24. Engel, *Women in Russia*, 211.
25. Ibid., 210–213.
26. Summerfield, *Women Workers*, 196.
27. Rupp, *Mobilizing Women*, 171.
28. Gail Warshofsky Lapidus, *Women in Soviet Society: Equality, Development, and Social Change* (Berkeley: U. of California Press, 1978), 130–131.
29. Summerfield, *Women Workers*, 67–98.
30. Engel, *Women in Russia*, 212.
31. Denise Riley, *War in the Nursery: Theories of the Child and Mother* (London: Virago, 1983), 93–108.

32. Martin Pugh, *Women and the Women's Movement in Britain, 1914–1959* (Houndmills: Macmillan, 1992), 264–293.

33. Kathleen Brockington, "Bombed in the London Blitz," transcribed from an interview by Harvinder Jauhal, August 1994, http://atschool. eduweb.co.uk/chatback/english/memories/blitz.html.

34. Jörg Friedrich, *The Fire: The Bombing of Germany, 1940–1945,* trans. Alison Brown (New York: Columbia U. Press, 2006), 434.

35. Margaret Freyer, quoted in "Bombing of Dresden," http://www. spartacus.schoolnet.co.uk/2WWdresden.html.

36. Gisela Bock, "Antinatalism, Maternity, and Paternity in National Socialist Racism," in Gisela Bock and Pat Thane, eds., *Maternity and Gender Policies: Women and the Rise of European Welfare* States (New York and London: Routledge, 1991), 233–255.

37. "Helene Melanie Lebel," United States Holocaust Memorial Museum, ID Cards, http://www.ushmm.org/wlc/idcard.

38. Heinrich Himmler, quoted in Joan Ringelheim, "Women and the Holocaust: A Reconsideration of Research," in Carol Rittner and John Roth, eds., *Different Voices: Women and the Holocaust* (New York: Paragon House, 1993), 374–405 (quotation 392). Cf. Bock, "Antinatalism, Maternity and Paternity in National Socialist Racism," 233–255.

39. Mary Felstiner, *To Paint her Life: Charlotte Salomon in the Nazi Era* (New York: Harper Collins, 1994), 205–206; quoted in Lenore J. Weitzman and Dalia Ofer, eds., "Introduction: The Role of Gender in the Holocaust," *Women in the Holocaust*, 1–18 (quotation 9).

40. Lucie Adelsberger, *Auschwitz: A Doctor's Story*, trans. Susan Ray (Boston: Northeastern U. Press, 1995), 12.

41. Yehuda Bauer, "Gisi Fleischmann," in Ofer and Weizmann, eds., *Women in the Holocaust*, 253–264.

42. David Sierakowiak, *The Diary of David Sierakowiak*, quoted in Michael Unger, "The Status and Plight of Women in the Lodz Ghetto," in Ofer and Weitzman, eds., *Women in the Holocaust*, 123–142 (quotation 139).

43. See Appendix to Rittner and Roth, eds., *Different Voices*, 406–418.

44. Gisella Perl, "A Doctor in Auschwitz," in Roth and Rittner, eds., *Different Voices*, 104–118 (quotation 115).

45. Primo Levi, *Survival in Auschwitz* (New York: Touchstone, 1996).

46. Adelsberger, *Auschwitz: A Doctor's Story*, 95–99.

47. Ruth Kluger, *Still Alive: A Holocaust Girlhood Remembered* (New York: Feminist Press, 2001); Judith Magyar Isaacson, *Seed of Sarah: Memoirs of a Survivor* (Urbana: U. of Illinois Press, 1990).

48. Charlotte Delbo, *None of Us Will Return,* excerpted in Rittner and Roth, eds., *Different Voices*, 100–103 (quotation 103).

49. Joan Ringelheim, "The Split between Gender and the Holocaust," in Ofer and Weitzmann, eds., *Women in the Holocaust*, 340–350.

50. Guenther Lewy, "The Travail of the Gypsies," *National Interest*, 57 (Fall 1999): 78–87; but see also Sybil Milton, "Holocaust: The Gypsies," in Samuel Totten, William S. Parsons, and Israel Charny, eds., *Century of*

Genocide: Eyewitness Accounts and Critical Views (New York: Garland Publishing, 1997).

51. Marie Sidi Stojka, "U.S. Holocaust Memorial Museum," http://www.ushmm.org/wlc/idcard.
52. Guenther Lewy, *The Nazi Persecution of the Gypsies* (Oxford: Oxford U. Press 2000), 162.
53. Ibid., 164–166.
54. Magdalena Kusserow, "United States Holocaust Memorial Museum," www.ushmm.org/clmedia/viewer/wlc/idcard.
55. "Dokumentation: Frauen gegen Frauen: Das Vernichtungslager Uckermark-Ravensbrück, January–April, 1945," in Angelika Ebbinghaus, ed., *Opfer und Täterinnen: Frauenbiographien im Nationalsozialismus* (Nördlingen: Franz Greno, 1987), 275–300.
56. "Herta Oberheuser im Kreuzverhör," in Ebbinghaus, ed., *Opfer und Täterinnen*, 260–273 (quotation 285).
57. Lenore J. Weitzman, "Living on the Aryan Side in Poland," in Ofer and Weitzman, eds., *Women in the Holocaust*, 187–222 (quotation 200).
58. Ibid., 212.
59. Renée Poznanski, "Women in the French-Jewish Underground," in Ofer and Weitzman, eds., *Women in the Holocaust*, 224–272.
60. "Magda Trocmé," in Rittner and Roth, eds., *Different Voices*, 309–316 (quotation 312).
61. De Grazia, *How Fascism Ruled Women*, 285.
62. Mordecai Paldiel, "The Path of the Righteous: Gentile Rescuers of Jews during the Holocaust," http://www.pbs.org/wgbh/pages/frontline/shtetl/righteous/gentilesbios.html.
63. Foley, *Women in France*, 223–252.
64. Atina Grossmann, "A Question of Silence: The Rape of German Women by Occupation Soldiers," in Robert G. Moeller, ed., *West Germany under Construction: Politics, Society, and Culture in the Adenauer Era* (Ann Arbor: University of Michigan Press, 1997), 33–52.

5   The Best of Both Worlds? Women in Western Europe in the Post-war Era, 1945–1970

1. Betty Friedan, *The Feminine Mystique* (New York: Norton, 1963).
2. Alva Myrdal and Viola Klein, *Women's Two Roles: Home and Work* (London: Routledge, 1956), xiii.
3. Iris von Roten, *Frauen im Laufgitter: Offene Worte zur Stellung der Frau* [1958], Mit einem Nachwort von Elisabeth Joris (Bern: eFeF-Verlag, 1996), 563.
4. Quoted in Susanna Woodtli, *Gleichberechtigung, Der Kampf um die politischen Rechte der Frau in der Schweiz* (Frauenfeld: Huber, 1983), 166.
5. Susan K. Foley, *Women in France since 1989: The Meanings of Difference* (New York: Palgrave, 2004), 235–263.
6. Eva Kolinsky, *Women in Contemporary Germany: Life, Work, and Politics* (New York: Berg, 1993), 45.

7. Robert G. Moeller, *Protecting Motherhood: Women and the Family in the Politics of Postwar West Germany* (Berkeley: U. of California Press, 1993).

8. Foley, *Women in France*, 255.

9. Lucia Chiavola Birnbaum, *Liberazione delle Donne: Feminism in Italy* (Middletown, CT: Wesleyan U. Press, 1986), 88–110.

10. Helmut Schelsky, *Wandlungen der deutschen Familie in der Gegenwart: Darstellung und Deutung einer empirisch-soziologischen Tatbestandaufnahme* (Stuttgart: Ferdinand Enke, 1967), 335–350.

11. B.R. Mitchell, *International Historical Statistics, Europe 1750–1988* (New York: Stockton Press, 1992), 90–114.

12. Claire Duchen, *Women's Rights and Women's Lives in France, 1944–1968* (London and New York: Routledge, 1994), 96–127.

13. John Bowlby, *Maternal Care and Mental Health* (Geneva: WHO, 1952); see also Denise Riley, *War in the Nursery: Theories of the Child and Mother* (London: Virago, 1983).

14. Benjamin Spock, *The Common Sense Book of Baby and Child Care* (New York: Duell, Sloan, and Pearce, 1946), 19.

15. Yvonne Schütze, *Die gute Mutter: Zur Geschichte des normativen Musters "Mutterliebe,"* (Bielefeld: Kleine Verlag, 1986), 86–102.

16. Gisela Kaplan, *Contemporary Western European Feminism* (New York: New York U. Press, 1992), 218.

17. Friedan, *The Feminine Mystique*.

18. Simone de Beauvoir, *The Second Sex* [1949] trans. and ed. H.M. Parshley (New York: A.A. Knopf, 1993).

19. Duchen, *Women's Rights and Women's Lives*, 117–146.

20. Ursula Barry, "Movement, Change and Reaction: The Struggle over Reproductive Rights in Ireland," in Ailbhe Smyth, ed., *The Abortion Papers: Ireland* (Dublin: Attic Press, 1992), 107–118.

21. See Dagmar Herzog, "Between Coitus and Commodification: Young West German Women and the Impact of the Pill," in Axel Schildt and Detlef Siegfried, eds., *Between Marx and Coca-Cola: Youth Cultures in Changing European Societies, 1960–1980* (New York: Berghahn Books, 2006), 261–286.

22. Lesley A. Hall, *Sex, Gender, and Social Change in Britain since 1889* (New York: St. Martin's, 2000), 168.

23. Évelyne Sullerot, *Women, Society, and Change*, trans. Margaret Scotford Archer (New York: McGraw Hill, 1971), 19.

24. Pearl Jephcott, *Married Women Working* (London: George Allen and Unwin, 1962), 19.

25. Ibid., 19.

26. Judith Hubback, *Wives who Went to College* (London: Heinemann, 1957), 53.

27. Kaplan, *Contemporary Western European Feminism*, 94.

28. Kolinsky, *Women in Contemporary Germany*, 128.

29. Aurora G. Morcillo, *True Catholic Womanhood: Gender and Ideology in Franco's Spain* (Dekalb: North Illinois U. Press, 2000), 94.

30. Sissela Bok, *Alva Myrdal: A Daughter's Memoir* (Reading, MA: Addison-Wesley, 1991), 201.
31. Myrdal and Klein, *Women's Two Roles*, 128.
32. The six original countries were France, the Netherlands, Belgium, Luxemburg, West Germany, and Italy.
33. Denmark, Ireland, and the United Kingdom joined in 1973; Greece in 1981; Spain and Portugal in 1986; Austria, Finland, and Sweden in 1995.
34. Foley, *Women in France*, 246; Eva Kolinsky, *Women in Contemporary Germany: Life, Work and Politics* (Providence: Berg, 1989), 185–188.
35. Ellen Furlough, "Making Mass Vacations: Tourism and Consumer Culture in France, 1930s to 1970s," *Comparative Studies in Society and History*, 40 (April 1998): 247–286.
36. Uta G. Poiger, "Rock 'n Roll, Female Sexuality, and the Cold War Battle over German Identities," in Robert G. Moeller, ed., *West Germany under Construction: Politics, Society and Culture in the Adenauer Era* (Ann Arbor: U. of Michigan Press, 1997), 413–444.
37. Viola Klein, *The Feminine Character: History of an Ideology* (Champaign-Urbana: U. of Illinois Press, 1972), 32.
38. Klein, *The Feminine Character*, 34.
39. De Beauvoir, *The Second Sex*.
40. Ibid., 267.
41. Penny Foster and Imogen Sutton, eds., *Daughters of de Beauvoir* (London: The Women's Press, 1989).
42. Roten, *Frauen im Laufgitter*, 19.
43. Ibid., 321.
44. Friedan, *The Feminine Mystique*.
45. Yvette Roudy, *À cause d'elles*, quoted in Duchen, *Women's Rights and Women's Live*, 76–77.
46. Joke Smit-Lezingen, *Wat is er met de vrouwenbeweging gebeurd?* (Amsterdam: Nigh & van Ditmar, 1989), 11–37.
47. Kaplan, *Contemporary Western European Feminism*, 13.

6 Too Emancipated? Women in the Soviet Union and Eastern Europe, 1945–1989

1. Christa Wolf, "In Touch," trans. Jeannette Clausen, in Edith Hoshino Altbach, Jeanette Clausen, Dagmar Schultz, and Naomi Stephan, eds., *German Feminism: Readings in Politics and Literature* (Albany: SUNY Press, 1984), 161–169 (quotation 166).
2. Ibid., 167.
3. *Time Magazine*, September 20, 1948.
4. Robert Levy, *Ana Pauker: The Rise and Fall of a Jewish Communist* (Berkeley: U. of California Press, 2001), 91–133 and 52–67.
5. Barbara Alpern Engel, *Women in Russia, 1700–2000* (Cambridge: Cambridge U. Press, 2004), 235.

6. Jiřina Siklová, "Are Women in Central and Eastern Europe Conservative?" in Nanette Funk and Magda Mueller, eds., *Gender Politics and Post-Communism* (New York and London: Routledge, 1993), 74–83.

7. Mary Ellen Fischer, "Women in Romanian Politics: Elena Ceauşescu, Pronatalism, and the Promotion of Women," in Sharon L. Wolchik and Alfred G. Meyer, eds., *Women, State, and Party in Eastern Europe* (Durham: Duke U. Press, 1985), 121–151 (quotation 126).

8. Ibid., 128.

9. John Kolsti, "From Courtyard to Cabinet: The Political Emergence of Albanian Women," in Wolchik and Meyer, eds., *Women, State, and Party in Eastern Europe*, 138–153.

10. Sharon Wolchik, "Introduction," in Wolchik and Meyer, eds., *Women, State, and Party*, 115–120.

11. Fischer, "Women in Romanian Politics," 123.

12. See her memoir of life in prison, Eva Kantůrková, *My Companions in the Bleak House* (New York: Woodstock, 1987).

13. Wilma Iggers, *Women of Prague: Ethnic Diversity and Social Change from the Eighteenth Century to the Present* (Providence and Oxford: Berghahn Books, 1995), 336–363.

14. Jiřina Šiklová, "Courage, Heroism, and the Postmodern Paradox," *Social Research* 71 (Spring 2004): 135–148.

15. Václav Havel *et al.*, *The Power of the Powerless: Citizens against the State in Central-Eastern Europe*, ed., John Keane (Armonk, NY: M.E. Sharpe, 1985).

16. Shana Penn, *Solidarity's Secret: The Women Who Defeated Communism in Poland* (Ann Arbor: U. of Michigan Press, 2005), 29–65 and 100–147.

17. Engel, *Women in Russia*, 237–243.

18. Slavenka Drakulić, *How We Survived Communism and Even Laughed* (New York: W.W. Norton, 1991), 30.

19. Dagmar Herzog, *Sex After Fascism: Memory and Morality in Twentieth-Century Germany* (Princeton: Princeton U. Press, 2005), 185–219.

20. Ibid., 86.

21. Engel, *Women in Russia*, 244.

22. Cristopher Tietze, "The Demographic Significance of Legal Abortion in Eastern Europe," *Demography* 1 (1964): 119–125 (figures 121 and 123).

23. Kevin J. Kinsella, "Changes in Life Expectancy, 1900–1990," *American Journal of Clinical Nutrition* 55 (1992): 1196–1202.

24. Myra Marx Ferree, "The Rise and Fall of 'Mommy Politics': Feminism and Unification in East Germany," *Feminist Studies* 19 (Spring 1993): 89–116.

25. Alena Heitlinger, "The Impact of the Transition from Communism on the Status of Women in the Czech and Slovak Republics," in Funk and Mueller, eds., *Gender Politics and Post-Communism*, 95–108.

26. Engel, *Women in Russia*, 238.

27. Donna Harsch, "Society, the State, and Abortion in East Germany, 1950–1972," *American Historical Review* 102 (1997): 53–84.

28. Robert J. McIntyre, "Demographic Policy and Sexual Equality: Value Conflicts and Policy Appraisal in Hungary and Romania," in Wolchik and Meyer, eds., *Women, State, and Party in Eastern Europe*, 270–285.

29. Josef Kalvoda, "The Gypsies of Czechoslovakia," in David Crowe and John Kolsti, eds., *The Gypsies of Eastern Europe* (Armonk: M.E. Sharpe, 1991), 93–117.

30. Engel, *Women in Russia*, 235–236.

31. Kolsti, "From Courtyard to Cabinet."

32. Sharon L. Wolchik, *Czechoslovakia in Transition: Politics, Economics, and Society* (London and New York: Pinter Publishers, 1991), 196–197.

33. Rózsa Kulczár, "The Socioeconomic Conditions of Women in Hungary," in Wolchik and Meyer, eds., *Women, State, and Party in Eastern Europe*, 195–213.

34. Ibid., 196; Renata Siemenska, "Women, Work, and Gender Equality in Poland: Reality and Social Perception," in Wolchik and Meyer, eds., *Women, State, and Party in Eastern Europe*, 305–322.

35. Ferree, "The Rise and Fall of 'Mommy Politics.'"

36. Ibid.

37. Document 7, Charter 77, in *White Paper on Czechoslovakia* (Paris: International Committee for the Support of Charter 77, 1977), 87–92 (quotation p. 88).

38. Patricia Herminghouse, "Legal Equality and Women's Reality in the German Democratic Republic," in Altbach, Clausen, Schulz, and Stephan, eds., *German Feminism*, 41–46.

39. Herminghouse, "Legal Equality and Women's Reality."

40. Charlotte Worgitzky, "I Quit," in Nancy Lukens and Dorothy Rosenberg, eds., *Daughters of Eve: Women's Writing from the German Democratic Republic*, trans. Dorothy Rosenberg and Nancy Lukens (Lincoln and London: U. of Nebraska Press, 1993), 51–60.

41. Imtraud Morgner, "Third Fruit of Bitterfield: The Tightrope," in Ibid.,137–142. See also Irmtraud Morgner, *The Life and Adventures of Trobadora Beatrice, as Chronicled by her Minstrel Laura: A Novel in Thirteen Books and Seven Intermezzos,* trans. Jeanette Clausen and Silke von der Emde (Lincoln: U. of Nebraska Press, 2000).

42. Christa Wolf. *The Quest for Christa T.*, trans. Christopher Middleton (New York: Farrar, Straus, and Giroux, 1979).

43. Christa Wolf, "Unter den Linden," in Christa Wolf, *"What Remains" and other Stories*, trans. Heike Schwarzbauer and Rick Takvorian (New York: Farrar and Giroux, 1993), 69–118.

44. Wolf, "In Touch," 166–167.

45. Ibid., 169.

46. Letter from Véra Chitilová to President Gustav Husák, October 8, 1975, in *White Paper on Czechoslovakia*, 176–178.

47. Drakulić, *How We Survived Communism*, 76–81.

48. Wolf, "What Remains," in Wolf, *What Remains*, 231–295.

49. Drakulić, *How We Survived Communism*, 111.

50. Wolf, "In Touch," 169.

7 The Personal and the Political: Women's Liberation in Western Europe, 1968–1990

1. Karen Offen, *European Feminisms, 1700–1950: A Political History* (Stanford: Stanford U. Press, 2000), 25–26.
2. Quoted in Claire Duchen, *Feminism in France, from May '68 to Mitterand* (London and New York: Routledge, 1988), 43.
3. Dorte Marie Søndergaard, "Die Frauenbewegung in Dänemark," in Autonome Frauenredaktion, ed., *Frauenbewegungen in der Welt, Band I: Westeuropa* (Hamburg: Argument-Verlag, 1988), 63–66.
4. Evelyn Mahon, "Frauenbewegung in Irland," in Ibid., 131–147.
5. Daniela C. Colombo, "The Italian Feminist Movement," in Jan Bradshaw, ed., *The Women's Liberation Movement: Europe and North America* (Oxford: Pergamon Press, 1982), 461–469.
6. "Lesben gemeinsam sind stark," in *Frauenjahrbuch '75: Herausgegeben und Hergestellt von Frankfurter Frauen* (Frankfurt: Verlag Roter Stern, 1975), 200–203 (quotation 202).
7. Quoted in Duchen, *Feminism in France*, 23.
8. B. Bryan, S. Dadzie, and S. Scafe, *The Heart of the Race: Black Women's Lives in Britain* (London: Virago, 1985), 149, quoted in Sue Bruley, *Women in Britain since 1900* (Houndmills: Macmillan, 1999), 154.
9. Bruley, *Women in Britain*, 147–158.
10. Monique Wittig, *Les Guérillères*, translated from the French by David Le Vay (New York: Viking Press, 1971).
11. Alice Schwarzer, *Der kleine Unterschied und seine grossen Folgen: Frauen über sich: Beginn einer Befreiung* (Frankfurt am Main: S. Fischer, 1975).
12. Lucia Chiavola Birnbaum, *Liberazione delle Donne: Feminism in Italy* (Middletown: Wesleyan U. Press, 1986), 160–161.
13. Maria Isabel Barreno, Maria Teresa Horta, and Maria Velho da Costa "Authors' Afterword," in Maria Isabel Barreno, Maria Teresa Horta, and Maria Velho da Costa, *The Three Marias: New Portuguese Letters*, trans. Helen R. Lane (New York: Doubleday, 1975), 336–337.
14. Helen R. Lane, "Translator's Preface," *New Portuguese Letters*, ix–xv.
15. Judith Barrington, "Women's Lib Hits London, 1972," *The Gay and Lesbian Review* (May–June 2003): 14–16 (quotation 15).
16. Duchen, *Feminism in France*, 32–39.
17. Gisela Kaplan, *Contemporary Western Feminism* (New York: New York U. Press, 1992), 16–17.
18. Quoted in Kaplan, *Contemporary Western Feminism*, 21.
19. Lee Ann Banaszak, "When Waves Collide: Cycles of Protest and the Swiss and American Women's Movement," *Political Research Quarterly* (December 1996): 839–860; and Susanna Woodtli, *Gleichberechtigung: Der Kampf um die politischen Rechte der Frau* (Zurich: Frauenfeld, 1982), 201–219.
20. Kaplan, *Contemporary Western Feminism*, 186–187.
21. Birnbaum, *Liberazione delle Donne*, 89.

22. Quoted in Duchen, *Feminism in France*, 12.
23. Susan K. Foley, *Women in France since 1789: The Meanings of Difference* (Houndmills: Palgrave Macmillan, 2004), 262–263.
24. Kaplan, *Contemporary Western Feminism*, 154–155.
25. Birnbaum, *Liberazione delle Donne*, 220–221.
26. Kaplan, *Contemporary Western Feminism*, 251.
27. Quoted in Birnbaum, *Liberazione delle Donne*, 134.
28. "Manifesto: Rivolta Femminile," in Paola Bono and Sandra Kemp, eds., *Italian Feminist Thought: A Reader* (Oxford: Basil Blackwell, 1991), 37–40 (quotation 37).
29. Verena Stephan, *Häutungen* (München: Frauenoffensive, 1975), 41.
30. Germaine Greer, *The Female Eunuch* (New York: Bantam, 1971).
31. "Manifesto Rivolta Femminile," 38.
32. Alexandra Bocchetti, "The Indecent Difference," in Bono and Kemp, eds., *Italian Feminist Thought*, 149–161 (quotation 159).
33. Wittig, *Les Guérillères*, 107.
34. See Toril Moi, ed., *French Feminist Thought: A Reader* (Oxford: Blackwell, 1987).
35. For a very useful summary of French feminist philosophy, see Duchen, *Feminism in France*, 67–101; more bibliographical references are given there.
36. For a selection of these writings, see Elaine Marks and Isabelle de Courtivron, eds., *New French Feminisms: An Anthology* (New York: Schocken Books, 1981).
37. Bono and Kemp, *Italian Feminist Thought*, 109–161.
38. Monique Wittig, *The Straight Mind and Other Essays*, Foreword by Louise Turcotte (Boston: Beacon Press, 1992), 32.
39. Eine Frau aus Berlin, "Ich will Kind, Mann, und Frauensolidarität," *Frauenjahrbuch '75*, 84–85.

8 Democracy without Women: The Post-Communist Transition, 1989–Present

1. William Wordsworth, "French Revolution: As it Appeared to Enthusiasts at its Commencement," in *William Wordsworth, The Complete Poetical Works*, with an introduction by John Morley (London: Macmillan, 1888).
2. Jiřna Šiklová, "Backlash," *Journal of Social Research* (Winter 1993): 737–750 (quotation 737).
3. Anastasia Posadskaya, ed., *Women in Russia: A New Era in Russian Feminism*, trans. Kate Clark (London and New York: Verso, 1994), 1–7 (quotation 1).
4. Myra Marx Ferree, " 'The Time of Chaos was the Best': Feminist Mobilization and Demobilization in East Germany," *Gender and Society* 8 (December 1994): 597–623 (quotation 597).
5. Posadskaya, *Women in Russia*, 1–7.

6. Zentraleinrichtung zur Forderung von Frauen-und Geschlecter-forschung, Freie Universität Berlin, Interview with Jiřina Šiklová, www.querellesnet.de/forum/forum3-1.html.

7. Ferree, "The Time of Chaos was the Best," 597.

8. Posadskaya, *Women in Russia*, 4–5.

9. For example, Brigitte Young, *Triumph of the Fatherland: German Unification and the Marginalization of Women* (Ann Arbor: U. of Michigan Press, 1999), 223–225.

10. Mary Ellen Fischer, "From Tradition and Ideology to Elections and Competition: The Changing Status of Women in Romanian Politics," in Marilyn Rueschemeyer, ed., *Women in the Politics of Post-communist Eastern Europe* (Armonk, NY: M.E. Sharpe, 1998), 168–195.

11. Olga Voronina, "The Mythology of Women's Emancipation in the USSR as the Foundation for a Policy of Discrimination," in Posadskaya, ed., *Women in Russia*, 37–56 (quotation 50).

12. Kira Reoutt, in Tatyana Mamonova, ed., *Women's Glasnost vs. Naglost: Stopping Russian Backlash* (Westport, CT: Bergin and Garvey, 1994), 83–89 (quotation 85).

13. Quoted in Barbara Einhorn, *Cinderella Goes to Market: Citizenship, Gender, and Women's Movements in East Central Europe* (London and New York: Verso, 1993), 158.

14. Jiřina Šiklová, "Why Western Feminism Isn't Working in the Czech Republic," *New Presence* 3 (1998): 8–9.

15. Marie Adamik, "Feminism and Hungary," in Nanette Funk and Magda Mueller, eds., *Gender Politics and Post-Communism: Reflections from Eastern Europe and the Former Soviet Union* (New York: Routledge, 1993), 207–212 (quotation 207).

16. Valentina Konstantinova, "No Longer Totalitarianism, But Not Yet Democracy: The Emergence of an Independent Women's Movement in Russia," in Posadskaya, ed., *Women in Russia*, 57–73 (quotation 71).

17. Ibid., 70.

18. Adamik, "Feminism and Hungary."

19. Young, *Triumph of the Fatherland*, 189.

20. Ibid., 189.

21. Daina Stukuls, "Body of the Nation: Mothering, Prostitution, and Women's Place in Postcommunist Latvia," *Slavic Review* 58 (Autumn 1999): 537–558.

22. Gorbachev quoted in Anastasia Posadskaya, "A Feminist Critique of Policy, Legislation, and Social Consciousness in Post-Socialist Russia," in Posadskaya, ed., *Women in Russia*, 168.

23. Voronina, "The Mythology of Women's Emancipation," 37–56 (quotation 49).

24. Einhorn, *Cinderella goes to Market*, 134.

25. Vida Kanopienè, "Women and the Economy," in Suzanne LaFont, ed., *Women in Transition: Voices from Lithuania* (Albany: SUNY Press, 1998), 68–80 (quotation 74).

26. Ferree, "The Time of Chaos was the Best," 614.

27. Sue Bridger and Rebecca Kay, "Gender and Generation in the New Russian Labour Market," in Hilary Pilkington, ed., *Gender, Generation and Identity in Contemporary Russia* (London and New York: Routledge), 1996, 21–38 (quotation 30).
28. Quoted in Bridger and Kay, "Gender and Generation," 31.
29. Stukuls, "Body of the Nation," 550.
30. Silva Meznaric, Mirjana Ule, "The Case of Slovenia," in Rueschemeyer, ed., *Women in the Politics of Communist Eastern Europe*, 202–214.
31. Dinah Dodds and Pam Allen-Thompson, *The Wall in My Backyard: East German Women in Transition* (Amherst: U. of Massachusetts Press, 1994), 32.
32. Dodds and Allen-Thompson, *The Wall in My Backyard*, 151.
33. Quoted in Einhorn, *Cinderella Goes to Market*, 168.
34. Ibid., 141.
35. Elżbieta H. Oleksy, "Plight in Common? Women's Studies in the New Democracies," *Outskirts Online Journal* 3 (November 1998).
36. Quoted in Voichita Nachescu, "Hierarchies of Difference: National Identity, Gay and Lesbian Rights, and the Church in Postcommunist Romania," in Aleksandar Štulhofer and Theo Sandfort, eds., *Sexuality and Gender in Post-communist Eastern Europe and Russia* (New York and London: Haworth Press, 2005), 57–77 (quotation 67).
37. Aleksandar Štulhofer and Theo Sandfort, eds., "Introduction," *Sexuality and Gender*, 1–25.
38. Lynne Attwood, "Young People, Sex and Sexual Identity," in Pilkington, ed., *Gender, Generation and Identity*, 5–120 (quotation 99).
39. Maria Korac, quoted in Einhorn, *Cinderella Goes to Market*, 172.
40. Stukuls, "The Body of the Nation."
41. Giedrè Purvaneckienè, "Women in the Domestic Domain," in LaFont, ed., *Women in Transition*, 48–59.
42. Štulhofer and Sandfort, *Sexuality and Gender*, 12.
43. Igor S. Kon, "Sexual Culture and Politics in Contemporary Russia," in Štulhofer and Sandfort, eds., *Sexuality and Gender*, 111–123.
44. Quoted in Einhorn, *Cinderella goes to Market*, 94.
45. Andrzej Kulczycki, "Abortion Policy in Postcommunist Europe: The Conflict in Poland," *Population and Development Review* 21 (September 1995): 471–505.
46. Evert Ketting, "Abortion in Europe: The East-West Divide," *Choices* 28 (2000): 1.
47. Young, *The Triumph of the Fatherland*, 171–188.
48. Gail Kligman, "Abortion and International Adoption in post-Ceauşescu Romania," *Feminist Studies* 18 (Summer 1992): 405–417.
49. Daniel McLaughlin, "Gypsies Fight for Justice over Forced Sterilization," *The Observer*, May 22, 2005.
50. Nachescu, "Hierarchies of Difference," 61.
51. Ibid., 73.
52. United Nations, *Monthly Bulletin of Statistics*, June 1997; U.S. Census Bureau International Database.

53. Einhorn, *Cinderella goes to Market*, 103–104.

54. Kon, "Sexual Culture," 121.

55. Angela Robson, "Rape: Weapon of War," *New Internationalist*, June, 1993.

56. Roy Gutman, "Rape Camps: Evidence Serb Leaders in Bosnia OKd Attacks," *Newsday*, April 19, 1993; Lene Hansen, "Gender, Nation, Rape: Bosnia and the Construction of Security," *International Feminist Journal of Politics* 3 (April 2001): 56–75.

57. Einhorn, *Cinderella Goes to Market*, 105–106.

58. Quoted in Robson, "Rape: Weapon of War."

59. Branka Andjelković, "Reflections on Nationalism and its Impact on Women in Serbia," in Rueschemeyer, ed., *Women in the Politics of Postcommunist Eastern Europe*, 235–248.

60. Konstantinova, "No Longer Totalitarianism."

61. Šiklová, "Why Western Feminism Isn't Working in the Czech Republic."

9 From Equal Rights to Gender Mainstreaming: Women in the European Union, 1980–Present

1. Anna Diamantopolou, "Women in Decision-Making," Aspasia Forum on Equal Opportunities in Italy and the Rest of Europe, Venice, November 15, 2003.

2. In 1980 the EU included France, Germany, Italy, Belgium, the Netherlands, Luxemburg, Great Britain, Ireland and Denmark. By 2006, Greece, Portugal, Spain, Sweden, Finland, Austria, Latvia, Lithuania, Estonia, Poland, the Czech Republic, Slovakia, Hungary, Slovenia, Romania, Bulgaria, Cyprus, and Malta had joined. In 2007, Romania and Bulgaria became the newest members. This chapter will also deal with neighboring countries such as Norway, which is not a member of the EU.

3. Kevin J. Kinsella, "Changes in Life Expectancy, 1900–1990," *American Journal of Clinical Nutrition* 55 (1992): 1196–1202.

4. Göran Therborn, *Between Sex and Power: Family in the World, 1900–2000* (London: Routledge, 2004), 230 and 285.

5. Agnès Hubert, "From Equal Pay to Parity Democracy: The Rocky Ride of Women's Policy in the European Union," in Jytte Klausen and Charles S. Maier, eds., *Has Liberalism Failed Women?: Assuring Equal Representation in Europe and the United States* (New York: Palgrave, 2001), 143–163.

6. "Gender Disparities," *Society* (September/October 2005), 2; *Eurostat*, March 8, 2006.

7. "Reports from around the World: Europe," *WIN News* 22 (1996): 59–66.

8. Colette Fagan and Brendan Burchell, *Gender, Jobs and Working Conditions in the European Union* (Dublin: European Foundation for the Improvement of Living and Working Conditions, 2002); statistics, 50.

9. Karen Christopher, "Welfare State Regimes and Mothers' Poverty," *Social Politics* (Spring 2002): 60–86.

10. For more on policies supporting mothers and child-rearing, see Christopher, "Welfare State Regimes."

11. Fagan and Burchell, *Gender, Jobs and Working Conditions*, 19.
12. Therborn, *Between Sex and Power*, 289.
13. Ibid., 195.
14. Ibid., 201.
15. Christopher Pissarides, Pietro Garibaldi, Claudia Olivetti, Barbara Petrongolo, and Étienne Wasmer, "Women in the Labor Force: How Well is Europe Doing?" in T. Boeri, D. del Boca and C. Pissarides, eds., *European Women at Work* (Oxford: Oxford U. Press, 2005), Table 2.1; Therborn, *Between Sex and Power*, 285.
16. *Women in Political Decision-Making Positions: Facts and Figures, 2000* (Berlin: FrauenComputerZentrumBerlin), 2000, 4; Jill Rubery, Mark Smith, Dominque Anxo and Lennart Flood, "The Future European Labor Supply: The Critical Role of the Family," *Feminist Economics* 7 (2001): 33–69.
17. European Parliament, Women's Rights Committee, Address by Commissioner Padraig Flynn, Brussels, February 16, 1999.
18. Gøsta Esping-Andersen with Duncan Gallie, Anton Hemerijk, and John Myles, *Why We Need a New Welfare State* (Oxford: Oxford U. Press, 2002), 74.
19. Kimberly Morgan, "Does Anyone Have a *Libre Choix?* Subversive Liberalism and the Politics of French Child Care Policy," in Sonya Michel and Rianne Mahon, eds., *Child Care Policy at the Crossroads: Gender and Welfare State Restructuring* (New York and London: Routledge, 2002), 143–167; Celia Valiente, "The Value of an Educational Emphasis: Child Care and Restructuring in Spain since 1975," in Michel and Mahon, eds., *Child Care Policy*, 57–70.
20. Jacqueline Heinen, "Ideology, Economics, and the Politics of Child Care in Poland before and after the Transition," in Michel and Mahon, eds., *Child Care Policy*, 72–92.
21. Esping-Andersen, *Why We Need a New Welfare State*, 95.
22. Nancy Fraser, "After the Family Wage: Gender Equity and the Welfare State," *Political Theory* 22 (November 1994): 591–618.
23. "Quality time Thrills Nordic Dads," *BBC News*, June 28, 2005.
24. "Ursula von der Leyen im Interview mit der Bild am Sontag" *Bild am Sontag*, April 16, 2006.
25. Dr. Gro Harlem Brundtland (1939), Leaders and Transformation in Developing Countries, http://www.unit.brandeis.edu/~dwilliam/profiles/brundtland.htm.
26. Alice Kessler-Harris, "A Conversation with Ida Blom," *Perspectives* 44 (December 2006): 6–11 (quotation 7).
27. *Women in Political Decision-Making Positions: Facts and Figures, 2000* (Berlin: FrauenComputerZentrumBerlin), 2000, 6.
28. Claire Duchen, "Feminism and the Party Debate in France," in Anna Bull, Hanna Diamond, and Rosalind Marsh, eds., *Feminisms and Women's Movements in Contemporary Europe* (Houndmills: St. Martin's, 2000), 152–165; Susan K. Foley, *Women in France since 1789: The Meanings of Difference* (New York: Palgrave, 2004), 267–287.

29. *Women in Political Decision-Making*, 18.
30. Lee Ann Banaszak, Karen Beckwith, and Dieter Rucht, "When Power Relocates: Interactive Changes in Women's Movements and States," in Karen Beckwith, and Dieter Rucht, eds., *Women's Movements Facing the Reconfigured State* (Cambridge: Cambridge U. Press, 2003), 1–28.
31. Ailbhe Smyth, "And Nobody Was Any the Wiser: Irish Abortion Rights and the European Union," in R. Amy Elman, ed., *Sexual Politics and the European Union: The New Feminist Challenge* (Providence and Oxford: Berghahn, 1996), 109–130.
32. Amy G. Mazur, "The Interplay: The Formation of Sexual Harassment Legislation in France and European Union Policy Initiatives," in Elman, ed., *Sexual Politics and the European Union*, 35–49.
33. Dorchen Leidtholdt, "Sexual Trafficking of Women in Europe: A Human Rights Crisis for the European Union," in Elman, ed., *Sexual Politics and the European Union*, 83–95.
34. "The Global View of Gay Marriage," *CBS News*, March 4, 2004.
35. ILGA-Europe, www.ilga-europe.org.
36. Chad Graham, "European Unions," *The Advocate*, May 15, 2004, 36–37.
37. Peter Schneider, "The New Berlin Wall," *The New York Times*, December 4, 2005.
38. Ayaan Hirsi Ali, *The Caged Virgin: An Emancipation Proclamation for Women and Islam* (New York: Free Press, 2004), 82.
39. Ibid.
40. Christine Delphy, "L'affaire du foulard: non à l'exclusion," *Sysyphe*, November 1, 2003.
41. Marlise Simons, "Muslim Women Take Charge of their Faith," *International Herald Tribune*, December 4, 2004.
42. Nadya Kassam, ed., *Telling it Like it Is: Young Asian Women Talk* (London: The Women's Press, 1997), 33.
43. Foley, *Women in France*, 274–287; Caroline Lambert, "French Women in Politics: The Long Road to Parity," *U.S.-France Analysis*, May 2001, 1–5.
44. Vlaams Blok, "Programma: Gezinspartij, ethische partij," http://www.vlaamsblok.be.
45. Dansk Folkeparti, "The Danish People's Party," http://www.dansk.folkeparti.dk; "Nordic Nasties," *The Economist*, December 16, 2006, 51.
46. Rosi Braidotti, "Gender and Power in a Post-nationalist European Union," *NORA* 3 (2004): 130–142.

Conclusion: Emancipation as Myth and Reality

1. Virginia Woolf, *A Room of One's Own* (New York: Harcourt, Brace, Jovanovich, 1929), 88.

Suggested Reading

These lists contain only a very few of the excellent works that are available. I have listed only works in English or English translation. Of course, there are a great many more in the languages of all the countries that this book covers. For a few suggestions, see the citations in the individual chapters.

Chapter 1

Allen, Ann Taylor. *Feminism and Motherhood in Western Europe, 1890–1970: The Maternal Dilemma*. New York: Palgrave Macmillan, 2005.

Brittain, Vera. *Testament of Youth: An Autobiographical Study of the Years 1900–1925* [1933]. New York: Penguin Books, 1994.

Daniel, Ute. *The War from Within: German Working-Class Women in the First World War*. Translated by Margaret Ries. Oxford and New York: Berg, 1997.

Darrow, Margaret. *French Women and the First World War*. Oxford and New York: Berg, 2000.

Davis, Belinda J. *Home Fires Burning: Food, Politics, and Everyday Life in World War I Berlin*. Chapel Hill: University of North Carolina Press, 2000.

Grayzel, Susan R. *Women's Identities at War: Gender, Motherhood, and Politics in Britain and France during the First World War*. Chapel Hill: University of North Carolina Press, 1999.

Jacobs, Aletta. *Memories: My Life as an International Leader in Health, Suffrage, and Peace*. Edited by Harriet Feinberg, translated by Annie Wright. New York: Feminist Press, 1996.

Pedersen, Susan. "Gender, Welfare and Citizenship in Britain during the Great War." *American Historical Review* 95 (October 1990): 983–1006.

Reilly, Catherine, ed. *Scars upon my Heart: Women's Poetry and Verse of the First World War*. London: Virago Press, 1981.

Schulte, Regine. "The Sick Warrior's Sister: Nursing during the First World War." Translated by Pamela Selwyn. In Lynn Abrams and Elizabeth Harvey, eds., *Gender Relations in German History: Power, Agency and Experience from the Sixteenth to the Twentieth Century*. Durham: Duke U. Press, 1997, 121–141.

Swanwick, Helena. *Women and War*. London: Union of Democratic Control, 1915.

Thom, Deborah. *Nice Girls and Rude Girls: Women Workers in World War I*. London: LB Tauris, 1998.

Women's Cooperative Guild, comp. *Maternity: Letters from Working Women*. London: G. Bell and Sons, Ltd., 1915.

Chapter 2

Allen, Ann Taylor. *Feminism and Motherhood in Western Europe, 1890–1970: The Maternal Dilemma*. New York: Palgrave Macmillan, 2005.

Beauvoir, Simone de. *Memoirs of a Dutiful Daughter*. Translated by James Kirkup. New York: Harper & Row, 1974.

Bock, Gisela and Pat Thane, eds. *Maternity and Gender Policies: Women and the Rise of European Welfare States, 1880s–1950s*. London and New York: Routledge, 1991.

Bridenthal, Renate. "Something Old, Something New: Women Between the Two World Wars." In Renate Bridenthal and Claudia Koonz, eds., *Becoming Visible: Women in European History*. Boston: Houghton Mifflin, 1977, 422–444.

Brittain, Vera. *Honourable Estate: A Novel of Transition*. New York: Macmillan, 1936.

Feinberg, Melissa. "Democracy and Its Limits: Gender and Rights in the Czech Lands, 1918–1938," *Nationalities Papers* 30 (December 2002): 553–570.

Hall, Lesley. *Sex, Gender, and Social Change in Britain since 1880*. New York: St. Martin's Press, 2000.

Herman, Sondra R. "Dialogue: Children, Feminism, and Power: Alva Myrdal and Swedish Reform, 1929–1956." *Journal of Women's History* 4 (Fall 1992): 82–112.

Jackson, Pauline Conroy. "Managing the Mothers: the Case of Ireland." In Jane Lewis, ed., *Women and Social Policies in Europe: Work, Family and the State*. Aldershot: Edward Elgar, 1993, 72–91.

Margueritte, Victor. *The Bachelor Girl*. Translated by Hugh Burnaby. New York: Knopf, 1923.

Offen, Karen. *European Feminisms, 1700–1950: A Political History*. Stanford: Stanford University. Press, 2000.

Pedersen, Susan. *Family, Dependence and the Origins of the Welfare State: Britain and France, 1914–1945*. Cambridge and New York: Cambridge University Press, 1993.

Petersen, Vibeke Rützou. *Women and Modernity in Weimar Germany: Reality and its Representation in Popular Fiction*. New York and Oxford: Berghahn Books, 2001.

Pugh, Martin. *Women and the Women's Movement in Britain 1914–1959*. Houndmills: Macmillan, 1992.

Reagin, Nancy. *Sweeping the German Nation: Domesticity and National Identity in Germany, 1870–1945*. New York: Cambridge University Press, 2007.

Roberts, Mary Louise. *Civilization without Sexes: Reconstructing Gender in Postwar France, 1917–1927*. Chicago: University of Chicago Press, 1994.

Scannell, Yvonne. "The Constitution and the Role of Women." In Brian Farrell, ed., *De Valera's Constitution and Ours*. Goldenbridge, Dublin: Gillard Macmillan, 1988, 123–136.

Swanwick, Helena. *The War in its Effect upon Women*. New York: Garland Publishing, 1971.

Chapter 3

Bock, Gisela. "Antinatalism, Maternity, and Paternity in National Socialist Racism." In Gisela Bock and Pat Thane, eds., *Maternity and Gender Policies: Women and the Rise of the European Welfare States, 1880s–1950s*. London and New York: Routledge, 1991, 233–255.

De Grazia, Victoria. *How Fascism Ruled Women: Italy, 1922–1945*. Berkeley: University of California Press, 1992.

Engel, Barbara Alpern. *Women in Russia, 1700–2000*. Cambridge: Cambridge University Press, 2004.

Ginzburg, Eugenia Semyonovna. *Journey into the Whirlwind*. Translated by Paul Stevenson and Max Hayward. New York: Harcourt, Brace, 1967.

Goldman, Wendy Z. *Women, the State, and Revolution: Soviet Family Policy and Social Life, 1917–1936*. Cambridge and New York: Cambridge University Press, 1993.

Kaplan, Marion A. *Between Dignity and Despair: Jewish Life in Nazi Germany*. New York: Oxford, 1998.

Kevin Passmore, ed. *Women, Gender, and Fascism in Europe, 1919–1945*. New Brunswick: Rutgers University Press, 2003.

Koonz, Claudia. *Mothers in the Fatherland: Women, the Family, and Nazi Politics*. New York: St. Martin's, 1987.

Lapidus, Gail Warshofsky. *Women in Soviet Society: Equality, Development, and Social Change*. Berkeley: University of California Press, 1978.

Lewy, Guenter. *The Nazi Persecution of the Gypsies*. Oxford and New York: Oxford University Press, 2000.

Mouton, Michelle. *From Nurturing the Nation to Purifying the Volk: Weimar and Nazi Family Policy, 1918–1945*. Cambridge and New York: Cambridge University Press, 2007.

Pine, Lisa. *Nazi Family Policy, 1933–1945*. Oxford and New York: Berg, 1997.

Reese, Dagmar. *Growing Up Female in Nazi Germany*. Translated by William Templer. Ann Arbor: University of Michigan Press, 2006.

Stephenson, Jill. *Women in Nazi Society*. New York: Barnes and Noble, 1975.

Thurston, Robert W. "The Soviet Family during the Great Terror, 1935–1941," *Soviet Studies* 43, 3 (1991): 553–574.

Chapter 4

Boehm, Philip, ed. *A Woman in Berlin: Eight Weeks in the Conquered City: A Diary*. New York: Metropolitan Books/Henry Holt, 2005.

Campbell, D'Ann. "Women in Combat: The World War II Experience in the United States, Great Britain, Germany and the Soviet Union." *The Journal of Military History* 57 (April 1993): 301–323.

Chickering, Roger and Stig Förster, eds. *A World at Total War: Global Conflict and the Politics of Destruction, 1937–1945*. Cambridge: Cambridge University Press, 1995.

Engel, Barbara Alpern. *Women in Russia, 1700–2000*. Cambridge: Cambridge University Press, 2004.

Felstiner, Mary Lowenthal. *To Paint her Life: Charlotte Salomon in the Nazi Era*. New York: Harper Collins, 1994.

Foley, Susan K. *Women in France since 1789: The Meanings of Difference*. Houndmills: Palgrave Macmillan, 2004.

Isaacson, Judith Magyar. *Seed of Sarah: Memoirs of a Survivor*. Urbana: University of Illinois Press, 1990.

Kluger, Ruth. *Still Alive: A Holocaust Girlhood Remembered*. New York: Feminist Press, 2001.

Ofer, Dalia and Lenore J. Weitzman, eds. *Women in the Holocaust*. New Haven: Yale University Press, 1998.

Riley, Denise. *War in the Nursery: Theories of the Child and Mother*. London: Virago, 1983.

Rittner, Carol and John Roth, eds. *Different Voices: Women and the Holocaust*. New York: Paragon House, 1993.

Rupp, Leila J. *Mobilizing Women for War: German and American Propaganda, 1939–1945*. Princeton: Princeton University Press, 1978.

Summerfield, Penny. *Women Workers in the Second World War: Production and Patriarchy in Conflict*. London and New York: Routledge, 1989.

Summerfield, Penny. "Women and War in the Twentieth Century." In June Purvis, ed., *Women's History: Britain, 1850–1945: An Introduction*. London: UCL Press, 1995, 307–332.

Chapter 5

Allen, Ann Taylor. *Feminism and Motherhood in Western Europe, 1890–1970: The Maternal Dilemma*. New York: Palgrave Macmillan, 2005.

Beauvoir, Simone de. *The Second Sex* [1949]. Translated and edited by H.M. Parshley. New York: A.A. Knopf, 1993.

Bok, Sissela. *Alva Myrdal: A Daughter's Memoir*. Reading, MA: Addison-Wesley, 1991.

Bowlby, John. *Maternal Care and Mental Health*. Geneva: WHO, 1952.

Duchen, Claire. *Women's Rights and Women's Lives in France, 1944–1968*. London and New York: Routledge, 1994.

Friedan, Betty. *The Feminine Mystique*. New York: Norton, 1963.

Furlough, Ellen. "Making Mass Vacations: Tourism and Consumer Culture in France, 1930s to 1970s." *Comparative Studies in Society and History*, 40 (April 1998): 247–286.

Myrdal, Alva and Viola Klein. *Women's Two Roles: Home and Work*. London: Routledge, 1956.

Foley, Susan K. *Women in France since 1989: The Meanings of Difference*. New York: Palgrave, 2004.

Hall, Lesley A. *Sex, Gender, and Social Change in Britain since 1889*. New York: St. Martin's, 2000.

Hardyment, Christina. *Perfect Parents: Baby-Care Advice Past and Present*. New York: Oxford, 1995.

Herzog, Dagmar. "Between Coitus and Commodification: Young West German Women and the Impact of the Pill." In Axel Schildt and Detlef

Siegfried, eds., *Between Marx and Coca-Cola: Youth Cultures in Changing European Societies, 1960–1980*. New York: Berghahn Books, 2006, 261–286.

Jephcott, Pearl. *Married Women Working*. London: George Allen and Unwin, 1962.

Kaplan, Gisela. *Contemporary Western European Feminism*. New York: New York University Press, 1992.

Klein, Viola. *The Feminine Character: History of an Ideology* [1946]. Champaign-Urbana: University of Illinois Press, 1972.

Kolinsky, Eva. *Women in Contemporary Germany: Life, Work, and Politics*. New York: Berg, 1993.

Morcillo, Aurora G. *True Catholic Womanhood: Gender and Ideology in Franco's Spain*. Dekalb: North Illinois University Press, 2000.

Poiger, Uta G. "Rock 'n Roll, Female Sexuality, and the Cold War Battle over German Identities." In Robert G. Moeller, ed., *West Germany under Construction: Politics, Society and Culture in the Adenauer Era*. Ann Arbor: University of Michigan Press, 1997, 413–444.

Wilson, Elizabeth. *Only Halfway to Paradise: Women in Post-War Britain, 1945–1968*. London and New York: Tavistock Publications, 1980.

Chapter 6

Altbach, Edith Hoshino, Jeanette Clausen, Dagmar Schultz, and Naomi Stephan, eds., *German Feminism: Readings in Politics and Literature*. Albany: State University of New York Press, 1984.

Drakulić, Slavenka. *How We Survived Communism and Even Laughed*. New York: W.W. Norton, 1991.

Ferree, Myra Marx. "The Rise and Fall of 'Mommy Politics' ": Feminism and Unification in (East) Germany. *Feminist Studies* (Spring 1993): 89–116.

Funk, Nanette and Magda Mueller, eds., *Gender Politics and Post-Communism*. New York and London: Routledge, 1993.

Harsch, Donna. *Revenge of the Domestic: Women, the Family, and Communism in the German Democratic Republic*. Princeton: Princeton University Press, 2007.

Havel, Václav *et al*. *The Power of the Powerless: Citizens against the State in Central-Eastern Europe*. Introduction by Steven Lukes, edited by John Keane. Armonk, NY: M.E. Sharpe, 1985.

Herzog, Dagmar. *Sex After Fascism: Memory and Morality in Twentieth-Century Germany*. Princeton: Princeton University Press, 2005.

Iggers, Wilma. *Women of Prague: Ethnic Diversity and Social Change from the Eighteenth Century to the Present*. Providence and Oxford: Berghahn Books, 1995.

Kalvoda, Josef. "The Gypsies of Czechoslovakia." In David Crowe and John Kolsti, eds., *The Gypsies of Eastern Europe*. Armonk: M.E. Sharpe, 1991, 93–117.

Lukens, Nancy and Dorothy Rosenberg, eds. *Daughters of Eve: Women's Writing from the German Democratic Republic*. Translated by Dorothy Rosenberg and Nancy Lukens. Lincoln, Nebraska, and London: University of Nebraska Press, 1993, 51–60.

Morgner, Irmtraud. *The Life and Adventures of Trobadora Beatrice, as Chronicled by her Minstrel Laura: A Novel in Thirteen Books and Seven Intermezzos.* Translated by Jeanette Clausen and Silke von der Emde. Lincoln: University of Nebraska Press, 2000.

Penn, Shana. *Solidarity's Secret, The Women Who Defeated Communism in Poland.* Ann Arbor: University of Michigan Press, 2005.

White Paper on Czechoslovakia. Paris: International Committee for the Support of Charter 77, 1977.

Wolchik, Sharon L. and Alfred G. Meyer, eds. *Women, State, and Party in Eastern Europe.* Durham: Duke University Press, 1985.

Wolchik, Sharon L. *Czechoslovakia in Transition: Politics, Economics, and Society.* London and New York: Pinter Publishers, 1991.

Wolf, Christa. *The Quest for Christa T.* Translated by Christopher Middleton. New York: Farrar, Straus, and Giroux, 1979.

Wolf, Christa. *"What Remains" and Other Stories.* Translated by Heike Schwarzbauer and Rick Takvorian. New York: Farrar, Strauss, and Giroux, 1993.

Chapter 7

Banaszak, Lee Ann. "When Waves Collide: Cycles of Protest and the Swiss and American Women's Movement." *Political Research Quarterly* (December 1996): 839–860.

Barreno, Maria Isabel, Maria Teresa Horta, and Maria Velho da Costa. *The Three Marias: New Portuguese Letters.* Translated by Helen R. Lane. New York: Doubleday, 1975.

Beauvoir, Simone de. *The Second Sex* [1949]. Translated by H.M. Parshley. New York: Vintage Books, 1989.

Birnbaum, Lucia Chiavola. *Liberazione delle Donne: Feminism in Italy.* Middletown: Wesleyan University Press, 1986.

Bono, Paola and Sandra Kemp, eds. *Italian Feminist Thought: A Reader.* Oxford: Basil Blackwell, 1991.

Bradshaw Jan, ed. *The Women's Liberation Movement: Europe and North America.* Oxford: Pergamon Press, 1982.

Bruley, Sue. *Women in Britain since 1900.* Houndmills: Macmillan, 1999.

Duchen, Claire. *Women's Rights and Women's Lives in France, 1944–1968.* London and New York: Routledge, 1994.

Kaplan Gisela. *Contemporary Western Feminism.* New York: New York University Press, 1992.

Marks, Elaine and Isabelle de Courtivron, eds. *New French Feminisms: An Anthology.* New York: Schocken Books, 1981.

Offen, Karen. *European Feminisms, 1700–1950: A Political History.* Stanford: Stanford University Press, 2000.

Wittig, Monique. *Les Guérillères.* Translated from the French by David Le Vay. New York: Viking Press, 1971.

Wittig, Monique. *The Straight Mind and Other Essays.* Foreword by Louise Turcotte. Boston: Beacon Press, 1992.

Chapter 8

Dodds, Dinah and Pam Allen-Thompson. *The Wall in My Backyard: East German Women in Transition*. Amherst: University of Massachusetts Press, 1994.

Einhorn, Barbara. *Cinderella Goes to Market: Citizenship, Gender, and Women's Movements in East Central Europe*. London and New York: Verso, 1993.

Ferree, Myra Marx. " 'The Time of Chaos was the Best': Feminist Mobilization and Demobilization in East Germany." *Gender and Society* 8 (December 1994): 597–623.

Funk, Nanette and Magda Mueller eds. *Gender Politics and Post-Communism: Reflections from Eastern Europe and the Former Soviet Union*. New York: Routledge, 1993.

Kligman, Gail. "Abortion and International Adoption in post-Ceauşescu Romania." *Feminist Studies* 18 (Summer 1992): 405–417.

Kulczycki, Andrzej. "Abortion Policy in Postcommunist Europe: The Conflict in Poland." *Population and Development Review* 21 (September 1995): 471–505.

LaFont, Suzanne, ed. *Women in Transition: Voices from Lithuania*. Albany: SUNY Press, 1998.

Mamonova, Tatyana, ed. *Women's Glasnost vs. Naglost: Stopping Russian Backlash*. Westport, CT: Bergin and Garvey, 1994.

Pilkington, Hilary, ed. *Gender, Generation and Identity in Contemporary Russia*. London and New York: Routledge, 1996.

Posadskaya, Anastasia, ed. *Women in Russia: A New Era in Russian Feminism*. Translated by Kate Clark. London and New York: Verso, 1994.

Rueschemeyer, Marilyn, ed. *Women in the Politics of Postcommunist Eastern Europe*. Armonk, NY: M.E. Sharpe, 1998.

Šiklová, Jiřina. "Backlash." *Journal of Social Research* (Winter 1993): 737–750.

Šiklová, Jiřina. "Courage, Heroism, and the Postmodern Paradox." *Social Research* 71 (Spring 2004): 135–148.

Stukuls, Daina. "Body of the Nation: Mothering, Prostitution, and Women's Place in Post-communist Latvia." *Slavic Review* 58 (Autumn 1999): 537–558.

Štulhofer, Aleksandr and Theo Sandfort, eds. *Sexuality and Gender in Postcommunist Eastern Europe and Russia*. New York and London: Haworth Press, 2005.

Young, Brigitte. *Triumph of the Fatherland: German Unification and the Marginalization of Women*. Ann Arbor: University of Michigan Press, 1999.

Chapter 9

Beck-Gernsheim, E. *Reinventing the Family*. Cambridge: Cambridge University Press, 2002.

Beckwith, Karen and Dieter Rucht, eds. *Women's Movements Facing the Reconfigured State*. Cambridge: Cambridge University Press, 2003.

Boeri, Tito, Daniela del Boca, and Christopher Pissarides, eds. *European Women at Work*. Oxford: Oxford University Press, 2005.

Braidotti, Rosi. "Gender and Power in a Post-nationalist European Union." *NORA* 3 (2004): 130–142.

Bull, Anna, Hanna Diamond, and Rosalind Marsh, eds. *Feminisms and Women's Movements in Contemporary Europe*. Houndmills: St. Martin's, 2000.

Christopher, Karen. "Welfare State Regimes and Mothers' Poverty." *Social Politics* (Spring 2002): 60–86.

Elman, R. Amy, ed. *Sexual Politics and the European Union: The New Feminist Challenge*. Providence and Oxford: Berghahn, 1996.

Esping-Andersen, Gøsta, with Duncan Gallie, Anton Hemerijk, and John Myles. *Why We Need a New Welfare State*. Oxford: Oxford University Press, 2002.

Fagan, Colette and Brendan Burchell. *Gender, Jobs and Working Conditions in the European Union*. Dublin: European Foundation for the Improvement of Living and Working Conditions, 2002.

Fraser, Nancy. "After the Family Wage: Gender Equity and the Welfare State." *Political Theory* 22 (November 1994): 591–618.

Lewis, Jane, ed. *Gender, Social Care and Welfare State Restructuring in Europe*. Aldershot: Ashgate, 1998.

Klausen, Jytte and Charles S. Maier, eds. *Has Liberalism Failed Women? Assuring Equal Representation in Europe and the United States*. New York: Palgrave Macmillan, 2001.

Michel, Sonya and Rianne Mahon, eds. *Child Care Policy at the Crossroads: Gender and Welfare State Restructuring*. New York and London: Routledge, 2002.

Therborn, Göran. *Between Sex and Power: Family in the World, 1900–2000*. London: Routledge, 2004.

Women in Political Decision-Making Positions: Facts and Figures, 2000. Berlin: FrauenComputerZentrumBerlin, 2000.

Index